THE wallflower

YAMATONADESHIKO SHICHIHENGE

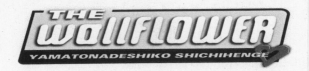

2

Tomoko Hayakawa

Translated and adapted by
David Ury

Lettered by
Dana Hayward

KC
KODANSHA
COMICS

The Wallflower volume 2 is a work of fiction. Names, characters, places, and incidents are the products of the author's imagination or are used fictitiously. Any resemblance to actual events, locales, or persons, living or dead, is entirely coincidental.

A Kodansha Comics Trade Paperback Original.

Published in the United States by Kodansha Comics, an imprint of Kodansha USA Publishing, LLC., New York.

Publication rights for this English edition arranged through Kodansha Ltd., Tokyo.

First published in Japan in 2001 by Kodansha Ltd., Tokyo, as *Yamatonadeshiko Shichihenge*, volume 2.

ISBN 978-1-61262-316-0

Printed in Canada.

www.kodanshacomics.com

9 8 7 6 5 4 3 2 1

Translator/Adapter—David Ury
Lettering—Dana Hayward
Cover Design—David Stevenson

Contents

A Note from the Author

I'M A "BEE"

PEOPLE KEEP SAYING THEY WANT TO SEE MY PICTURE.

♥ Lately, my life has been really hectic. Everybody was so worked up about Y2K*, but now, several months have already passed. I was all excited about Volume 1, and now, suddenly, Volume 2 is coming out. I'm gonna keep working hard, so please keep following the adventures of Sunako and the "Creatures of the Light."

—Tomoko Hayakawa

*Editor's note: This volume was originally published in Japan in March 2001, hence the reference to Y2K. . . .

Honorifics Explained

Throughout the Kodansha Comics books, you will find Japanese honorifics left intact in the translations. For those not familiar with how the Japanese use honorifics and, more important, how they differ from American honorifics, we present this brief overview.

Politeness has always been a critical facet of Japanese culture. Ever since the feudal era, when Japan was a highly stratified society, use of honorifics—which can be defined as polite speech that indicates relationship or status—has played an essential role in the Japanese language. When addressing someone in Japanese, an honorific usually takes the form of a suffix attached to one's name (example: "Asuna-san"), is used as a title at the end of one's name, or appears in place of the name itself (example: "Negi-sensei," or simply "Sensei!").

Honorifics can be expressions of respect or endearment. In the context of manga and anime, honorifics give insight into the nature of the relationship between characters. Many English translations leave out these important honorifics and therefore distort the feel of the original Japanese. Because Japanese honorifics contain nuances that English honorifics lack, it is our policy at Kodansha Comics not to translate them. Here, instead, is a guide to some of the honorifics you may encounter in Kodansha Comics.

-san: This is the most common honorific and is equivalent to Mr., Miss, Ms., or Mrs. It is the all-purpose honorific and can be used in any situation where politeness is required.

-sama: This is one level higher than "-san" and is used to confer great respect.

-dono: This comes from the word "tono," which means "lord." It is an even higher level than "-sama" and confers utmost respect.

-kun: This suffix is used at the end of boys' names to express famil-
iarity or endearment. It is also sometimes used by men among
friends, or when addressing someone younger or of a lower
station.

-chan: This is used to express endearment, mostly toward girls. It is
also used for little boys, pets, and even among lovers. It gives
a sense of childish cuteness.

Bozu: This is an informal way to refer to a boy, similar to the English
terms "kid" and "squirt."

**Sempai/
Senpai:** This title suggests that the addressee is one's senior in a
group or organization. It is most often used in a school set-
ting, where underclassmen refer to their upperclassmen as
"sempai." It can also be used in the workplace, such as when a
newer employee addresses an employee who has seniority in
the company.

Kohai: This is the opposite of "sempai" and is used toward underclassmen in school or newcomers in the workplace. It connotes
that the addressee is of a lower station.

Sensei: Literally meaning "one who has come before," this title is used
for teachers, doctors, or masters of any profession or art.

-[blank]: This is usually forgotten in these lists, but it is perhaps the
most significant difference between Japanese and English. The
lack of honorific means that the speaker has permission to address the person in a very intimate way. Usually, only family,
spouses, or very close friends have this kind of permission.
Known as *yobisute*, it can be gratifying when someone who
has earned the intimacy starts to call one by one's name without an honorific. But when that intimacy hasn't been earned,
it can be very insulting.

THE wallflower

YAMATONADESHIKO SHICHIHENGE

ヤマトナデシコ七変化♡

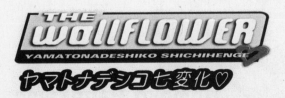

Chapter 6
Sunako, They're Calling You.

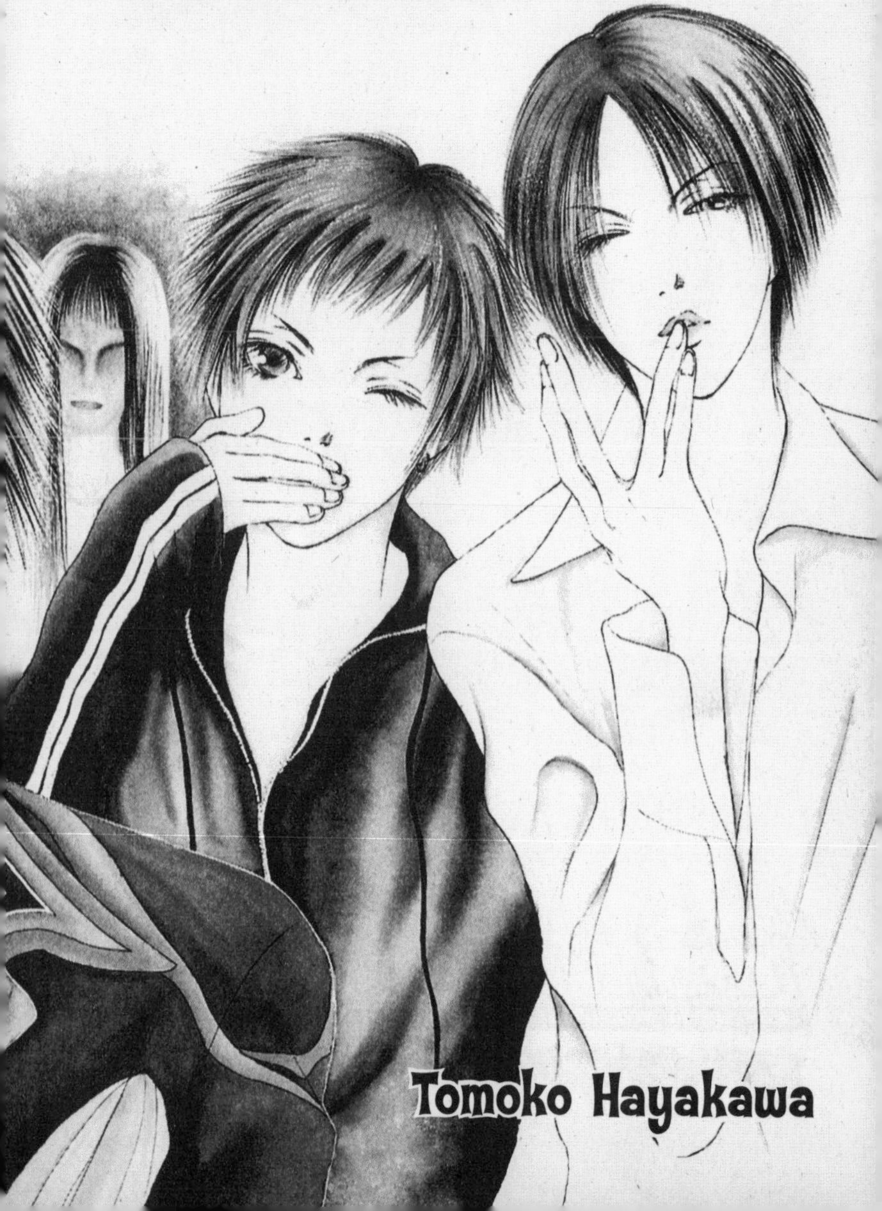
Tomoko Hayakawa

THE wallflower
YAMATONADESHIKO SHICHIHENGE

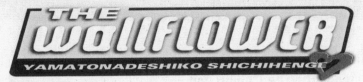

♥ BOOK 2 ♥

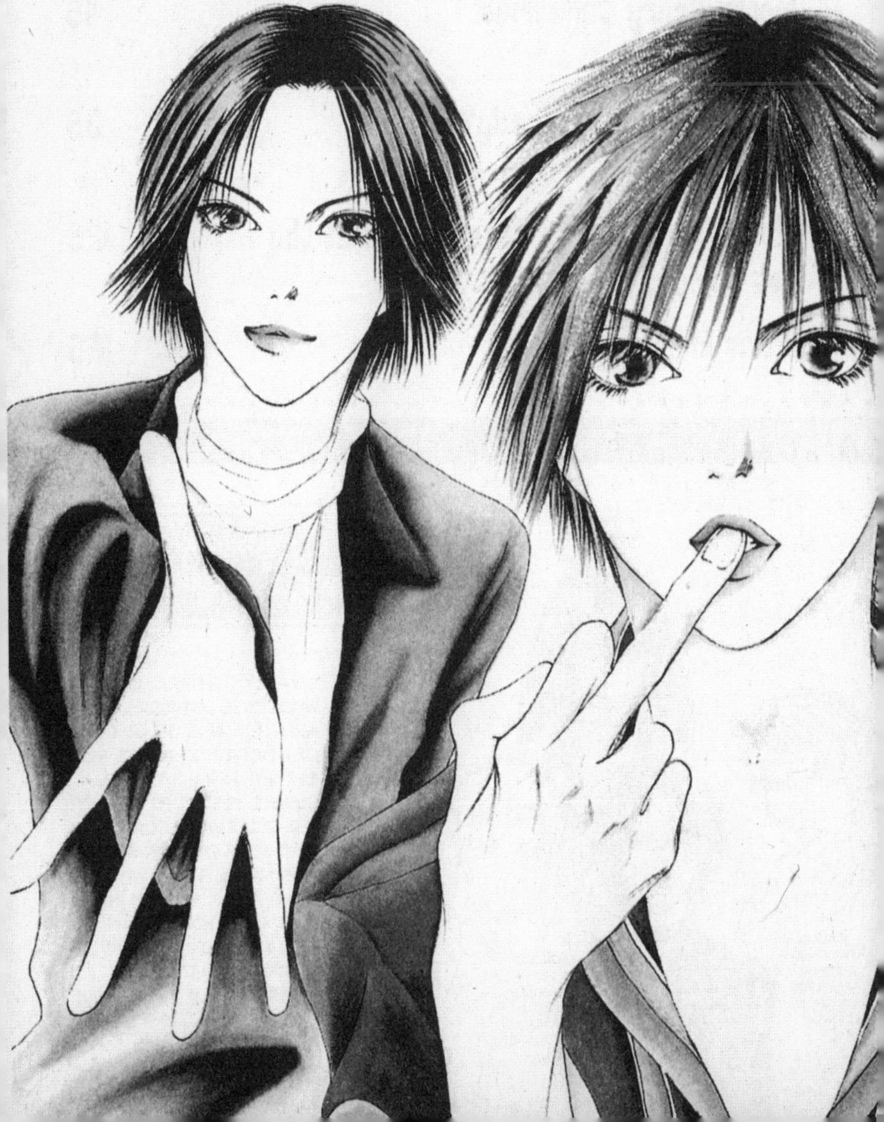

CONTENTS

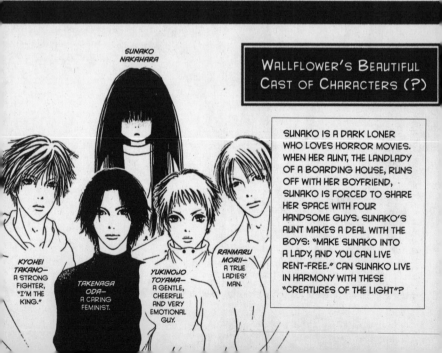

WALLFLOWER'S BEAUTIFUL CAST OF CHARACTERS (?)

SUNAKO NAKAHARA
RANMARU MORII— A TRUE LADIES' MAN.
YUKINOJO TOYAMA— A GENTLE, CHEERFUL AND VERY EMOTIONAL GUY.
TAKENAGA ODA— A CARING FEMINIST.
KYOHEI TAKANO— A STRONG FIGHTER, "I'M THE KING."

SUNAKO IS A DARK LONER WHO LOVES HORROR MOVIES. WHEN HER AUNT, THE LANDLADY OF A BOARDING HOUSE, RUNS OFF WITH HER BOYFRIEND, SUNAKO IS FORCED TO SHARE HER SPACE WITH FOUR HANDSOME GUYS. SUNAKO'S AUNT MAKES A DEAL WITH THE BOYS: "MAKE SUNAKO INTO A LADY, AND YOU CAN LIVE RENT-FREE." CAN SUNAKO LIVE IN HARMONY WITH THESE "CREATURES OF THE LIGHT"?

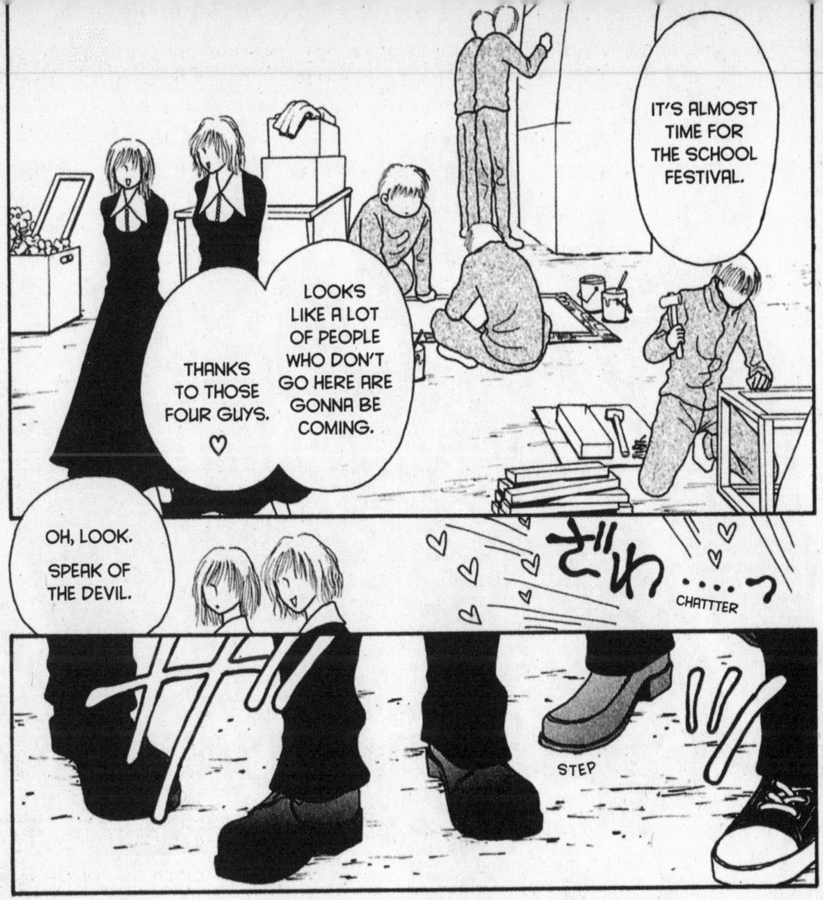
IT'S ALMOST TIME FOR THE SCHOOL FESTIVAL.
LOOKS LIKE A LOT OF PEOPLE WHO DON'T GO HERE ARE GONNA BE COMING.
THANKS TO THOSE FOUR GUYS. ♥
ざわ....っ
CHATTTER
OH, LOOK. SPEAK OF THE DEVIL.
STEP

HELLO.

THANK YOU FOR BUYING KODANSHA COMICS, ♥ AND THANKS FOR ALL YOUR LETTERS. ♥

I THINK I'LL USE THIS SPACE TO TAKE A BEHIND-THE-SCENES PEEK AT *THE WALLFLOWER*. PLEASE JOIN ME IF YOU HAVE TIME. THE DAY BEFORE MY DEADLINE FOR THIS BOOK WAS THE BEST DAY OF MY LIFE. I WAS GOING CRAZY, AND MY HEAD WAS SPINNING, BUT I FINISHED IT. (FOR A MORE DETAILED ACCOUNT, PLEASE READ THE BONUS MANGA.)

SUNAKO'S EXTREME SWEATING AT THE END OF THE BOOK REALLY CAN HAPPEN. WHEN PEOPLE GET SEVERELY NERVOUS, THEY SWEAT JUST LIKE THAT.

THANKS TO EVERYBODY WHO HELPED ME ON THIS BOOK.
CHITOSE SAKURA, MACHIKO SAKURA AND THE GENIUS HANA-CHAN.

I LOVE THE NEWS CLIPPINGS YOU GUYS SEND TOO. IT MIGHT TAKE ME A WHILE, BUT I'LL TRY TO WRITE BACK TO EVERYONE.

THE BEAUTIFUL BACKGROUNDS, THE SKELETONS AND THE BLOOD AND GUTS WERE ALL DRAWN BY THAT GENIUS HANA-CHAN.

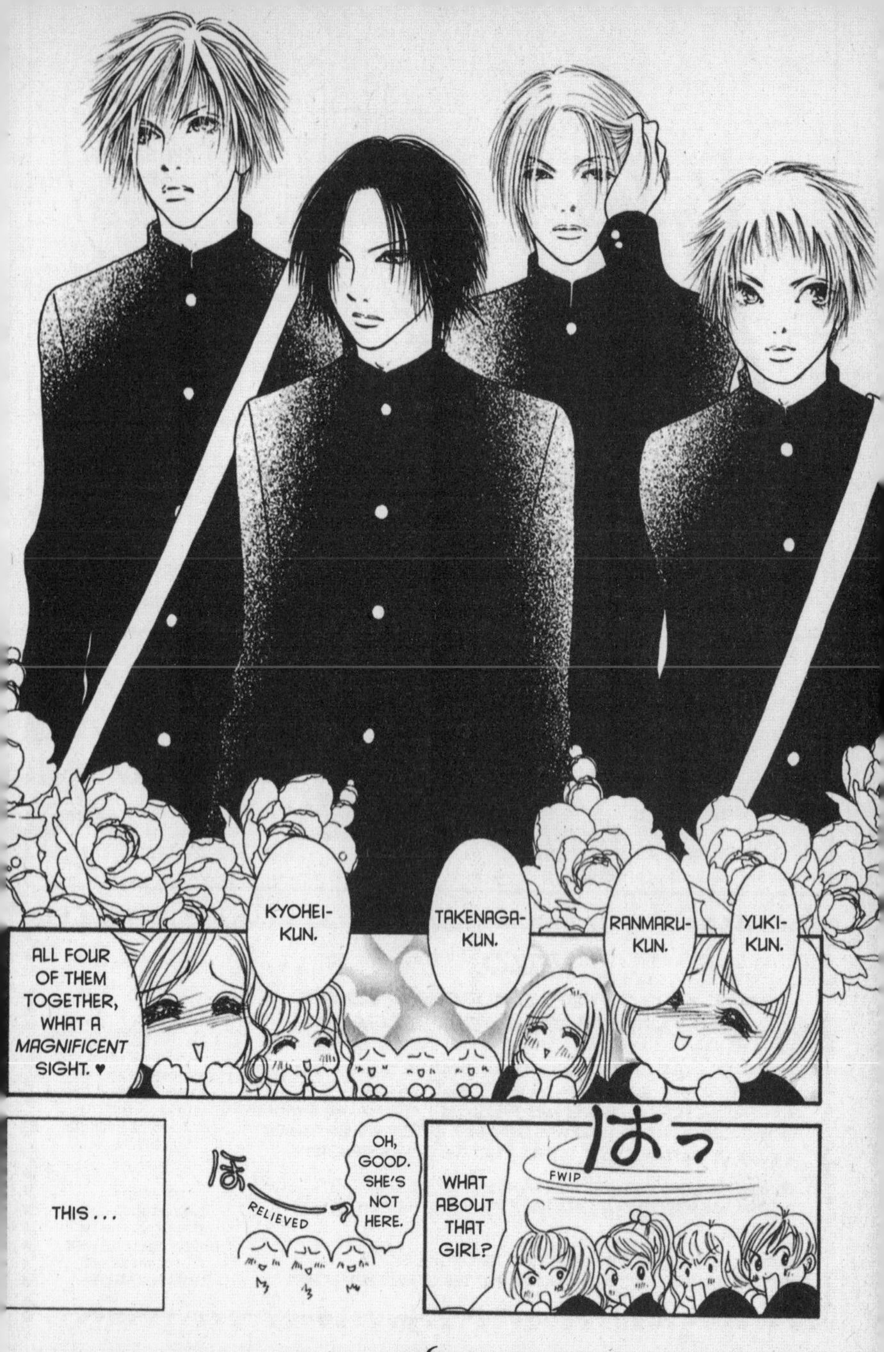
YUKI-KUN.
RANMARU-KUN.
TAKENAGA-KUN.
KYOHEI-KUN.
ALL FOUR OF THEM TOGETHER, WHAT A *MAGNIFICENT* SIGHT. ♥
はっ
FWIP
WHAT ABOUT THAT GIRL?
ほ—
RELIEVED
OH, GOOD. SHE'S NOT HERE.
THIS...

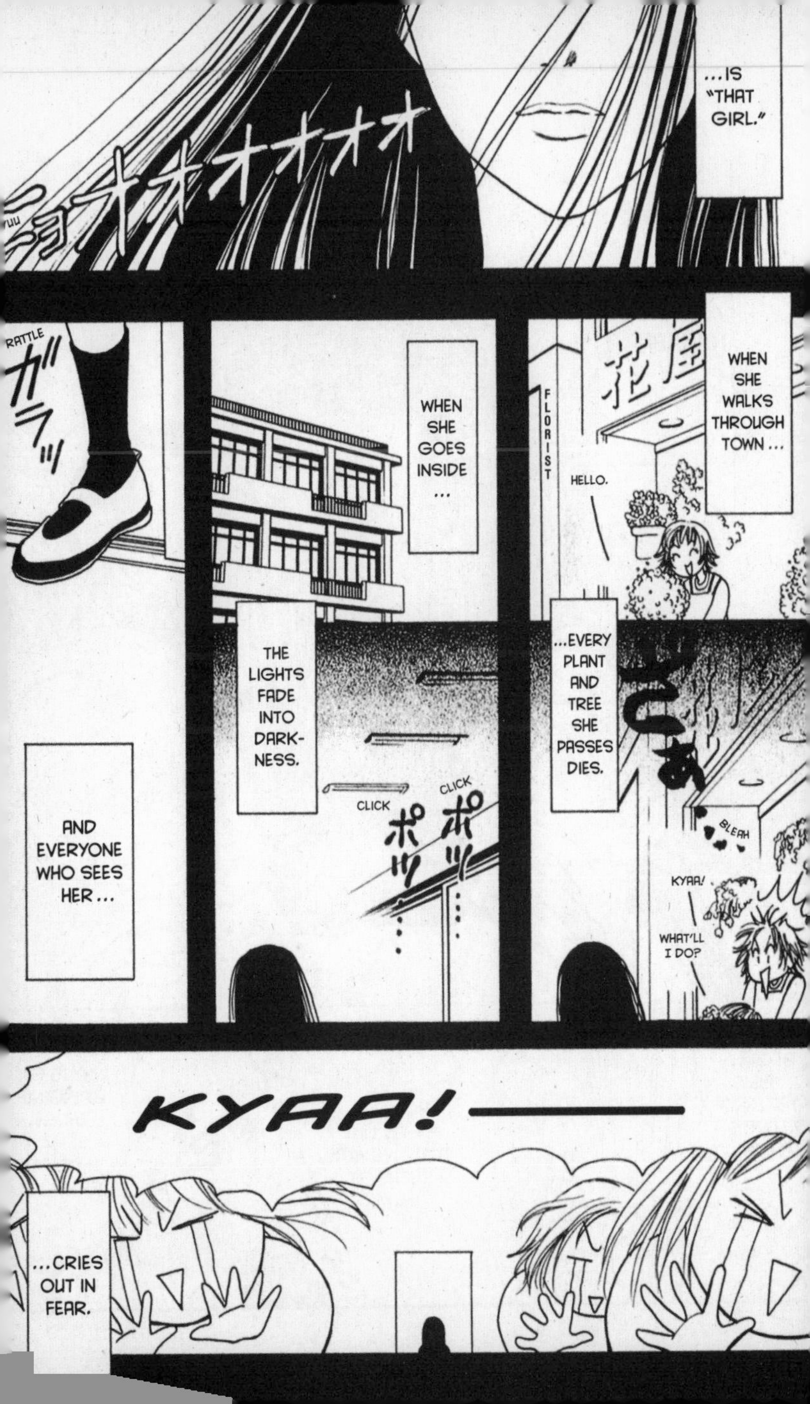

...IS "THAT GIRL."
YUU
WHEN SHE WALKS THROUGH TOWN...
FLORIST
HELLO.
...EVERY PLANT AND TREE SHE PASSES DIES.
BLEAH
KYAA!
WHAT'LL I DO?
WHEN SHE GOES INSIDE...
THE LIGHTS FADE INTO DARKNESS.
CLICK
CLICK
RATTLE
AND EVERYONE WHO SEES HER...
KYAA!—
...CRIES OUT IN FEAR.

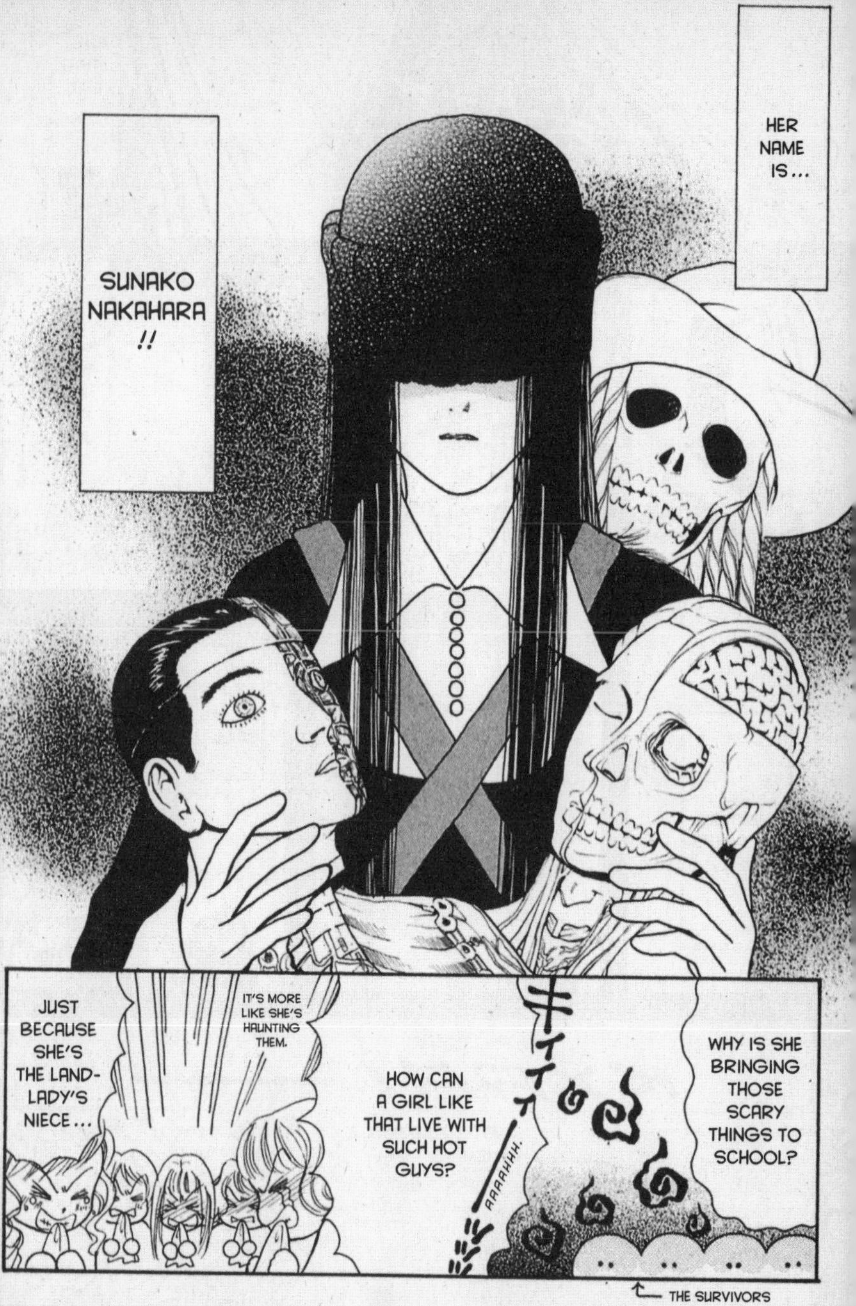
HER NAME IS...
SUNAKO NAKAHARA !!
WHY IS SHE BRINGING THOSE SCARY THINGS TO SCHOOL?
AAAAHHH.
HOW CAN A GIRL LIKE THAT LIVE WITH SUCH HOT GUYS?
IT'S MORE LIKE SHE'S HAUNTING THEM.
JUST BECAUSE SHE'S THE LAND-LADY'S NIECE...
THE SURVIVORS

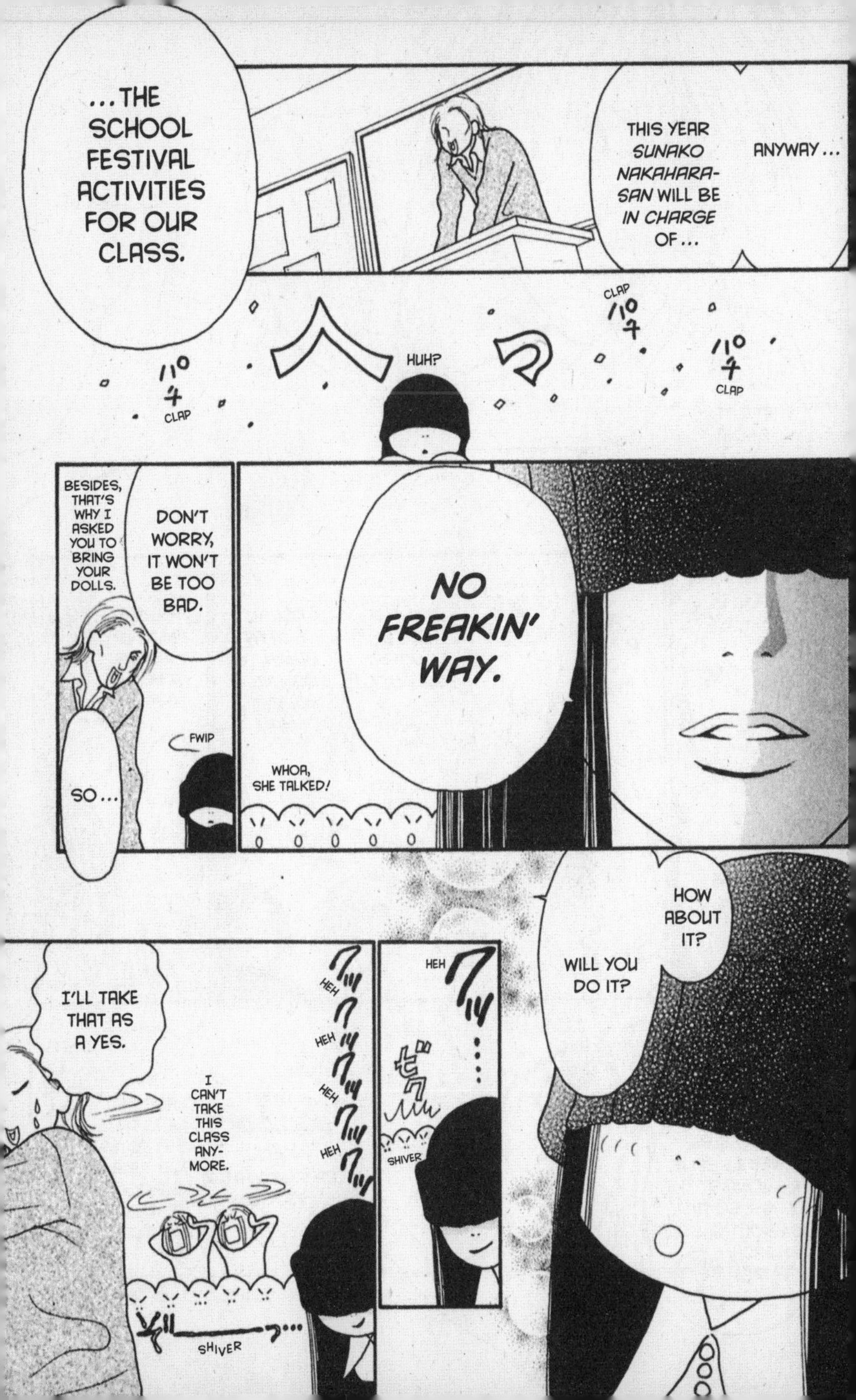
ANYWAY...
THIS YEAR SUNAKO NAKAHARA-SAN WILL BE IN CHARGE OF...
...THE SCHOOL FESTIVAL ACTIVITIES FOR OUR CLASS.
CLAP
CLAP
CLAP
HUH?
NO FREAKIN' WAY.
WHOA, SHE TALKED!
DON'T WORRY, IT WON'T BE TOO BAD.
BESIDES, THAT'S WHY I ASKED YOU TO BRING YOUR DOLLS.
FWIP
SO...
HOW ABOUT IT?
WILL YOU DO IT?
HEH
SHIVER
HEH
HEH
HEH
HEH
I CAN'T TAKE THIS CLASS ANYMORE.
I'LL TAKE THAT AS A YES.
SHIVER

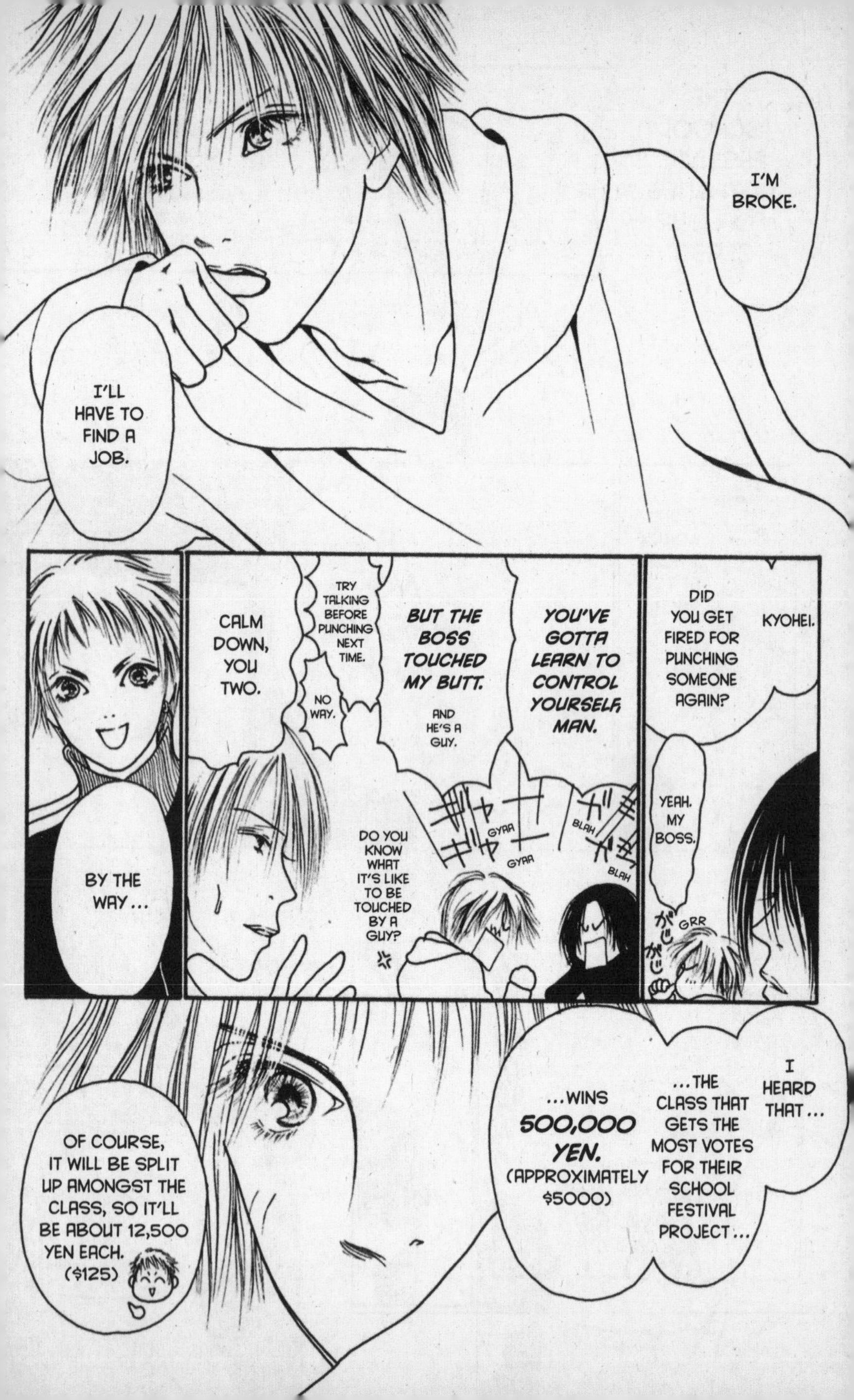
I'M BROKE.
I'LL HAVE TO FIND A JOB.
KYOHEI.
DID YOU GET FIRED FOR PUNCHING SOMEONE AGAIN?
YEAH. MY BOSS.
GRR
YOU'VE GOTTA LEARN TO CONTROL YOURSELF, MAN.
BUT THE BOSS TOUCHED MY BUTT.
AND HE'S A GUY.
TRY TALKING BEFORE PUNCHING NEXT TIME.
NO WAY.
CALM DOWN, YOU TWO.
BLAH BLAH
GYAA GYAA
DO YOU KNOW WHAT IT'S LIKE TO BE TOUCHED BY A GUY?
BY THE WAY...
I HEARD THAT...
...THE CLASS THAT GETS THE MOST VOTES FOR THEIR SCHOOL FESTIVAL PROJECT...
...WINS 500,000 YEN. (APPROXIMATELY $5000)
OF COURSE, IT WILL BE SPLIT UP AMONGST THE CLASS, SO IT'LL BE ABOUT 12,500 YEN EACH. ($125)

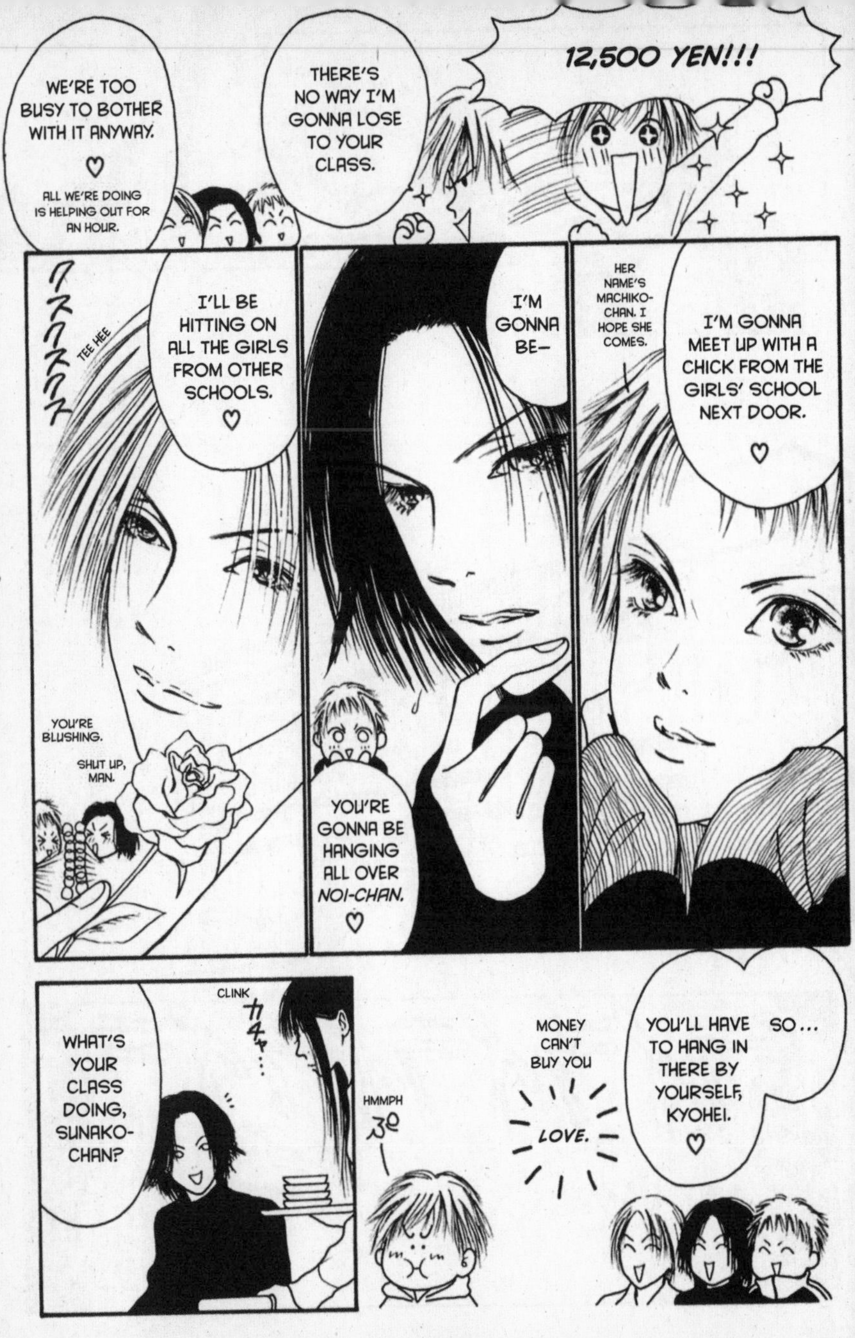
12,500 YEN!!!
THERE'S NO WAY I'M GONNA LOSE TO YOUR CLASS.
WE'RE TOO BUSY TO BOTHER WITH IT ANYWAY. ♡
ALL WE'RE DOING IS HELPING OUT FOR AN HOUR.
I'M GONNA MEET UP WITH A CHICK FROM THE GIRLS' SCHOOL NEXT DOOR. ♡
HER NAME'S MACHIKO-CHAN. I HOPE SHE COMES.
I'M GONNA BE—
YOU'RE GONNA BE HANGING ALL OVER *NOI-CHAN.* ♡
I'LL BE HITTING ON ALL THE GIRLS FROM OTHER SCHOOLS. ♡
TEE HEE
YOU'RE BLUSHING.
SHUT UP, MAN.
SO...
YOU'LL HAVE TO HANG IN THERE BY YOURSELF, KYOHEI. ♡
MONEY CAN'T BUY YOU
LOVE.
HMMPH
CLINK
WHAT'S YOUR CLASS DOING, SUNAKO-CHAN?

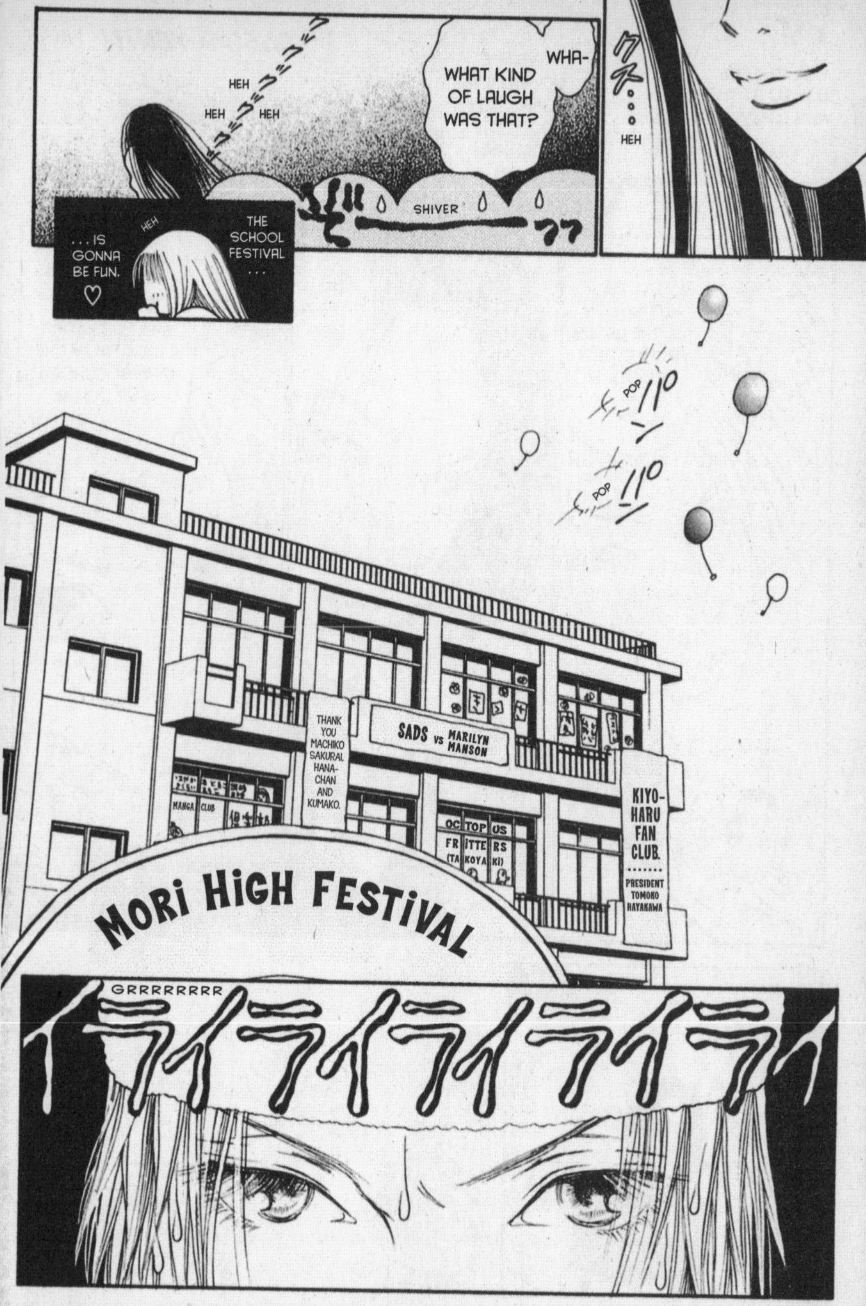
HEH
WHA-
WHAT KIND OF LAUGH WAS THAT?
HEH HEH HEH
SHIVER
THE SCHOOL FESTIVAL . . .
HEH
. . . IS GONNA BE FUN. ♡
POP
POP
KIYO-HARU FAN CLUB. PRESIDENT TOMOKO HAYAKAWA
SADS vs MARILYN MANSON
THANK YOU MACHIKO SAKURAI, HANA-CHAN AND KUMAKO.
OCTOPUS FRITTERS (TAKOYAKI)
MANGA CLUB
MORI HIGH FESTIVAL
GRRRRRRRR

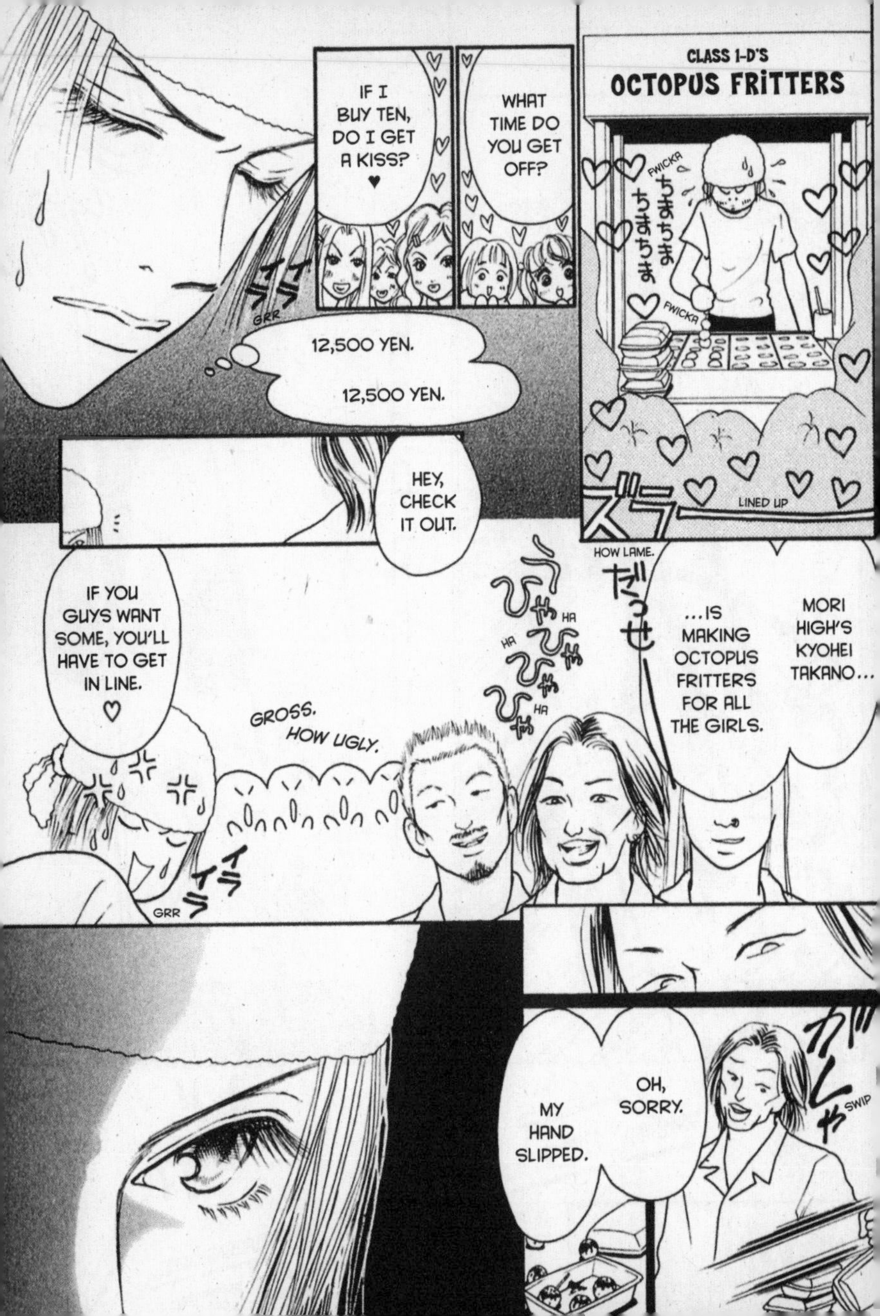
CLASS 1-D'S
OCTOPUS FRITTERS
FWICKA
FWICKA
LINED UP
WHAT TIME DO YOU GET OFF?
IF I BUY TEN, DO I GET A KISS? ♥
GRR
12,500 YEN.
12,500 YEN.
HEY, CHECK IT OUT.
MORI HIGH'S KYOHEI TAKANO...
...IS MAKING OCTOPUS FRITTERS FOR ALL THE GIRLS.
HOW LAME.
HA
HA
HA
GROSS.
HOW UGLY.
IF YOU GUYS WANT SOME, YOU'LL HAVE TO GET IN LINE. ♡
GRR
OH, SORRY.
MY HAND SLIPPED.
SWIP

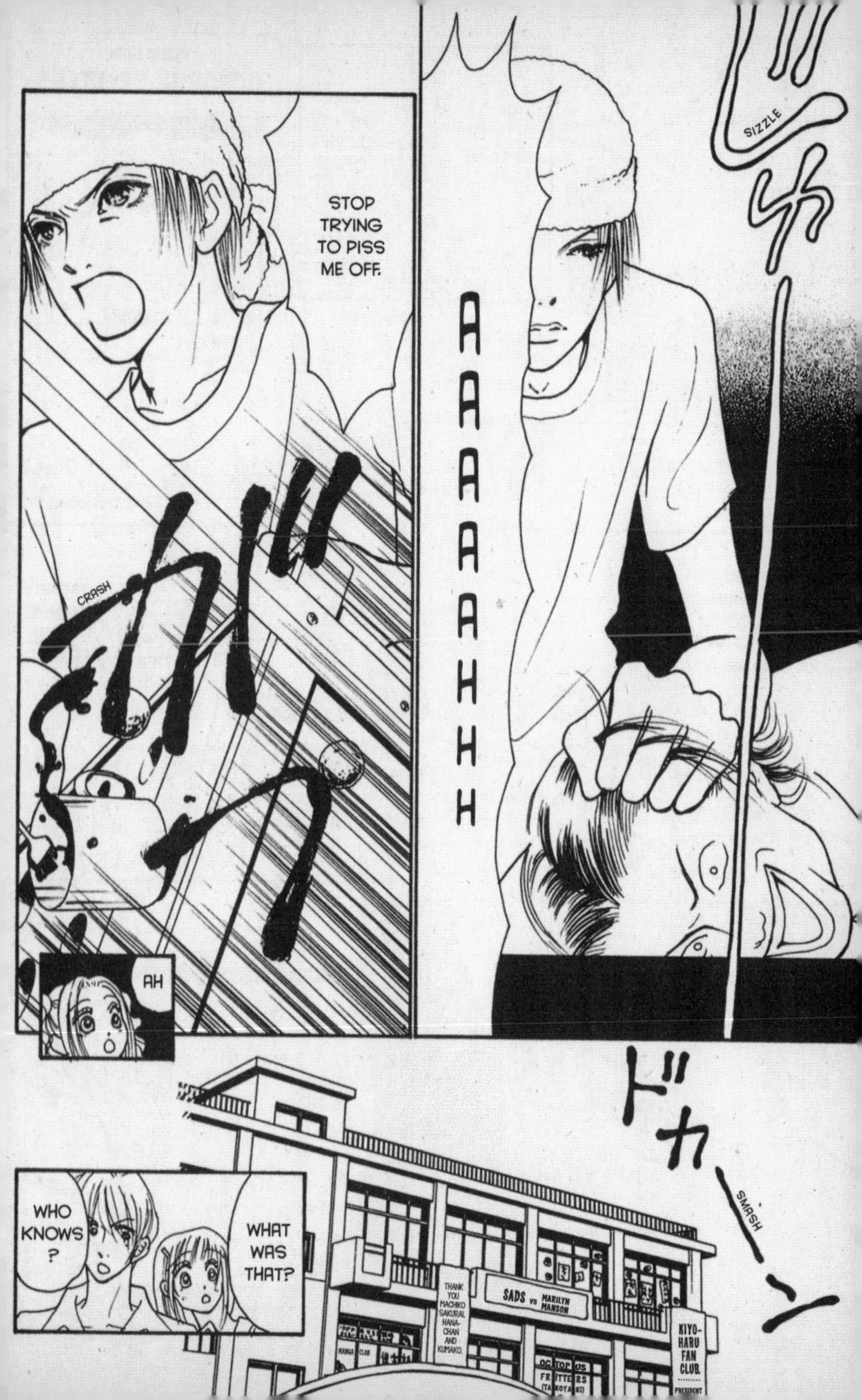
SIZZLE
AAAAAAHHH
STOP TRYING TO PISS ME OFF.
CRASH
AH
SMASH
KIYO-HARU FAN CLUB.
PRESIDENT
OCTOPUS FRITTERS (TAKOYAKI)
SADS vs MARILYN MANSON
THANK YOU MACHIKO SAKURAI, HANA-CHAN AND KUMAKO.
MANGA CLUB
WHAT WAS THAT?
WHO KNOWS?

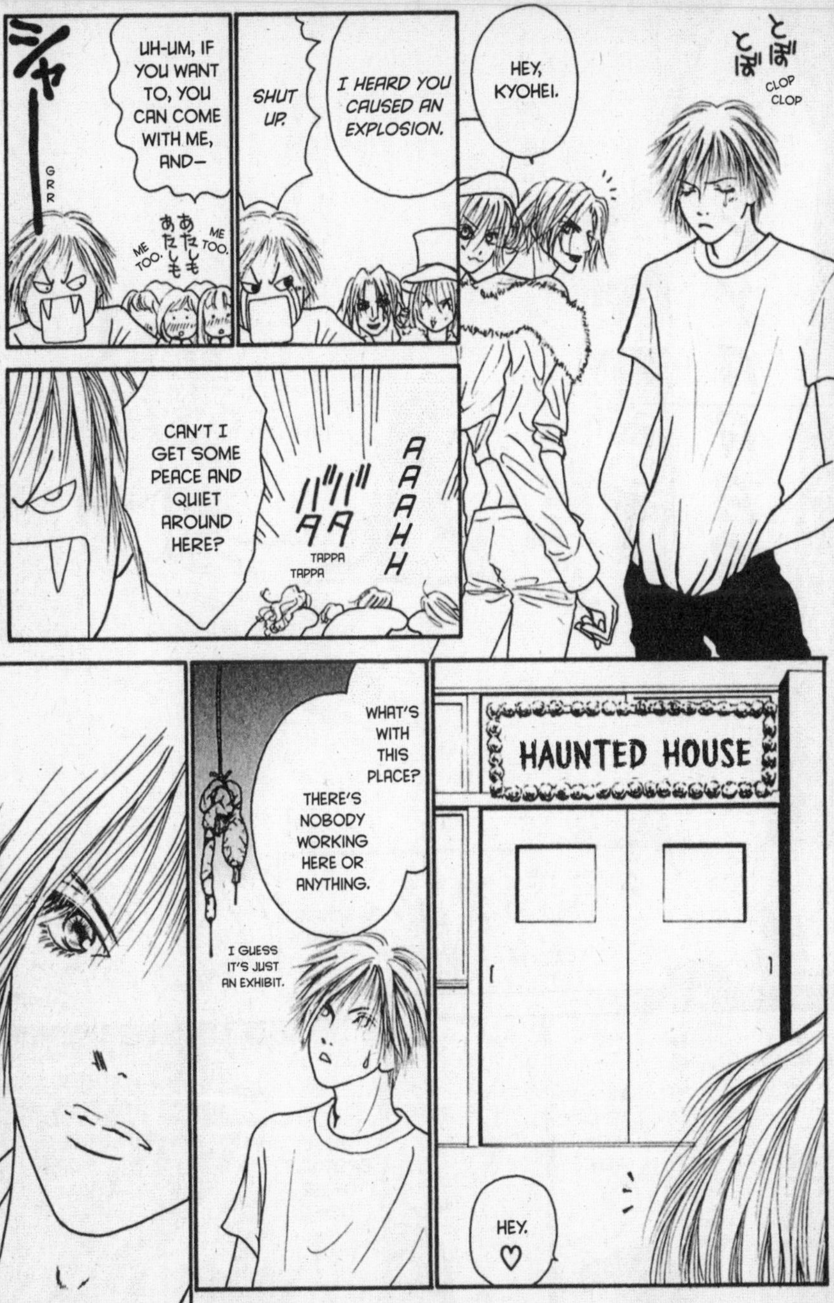
とぼとぼ
CLOP CLOP
HEY, KYOHEI.
I HEARD YOU CAUSED AN EXPLOSION.
SHUT UP.
UH-UM, IF YOU WANT TO, YOU CAN COME WITH ME, AND—
あたしもあたしも
ME TOO. ME TOO.
シャー
GRR
CAN'T I GET SOME PEACE AND QUIET AROUND HERE?
AAAAHH
バタバタ
TAPPA TAPPA
HAUNTED HOUSE
HEY. ♡
WHAT'S WITH THIS PLACE? THERE'S NOBODY WORKING HERE OR ANYTHING.
I GUESS IT'S JUST AN EXHIBIT.

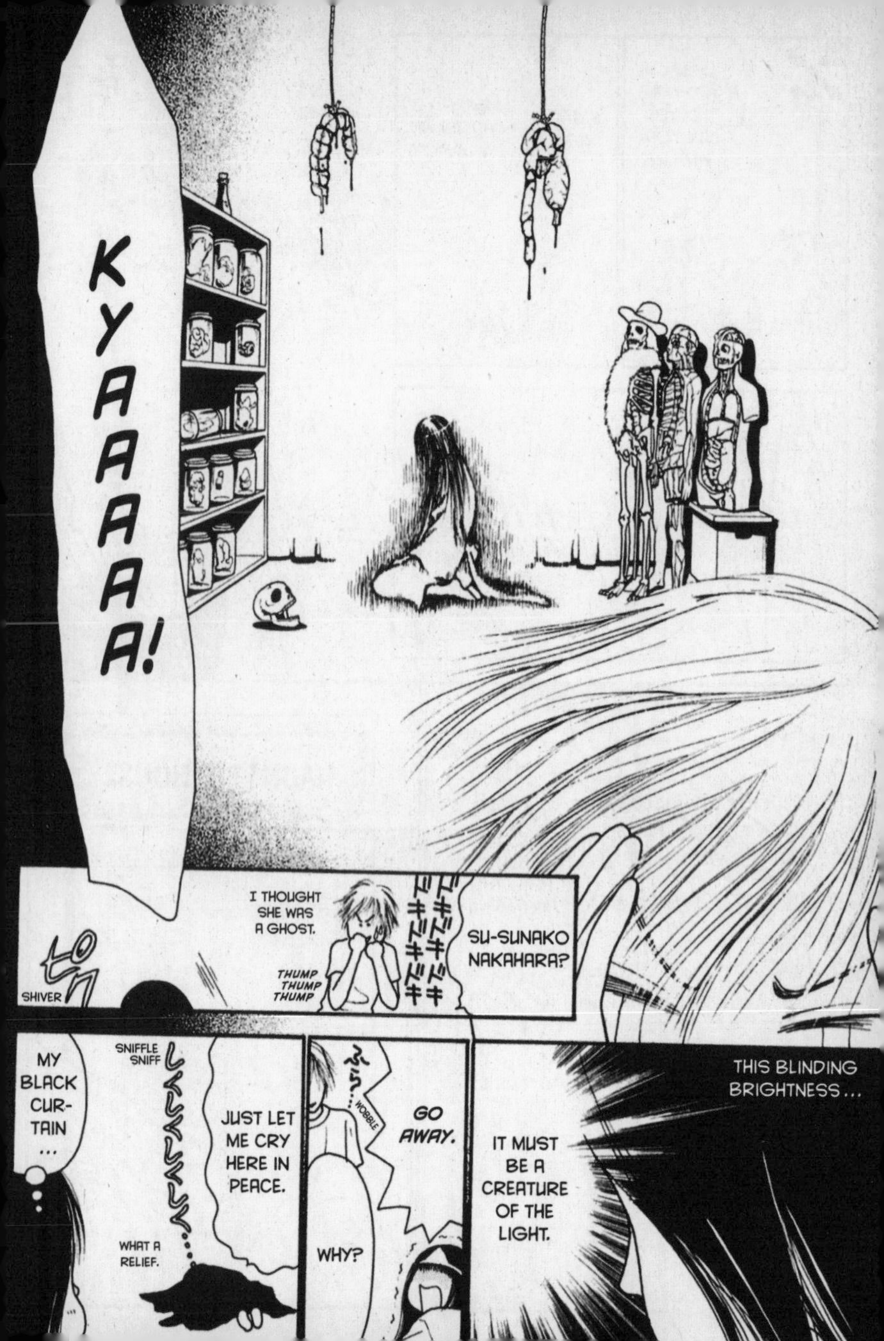
KYAAAAAA!
SU-SUNAKO NAKAHARA?
ドキドキドキ
ドキドキドキ
THUMP THUMP THUMP
I THOUGHT SHE WAS A GHOST.
ピク
SHIVER
THIS BLINDING BRIGHTNESS…
IT MUST BE A CREATURE OF THE LIGHT.
GO AWAY.
ふら…
WOBBLE
WHY?
JUST LET ME CRY HERE IN PEACE.
しくしくしくしく…
SNIFFLE SNIFF
WHAT A RELIEF.
MY BLACK CUR-TAIN …

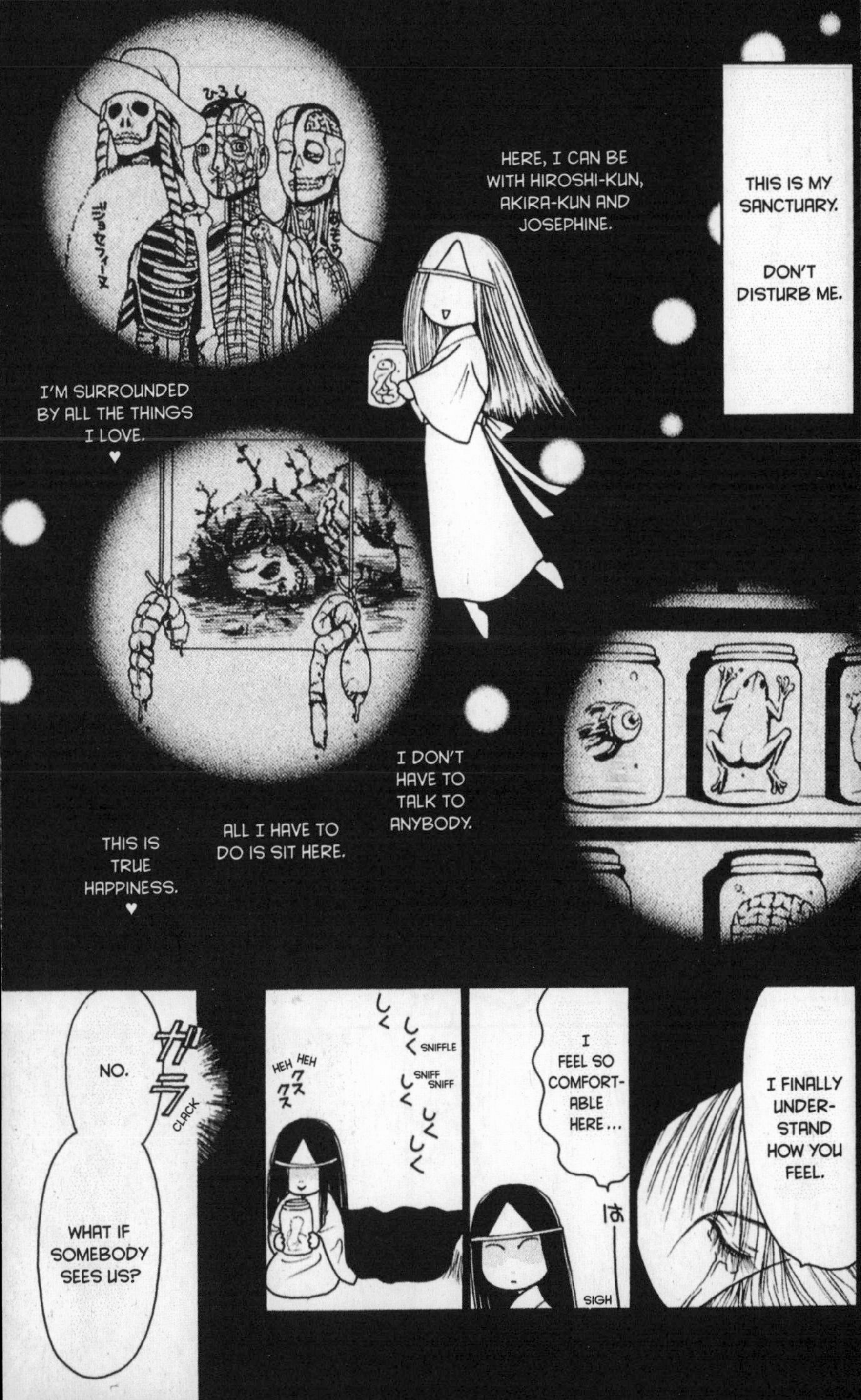

THIS IS MY SANCTUARY.
DON'T DISTURB ME.
HERE, I CAN BE WITH HIROSHI-KUN, AKIRA-KUN AND JOSEPHINE.
I'M SURROUNDED BY ALL THE THINGS I LOVE. ♥
I DON'T HAVE TO TALK TO ANYBODY.
ALL I HAVE TO DO IS SIT HERE.
THIS IS TRUE HAPPINESS. ♥
I FINALLY UNDERSTAND HOW YOU FEEL.
I FEEL SO COMFORTABLE HERE...
は
SIGH
しく しく
SNIFFLE
しく しく
SNIFF SNIFF
しく しく
クスクス
HEH HEH
ガラ
CLACK
NO.
WHAT IF SOMEBODY SEES US?

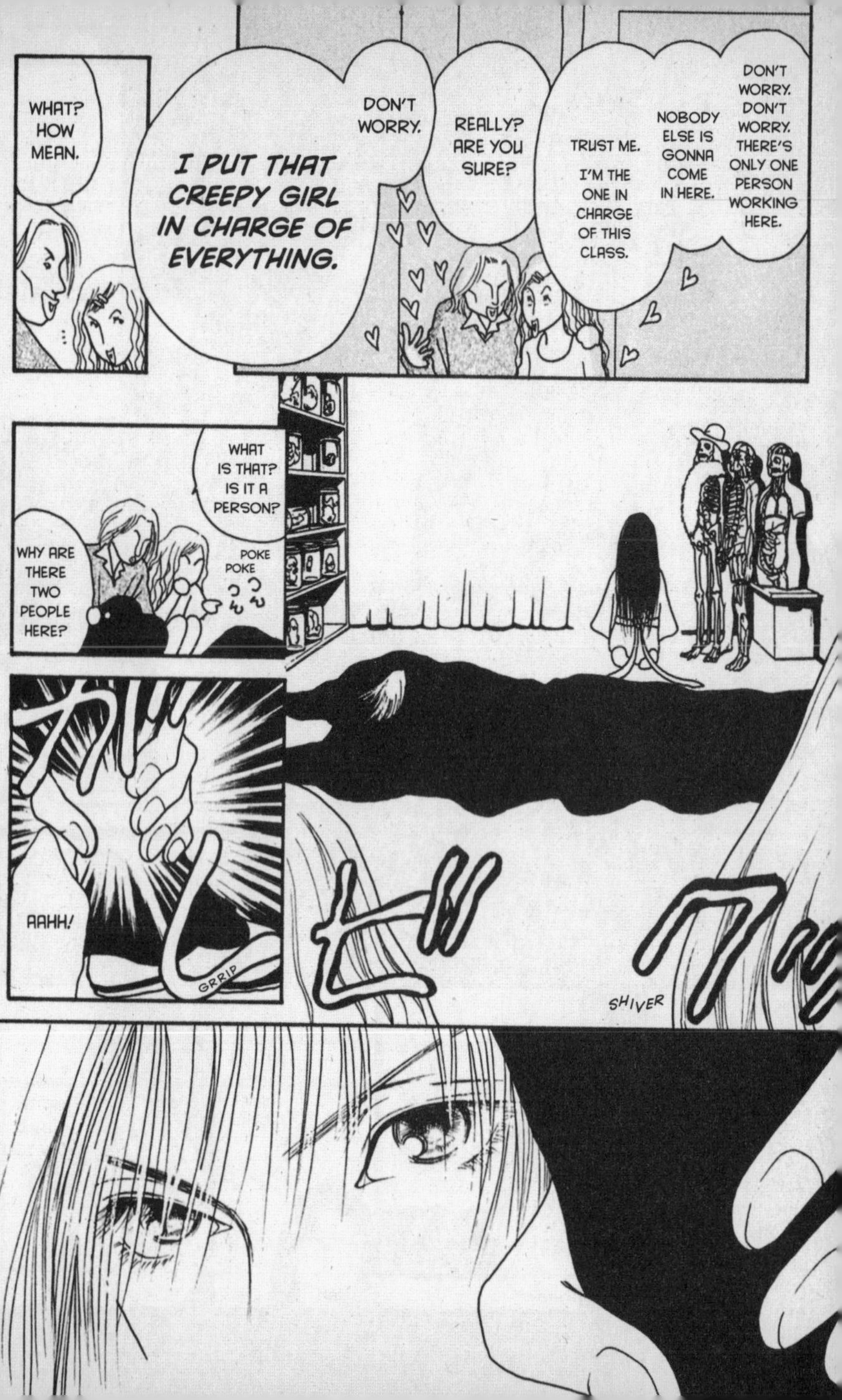
DON'T WORRY. DON'T WORRY. THERE'S ONLY ONE PERSON WORKING HERE.
NOBODY ELSE IS GONNA COME IN HERE.
TRUST ME. I'M THE ONE IN CHARGE OF THIS CLASS.
REALLY? ARE YOU SURE?
DON'T WORRY.
I PUT THAT CREEPY GIRL IN CHARGE OF EVERYTHING.
WHAT? HOW MEAN.
WHAT IS THAT? IS IT A PERSON?
POKE POKE
WHY ARE THERE TWO PEOPLE HERE?
SHIVER
AAHH!
GRRIP

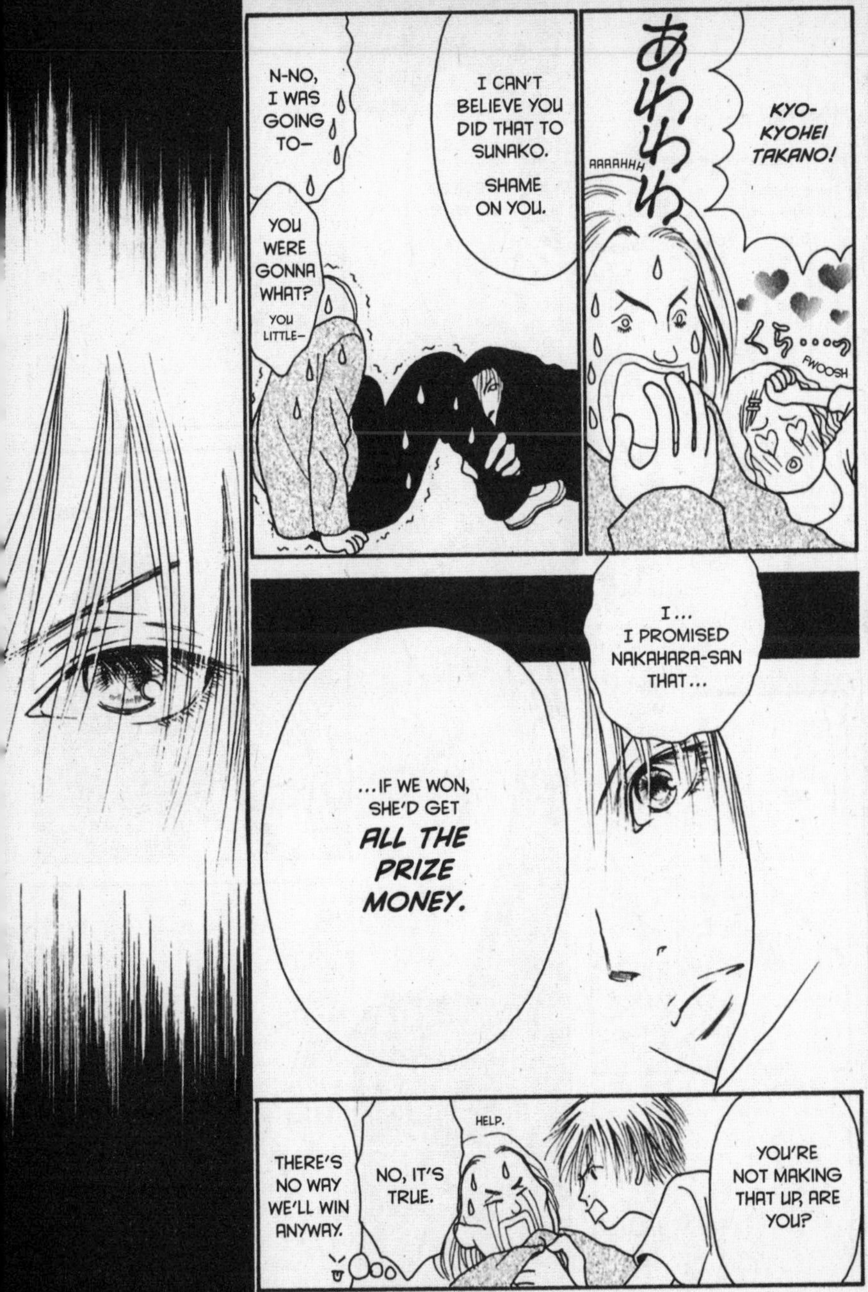

あわわ
AAAAHHH
KYO-KYOHEI TAKANO!
くら…っ
FWOOSH
I CAN'T BELIEVE YOU DID THAT TO SUNAKO.
SHAME ON YOU.
N-NO, I WAS GOING TO—
YOU WERE GONNA WHAT?
YOU LITTLE—
I... I PROMISED NAKAHARA-SAN THAT...
...IF WE WON, SHE'D GET ALL THE PRIZE MONEY.
YOU'RE NOT MAKING THAT UP, ARE YOU?
HELP.
NO, IT'S TRUE.
THERE'S NO WAY WE'LL WIN ANYWAY.

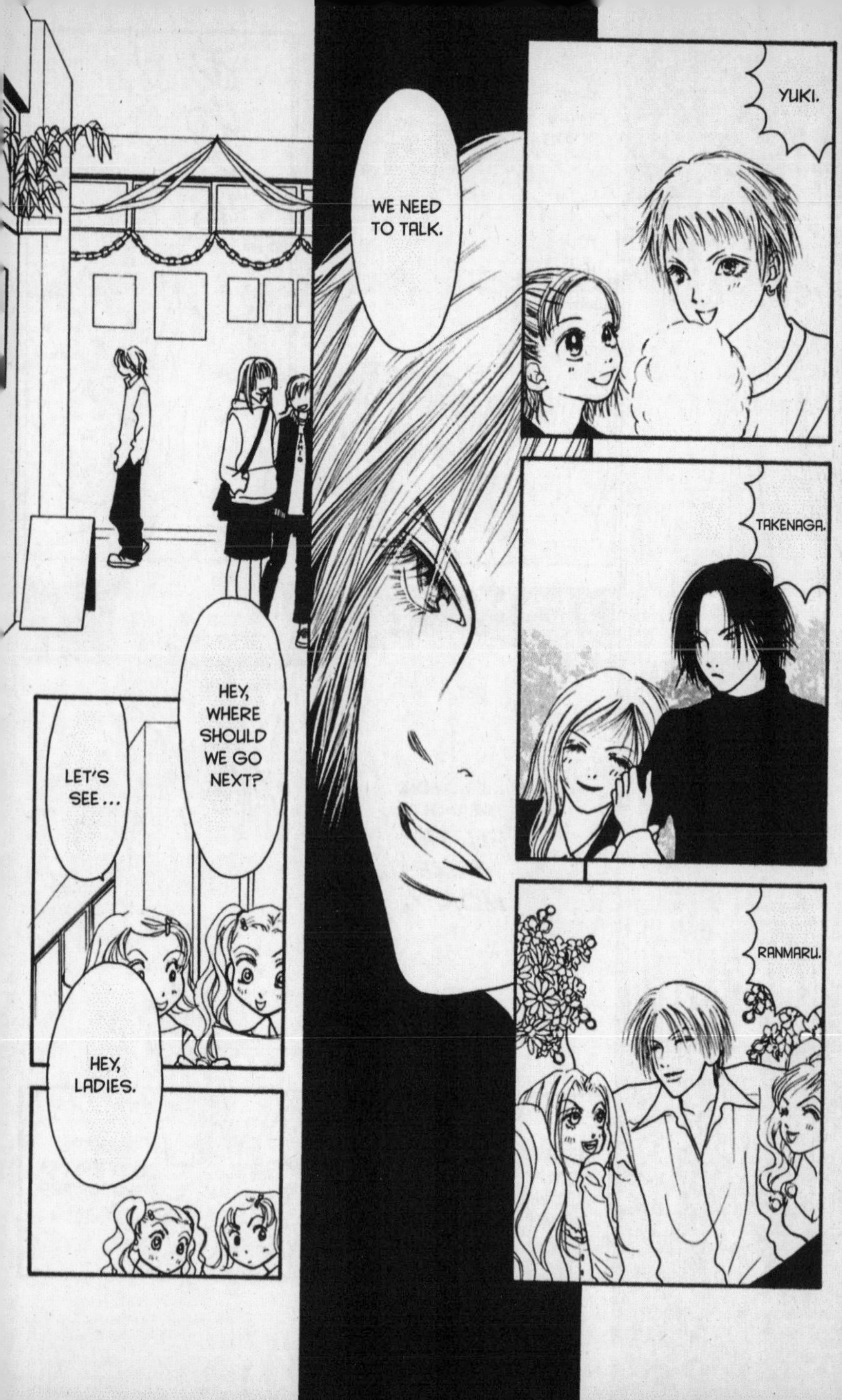
YUKI.
TAKENAGA.
RANMARU.
WE NEED TO TALK.
HEY, WHERE SHOULD WE GO NEXT?
LET'S SEE...
HEY, LADIES.

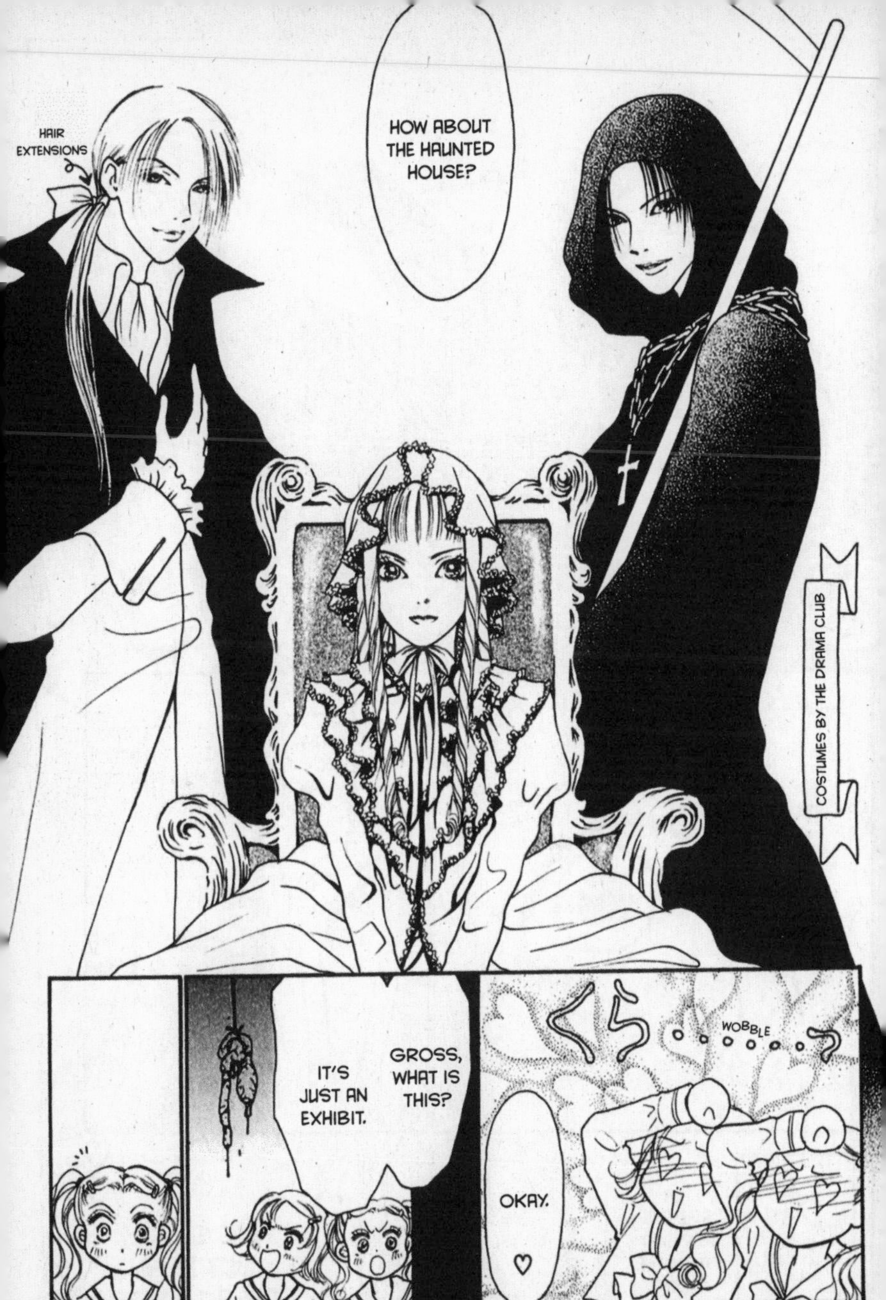

HOW ABOUT THE HAUNTED HOUSE?
COSTUMES BY THE DRAMA CLUB
HAIR EXTENSIONS
くら
WOBBLE
OKAY. ♥
GROSS, WHAT IS THIS?
IT'S JUST AN EXHIBIT.

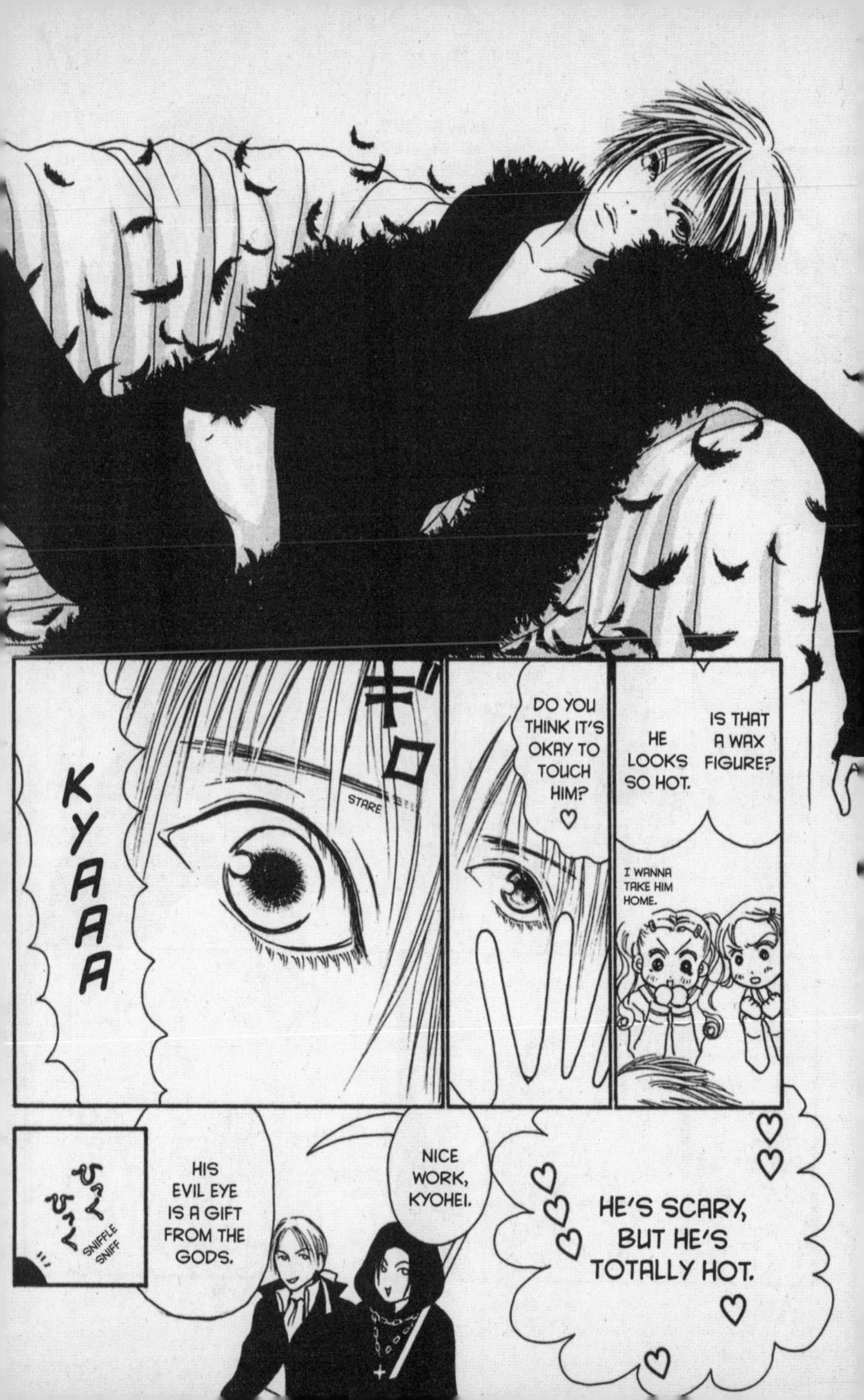
IS THAT A WAX FIGURE?
HE LOOKS SO HOT.
I WANNA TAKE HIM HOME.
DO YOU THINK IT'S OKAY TO TOUCH HIM? ♡
STARE
KYAAA
HE'S SCARY, BUT HE'S TOTALLY HOT.
NICE WORK, KYOHEI.
HIS EVIL EYE IS A GIFT FROM THE GODS.
SNIFFLE SNIFF

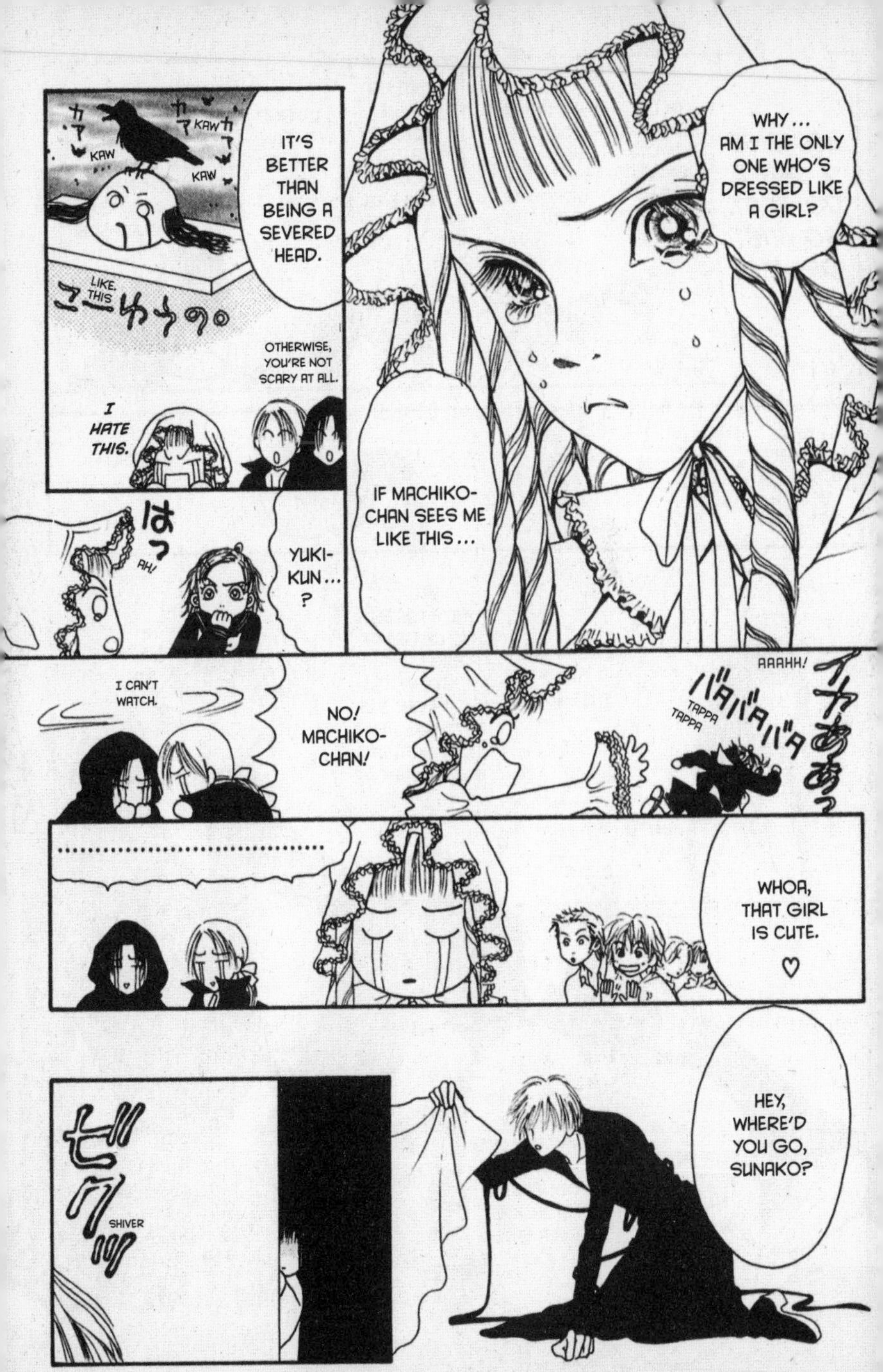
WHY... AM I THE ONLY ONE WHO'S DRESSED LIKE A GIRL?
IF MACHIKO-CHAN SEES ME LIKE THIS...
KAW
KAW
KAW
IT'S BETTER THAN BEING A SEVERED HEAD.
LIKE THIS.
OTHERWISE, YOU'RE NOT SCARY AT ALL.
I HATE THIS.
YUKI-KUN...?
AH!
AAAHH!
TAPPA TAPPA
NO! MACHIKO-CHAN!
I CAN'T WATCH.
WHOA, THAT GIRL IS CUTE. ♡
....
HEY, WHERE'D YOU GO, SUNAKO?
SHIVER

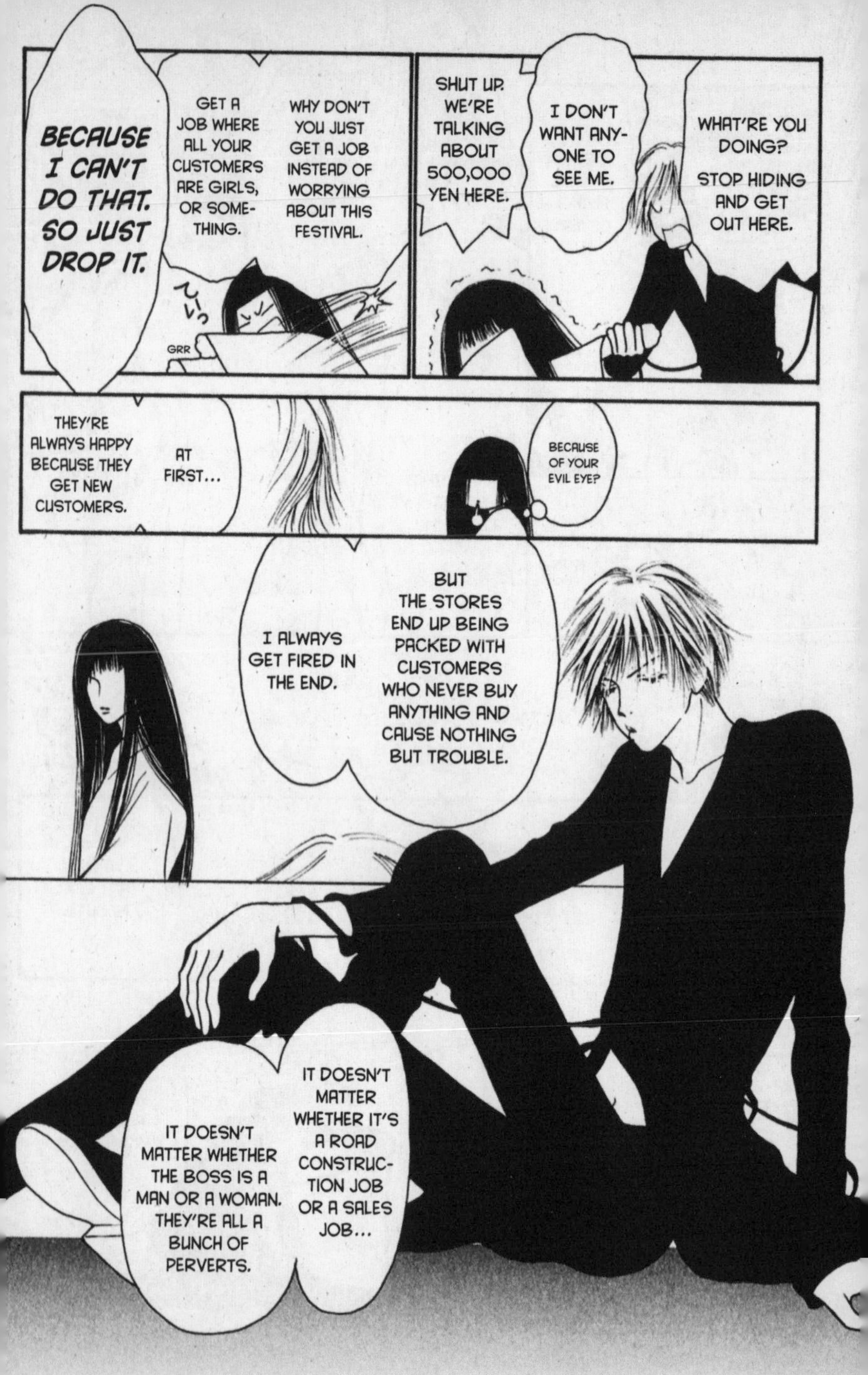
WHAT'RE YOU DOING?
STOP HIDING AND GET OUT HERE.
I DON'T WANT ANYONE TO SEE ME.
SHUT UP. WE'RE TALKING ABOUT 500,000 YEN HERE.
WHY DON'T YOU JUST GET A JOB INSTEAD OF WORRYING ABOUT THIS FESTIVAL.
GET A JOB WHERE ALL YOUR CUSTOMERS ARE GIRLS, OR SOMETHING.
GRR
BECAUSE I CAN'T DO THAT. SO JUST DROP IT.
BECAUSE OF YOUR EVIL EYE?
AT FIRST...
THEY'RE ALWAYS HAPPY BECAUSE THEY GET NEW CUSTOMERS.
BUT THE STORES END UP BEING PACKED WITH CUSTOMERS WHO NEVER BUY ANYTHING AND CAUSE NOTHING BUT TROUBLE.
I ALWAYS GET FIRED IN THE END.
IT DOESN'T MATTER WHETHER IT'S A ROAD CONSTRUCTION JOB OR A SALES JOB...
IT DOESN'T MATTER WHETHER THE BOSS IS A MAN OR A WOMAN. THEY'RE ALL A BUNCH OF PERVERTS.

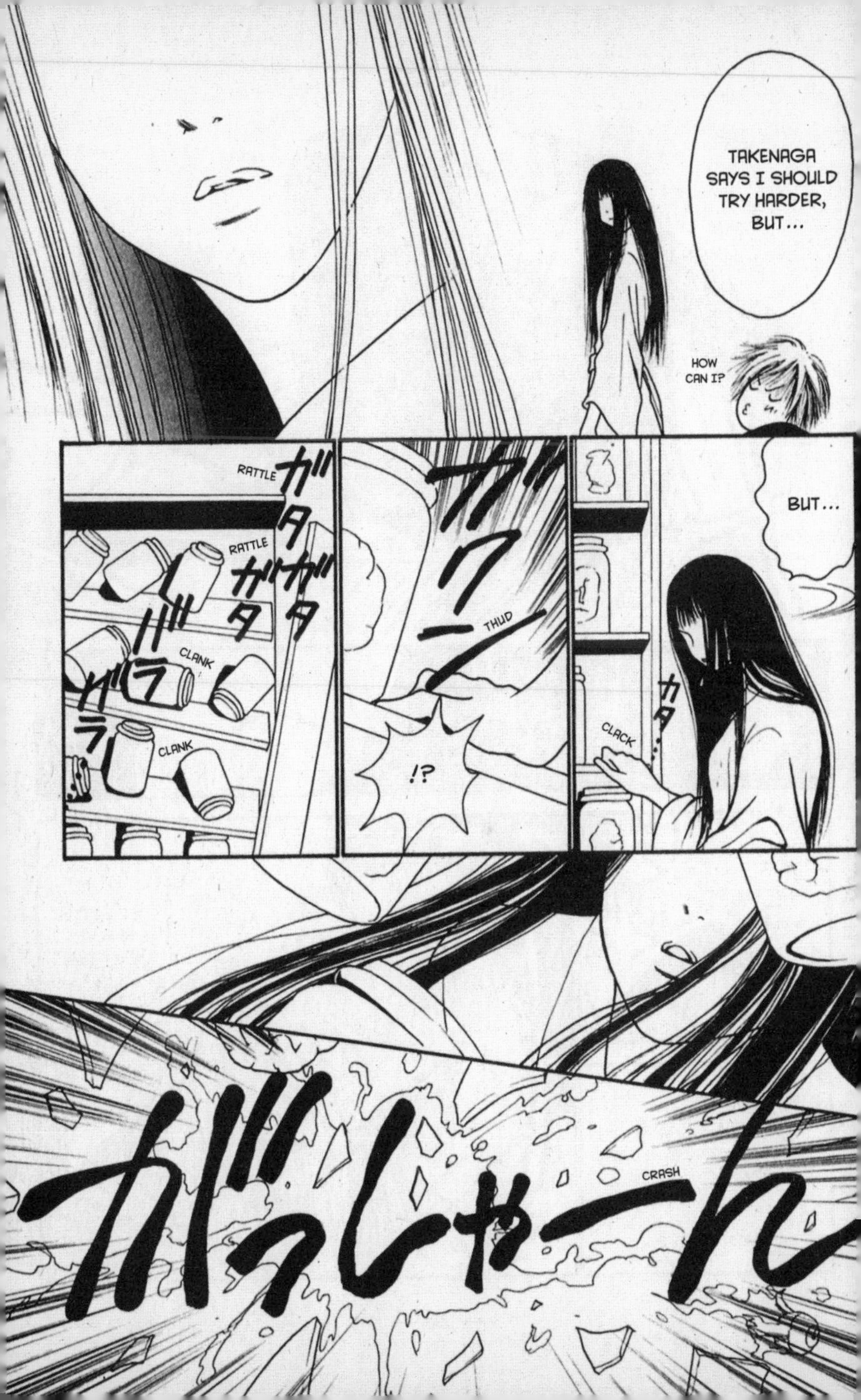
TAKENAGA SAYS I SHOULD TRY HARDER, BUT...
HOW CAN I?
BUT...
CLACK
THUD
!?
RATTLE
RATTLE
CLANK
CLANK
CRASH

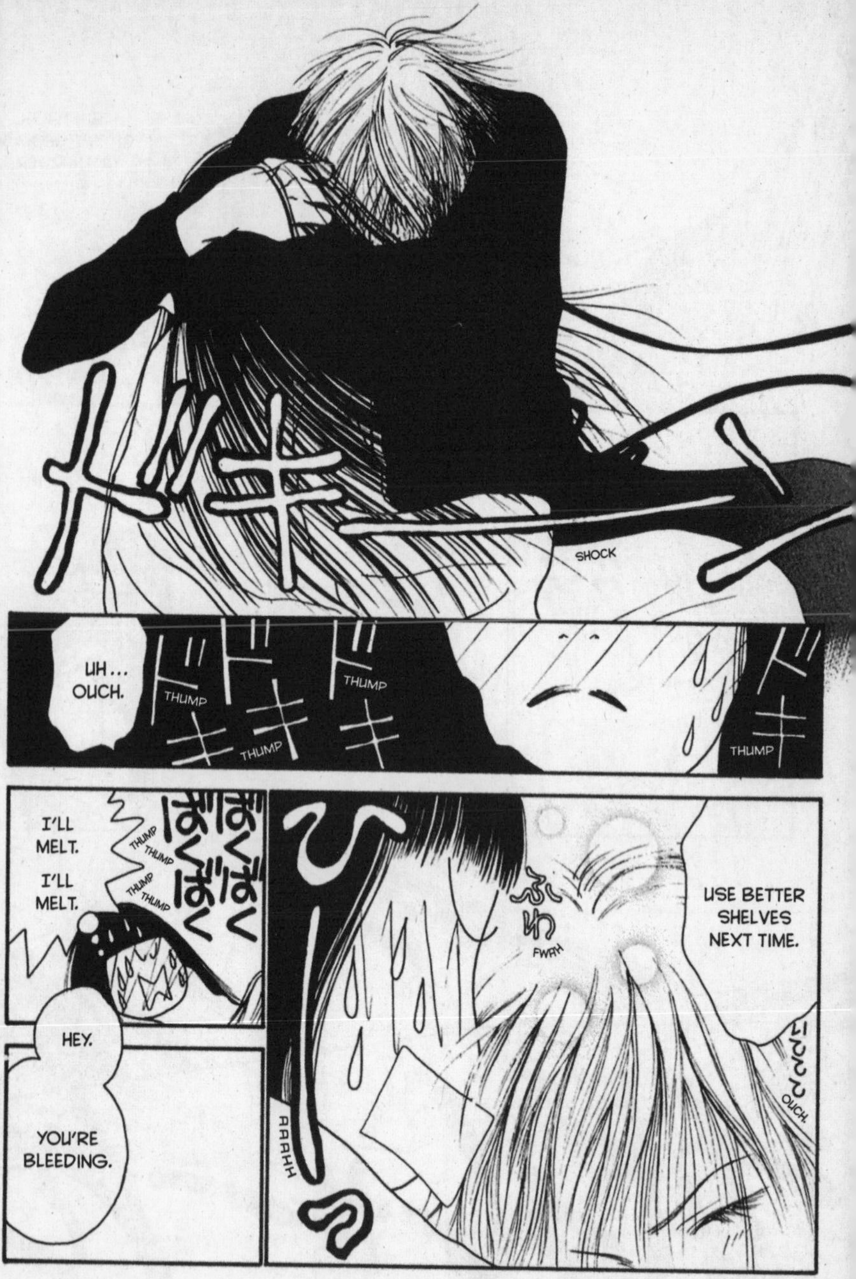
SHOCK
THUMP
THUMP
THUMP
THUMP
UH... OUCH.
USE BETTER SHELVES NEXT TIME.
OUCH.
FWAH
AAAHH
THUMP THUMP THUMP THUMP
I'LL MELT.
I'LL MELT.
HEY.
YOU'RE BLEEDING.

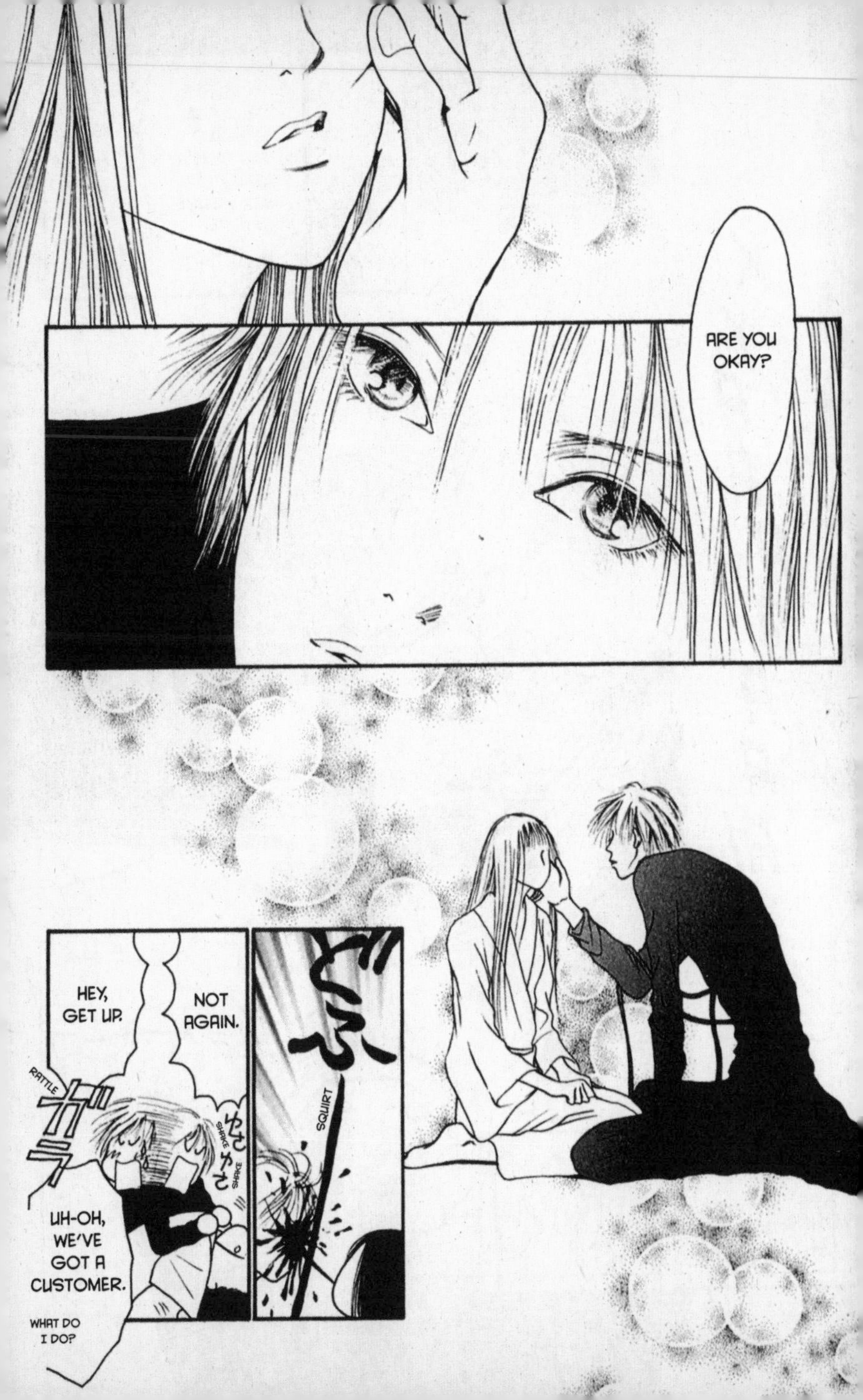
ARE YOU OKAY?
SQUIRT
NOT AGAIN.
HEY, GET UP.
RATTLE
SHAKE SHAKE
UH-OH, WE'VE GOT A CUSTOMER.
WHAT DO I DO?

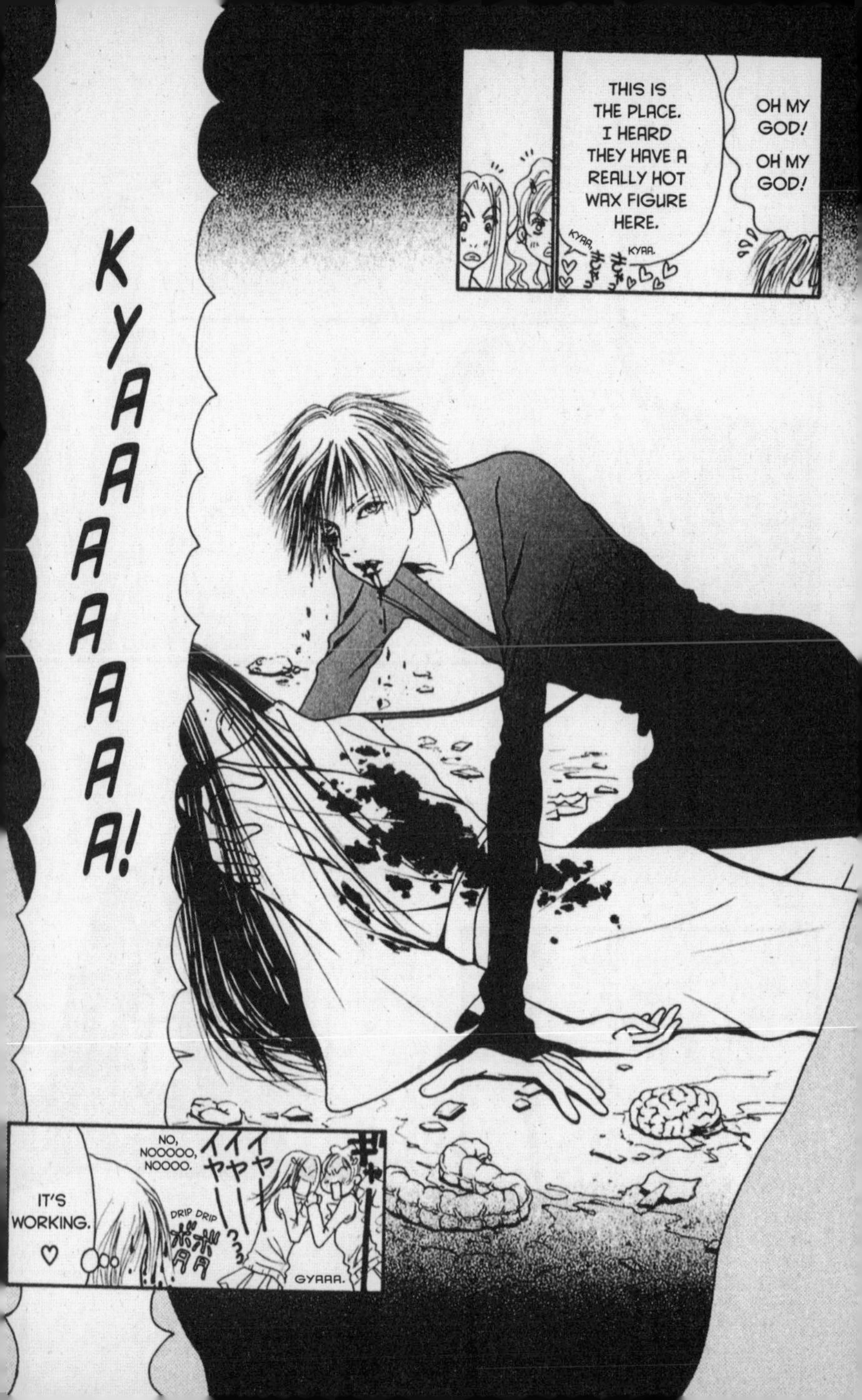
OH MY GOD! OH MY GOD!
THIS IS THE PLACE. I HEARD THEY HAVE A REALLY HOT WAX FIGURE HERE.
KYAA.
KYAA.
KYAAAAAAAAA!
NO, NOOOOO, NOOOO.
DRIP DRIP
GYAAA.
IT'S WORKING. ♡

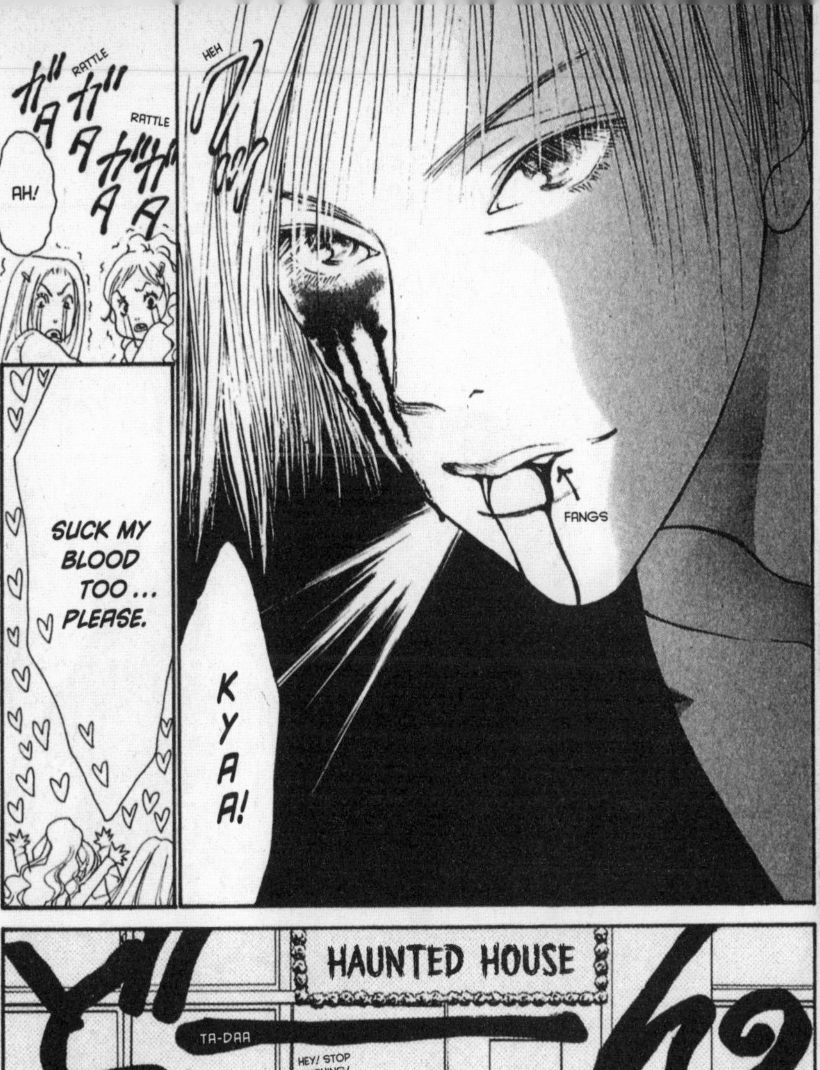
HEH
FANGS
KYAA!
RATTLE
RATTLE
AH!
SUCK MY BLOOD TOO... PLEASE.
HAUNTED HOUSE
TA-DAA
HEY! STOP PUSHING!
SHUFFLE
SHUFFLE

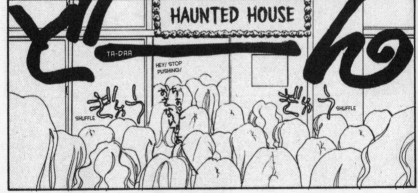

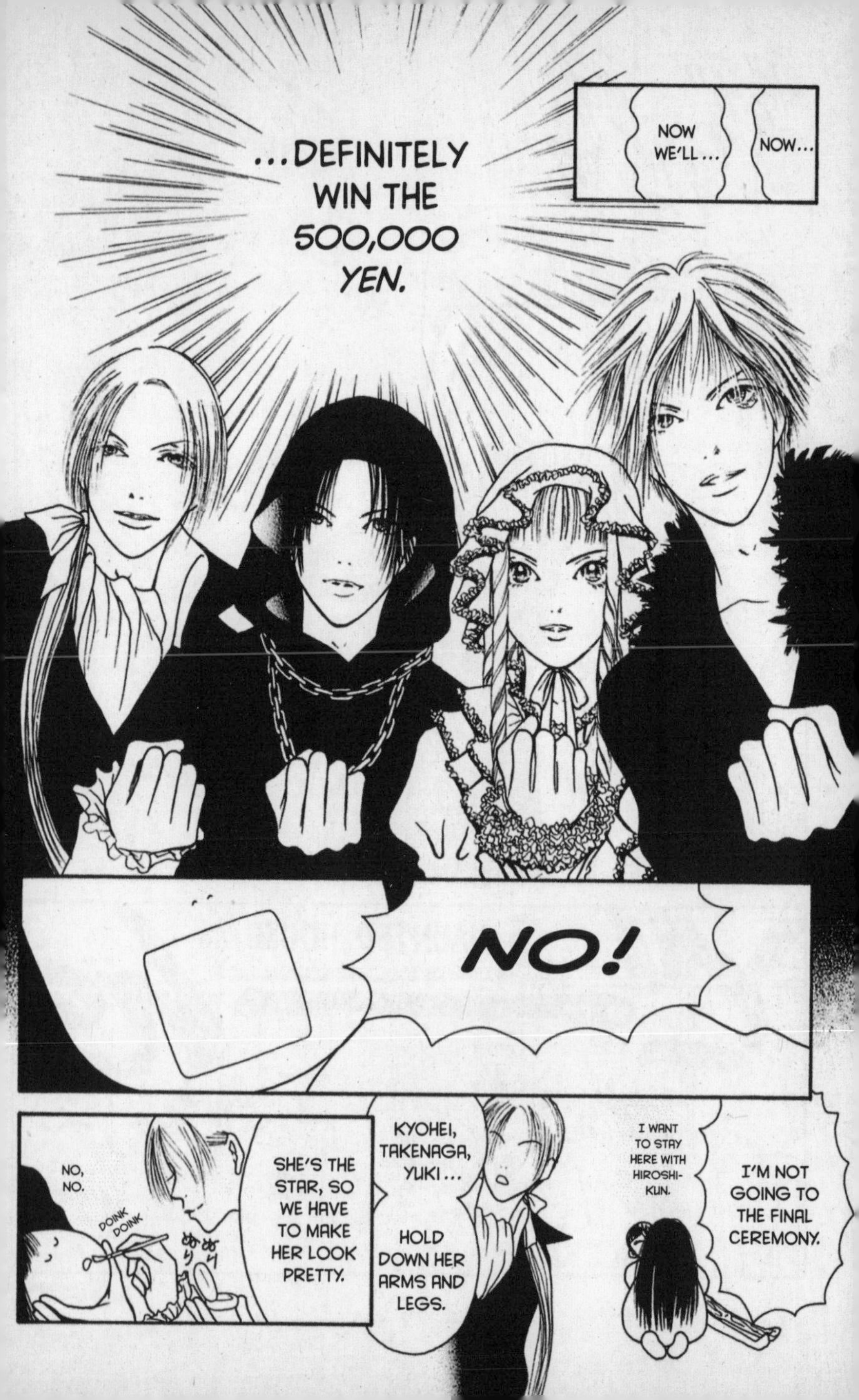
NOW...
NOW WE'LL...
...DEFINITELY WIN THE 500,000 YEN.
NO!
I'M NOT GOING TO THE FINAL CEREMONY.
I WANT TO STAY HERE WITH HIROSHI-KUN.
KYOHEI, TAKENAGA, YUKI...
HOLD DOWN HER ARMS AND LEGS.
SHE'S THE STAR, SO WE HAVE TO MAKE HER LOOK PRETTY.
NO, NO.
DOINK DOINK

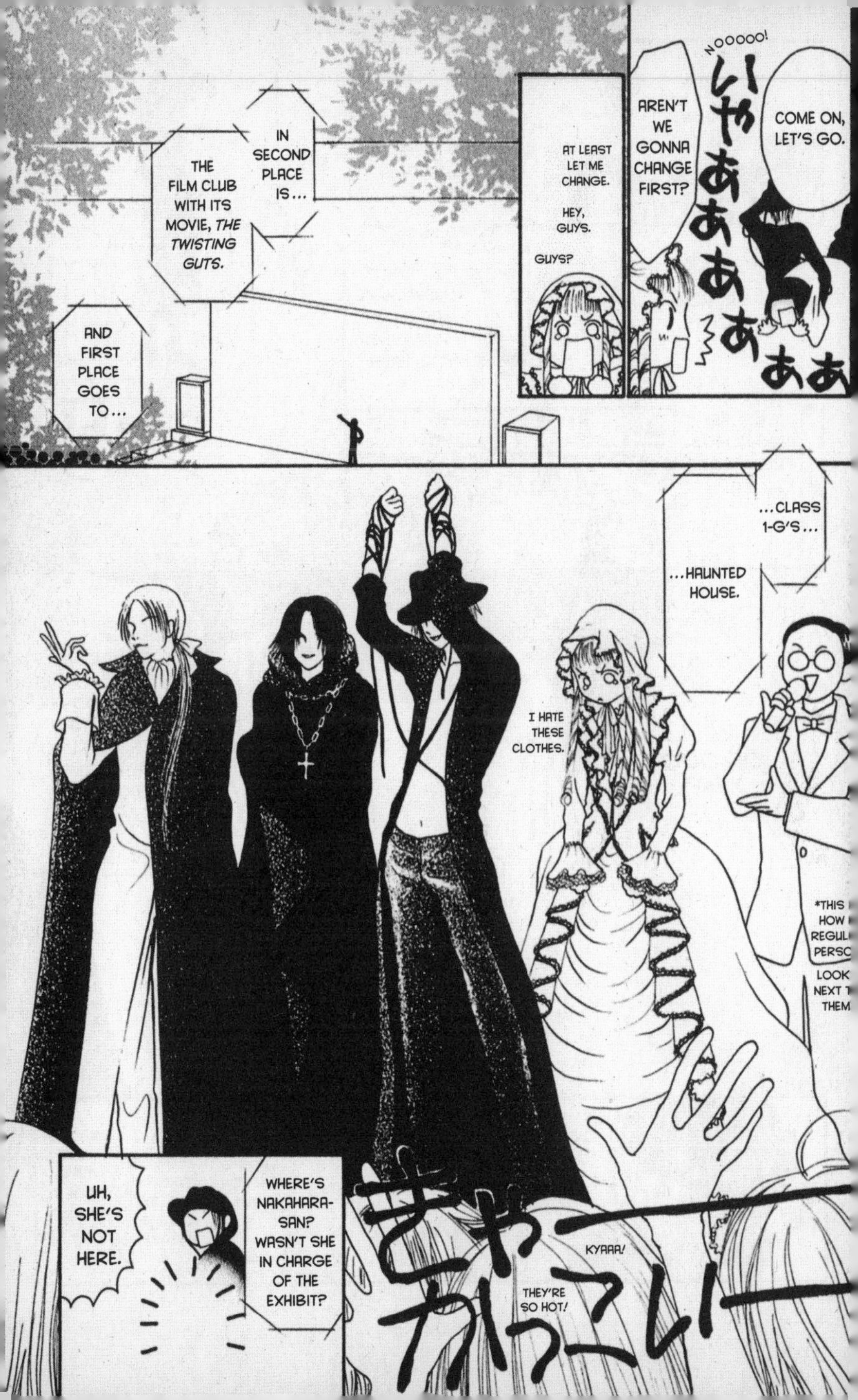
COME ON, LET'S GO.
NOOOOO!
いやあああああ
AREN'T WE GONNA CHANGE FIRST?
AT LEAST LET ME CHANGE.
HEY, GUYS.
GUYS?
IN SECOND PLACE IS...
THE FILM CLUB WITH ITS MOVIE, *THE TWISTING GUTS.*
AND FIRST PLACE GOES TO...
...CLASS 1-G'S...
...HAUNTED HOUSE.
I HATE THESE CLOTHES.
*THIS
HOW
REGUL
PERSO
LOOK
NEXT T
THEM
きゃー
かっこいー
KYAAA!
THEY'RE SO HOT!
WHERE'S NAKAHARA-SAN? WASN'T SHE IN CHARGE OF THE EXHIBIT?
UH, SHE'S NOT HERE.

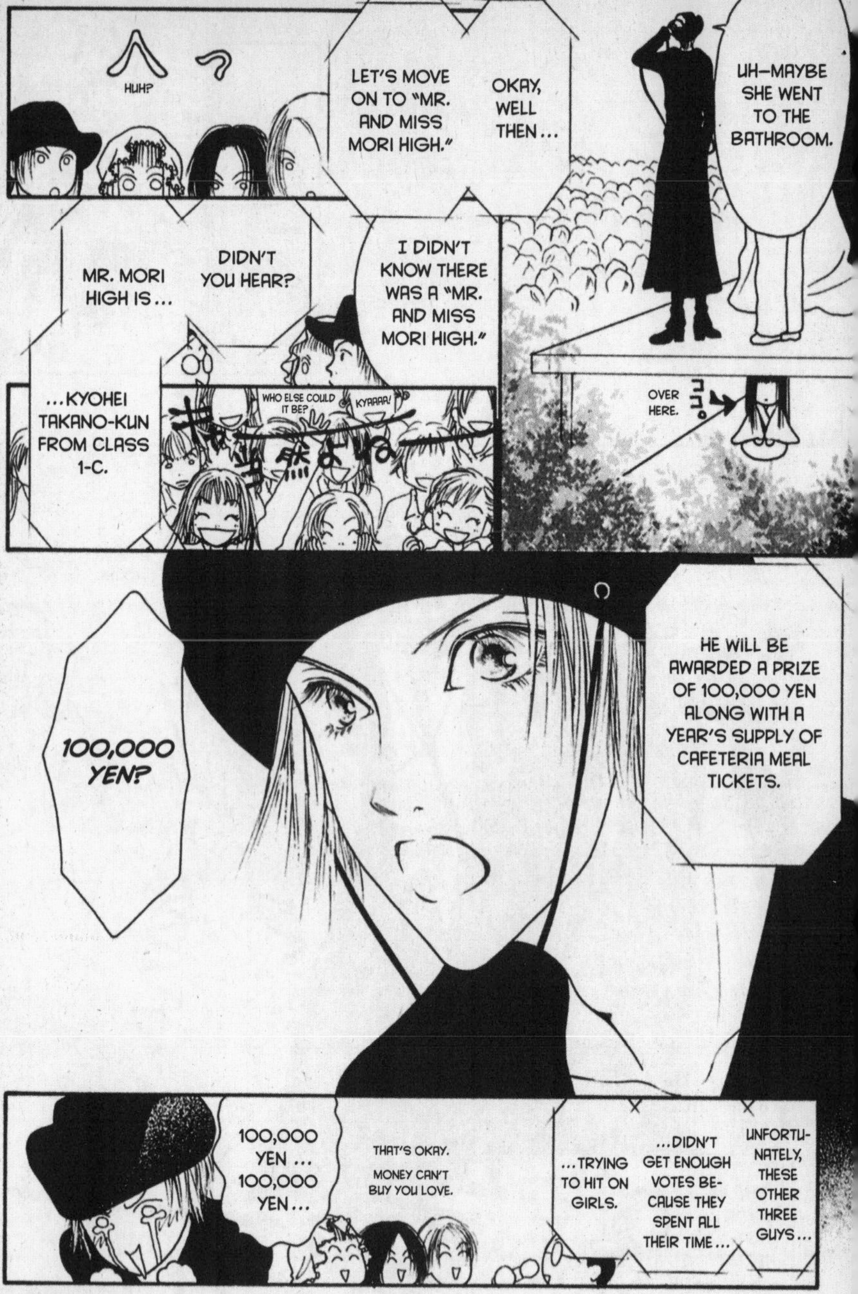
UH—MAYBE SHE WENT TO THE BATHROOM.
OVER HERE.
OKAY, WELL THEN...
LET'S MOVE ON TO "MR. AND MISS MORI HIGH."
HUH?
I DIDN'T KNOW THERE WAS A "MR. AND MISS MORI HIGH."
DIDN'T YOU HEAR?
MR. MORI HIGH IS...
...KYOHEI TAKANO-KUN FROM CLASS 1-C.
KYAAAA!
WHO ELSE COULD IT BE?
HE WILL BE AWARDED A PRIZE OF 100,000 YEN ALONG WITH A YEAR'S SUPPLY OF CAFETERIA MEAL TICKETS.
100,000 YEN?
UNFORTUNATELY, THESE OTHER THREE GUYS...
...DIDN'T GET ENOUGH VOTES BECAUSE THEY SPENT ALL THEIR TIME...
...TRYING TO HIT ON GIRLS.
THAT'S OKAY. MONEY CAN'T BUY YOU LOVE.
100,000 YEN... 100,000 YEN...

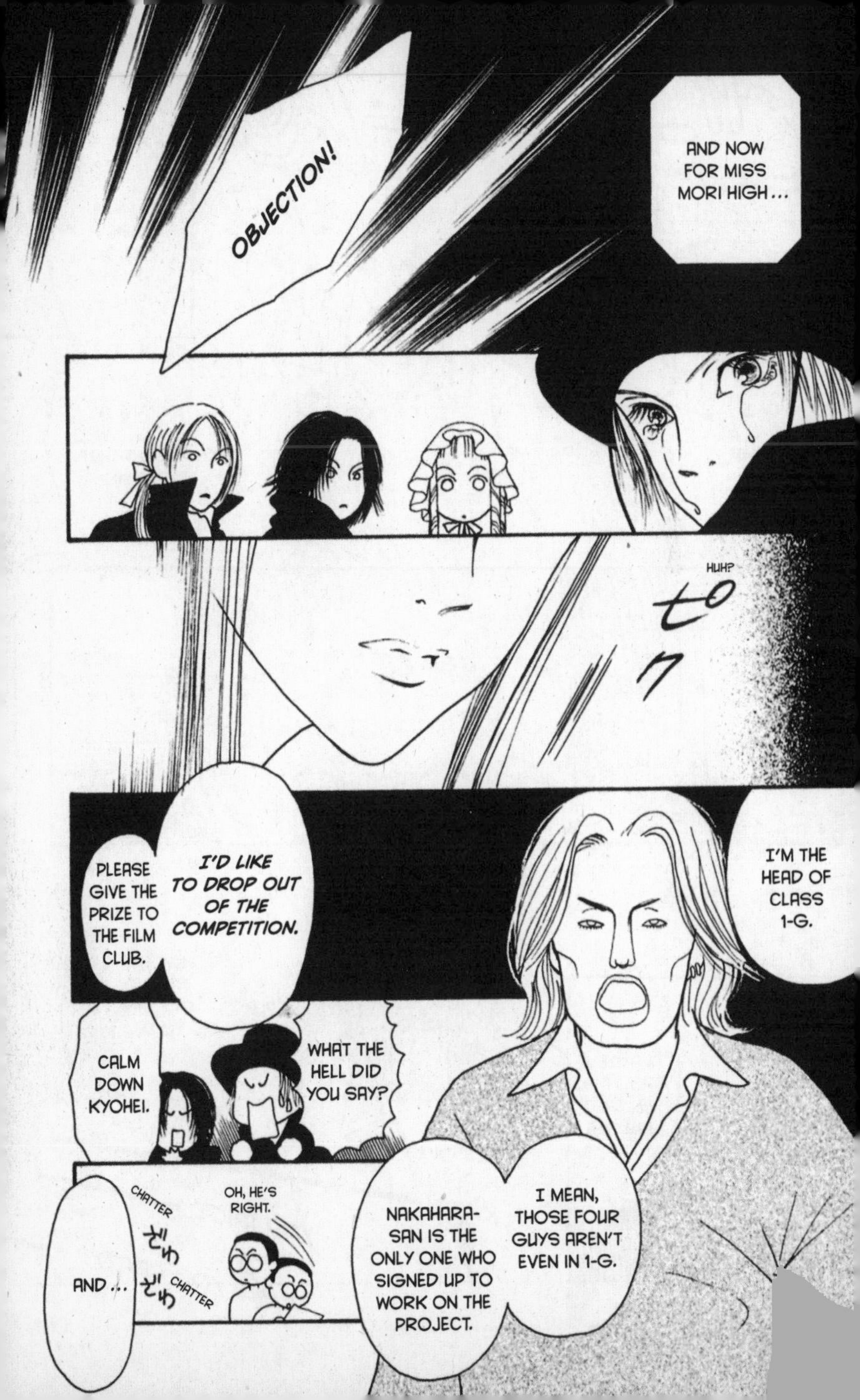

AND NOW FOR MISS MORI HIGH...
OBJECTION!
HUH?
I'M THE HEAD OF CLASS 1-G.
I'D LIKE TO DROP OUT OF THE COMPETITION.
PLEASE GIVE THE PRIZE TO THE FILM CLUB.
WHAT THE HELL DID YOU SAY?
CALM DOWN KYOHEI.
I MEAN, THOSE FOUR GUYS AREN'T EVEN IN 1-G.
NAKAHARA-SAN IS THE ONLY ONE WHO SIGNED UP TO WORK ON THE PROJECT.
OH, HE'S RIGHT.
CHATTER
CHATTER
AND...

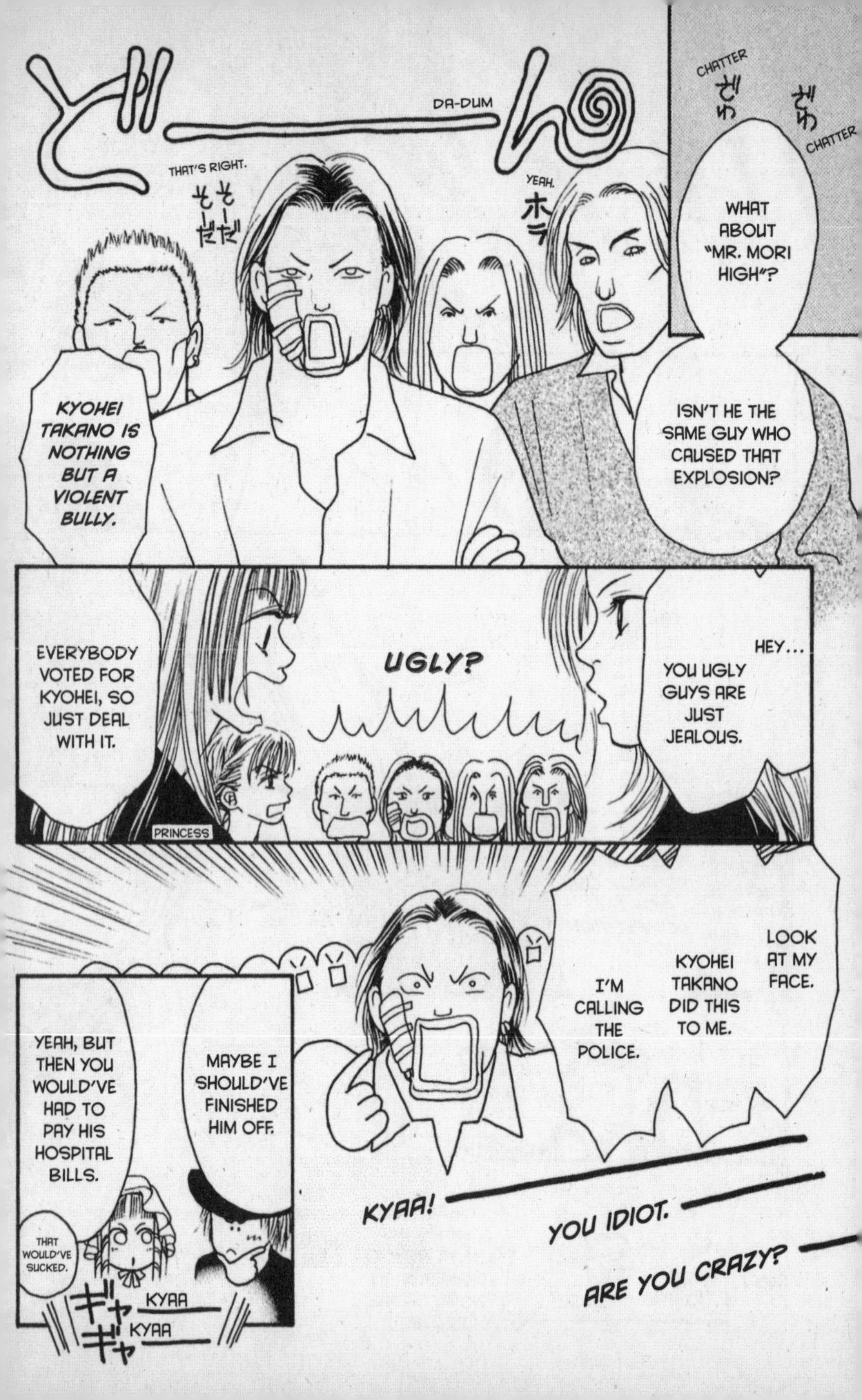

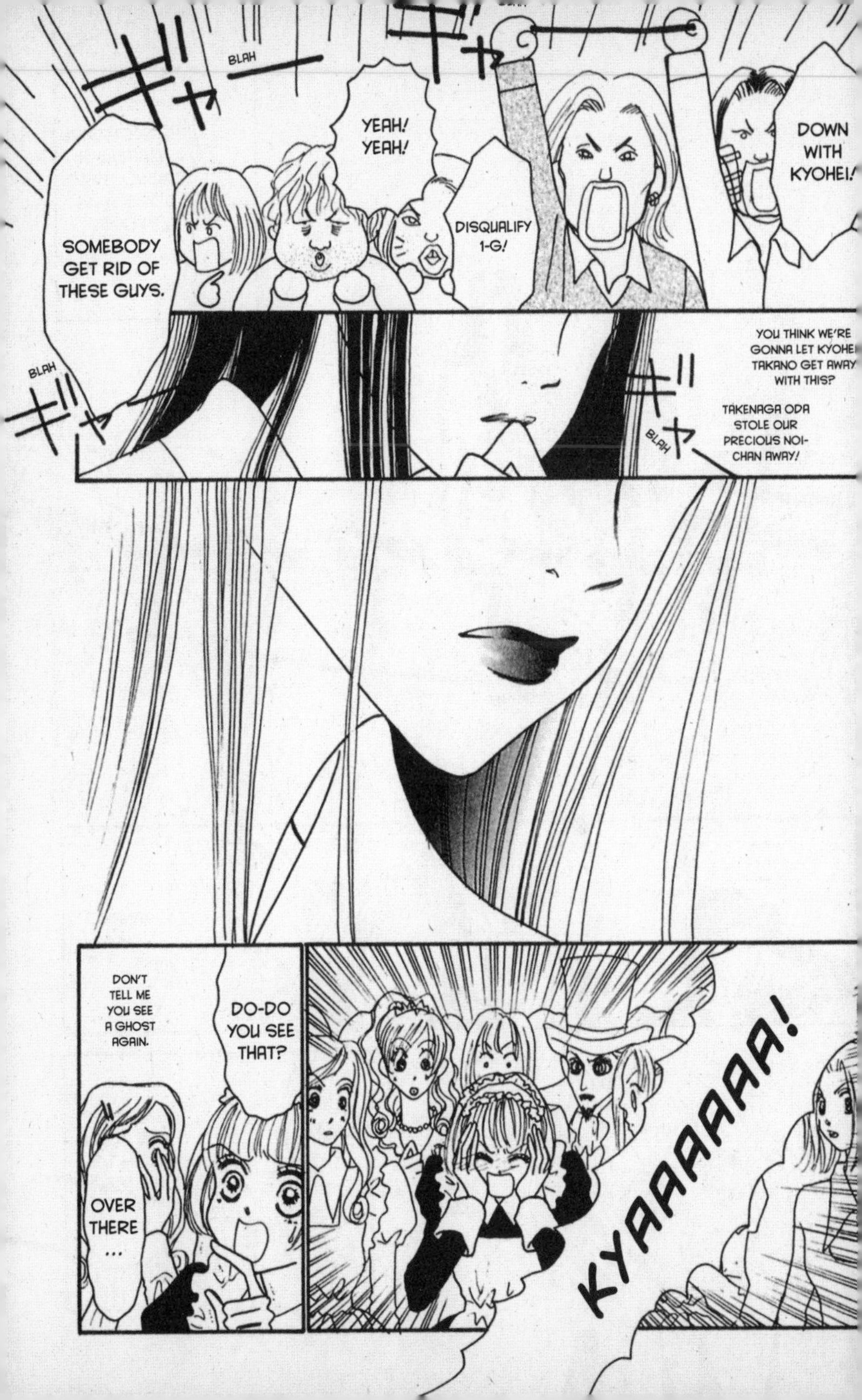
DOWN WITH KYOHEI!
DISQUALIFY 1-G!
YEAH! YEAH!
BLAH
SOMEBODY GET RID OF THESE GUYS.
YOU THINK WE'RE GONNA LET KYOHEI TAKANO GET AWAY WITH THIS?
TAKENAGA ODA STOLE OUR PRECIOUS NOI-CHAN AWAY!
BLAH
BLAH
KYAAAAAA!
DO-DO YOU SEE THAT?
DON'T TELL ME YOU SEE A GHOST AGAIN.
OVER THERE ...

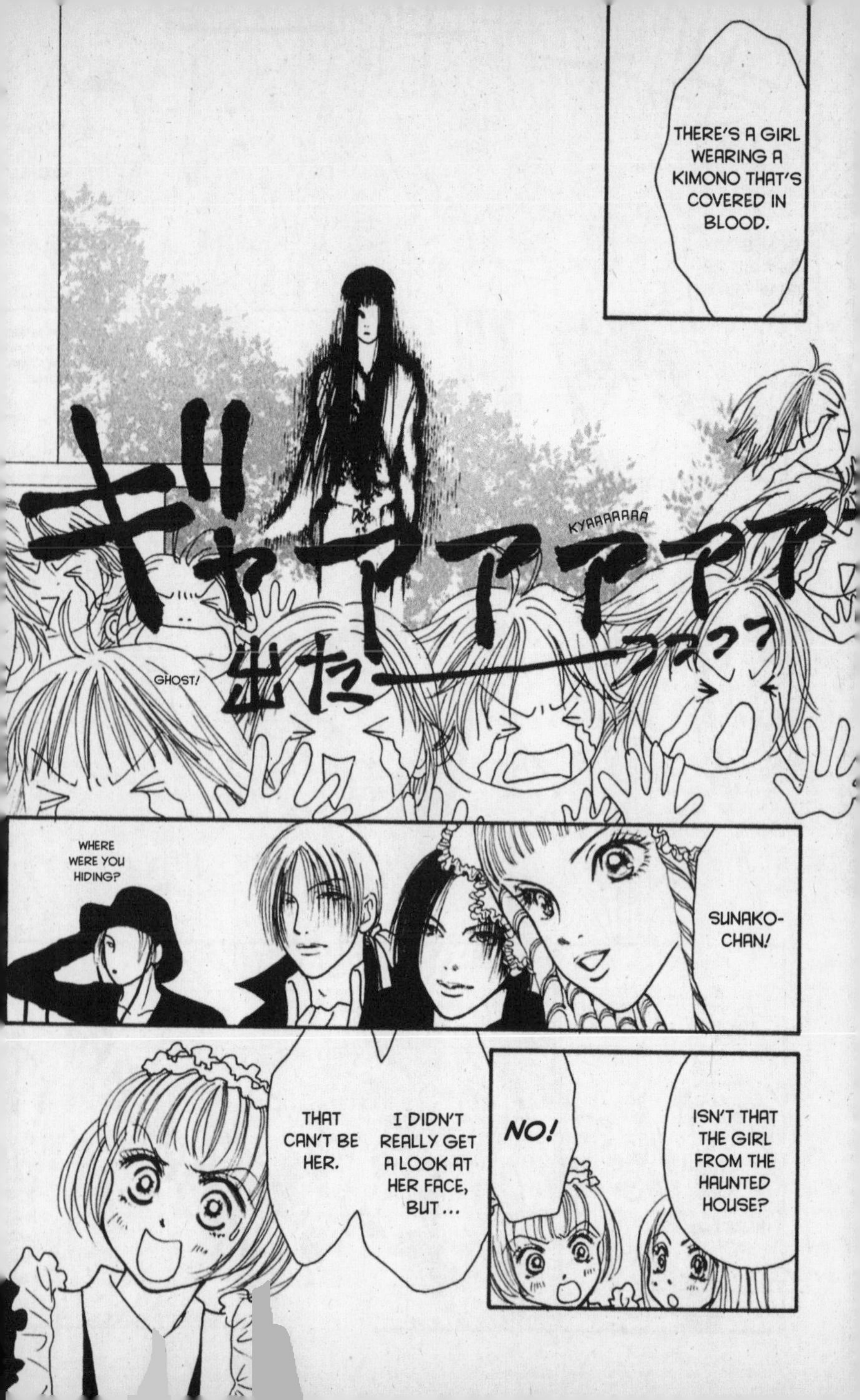
THERE'S A GIRL WEARING A KIMONO THAT'S COVERED IN BLOOD.
ギャアアアアー
KYAAAAAAA
出たーーッッッ
GHOST!
SUNAKO-CHAN!
WHERE WERE YOU HIDING?
ISN'T THAT THE GIRL FROM THE HAUNTED HOUSE?
NO!
I DIDN'T REALLY GET A LOOK AT HER FACE, BUT ...
THAT CAN'T BE HER.

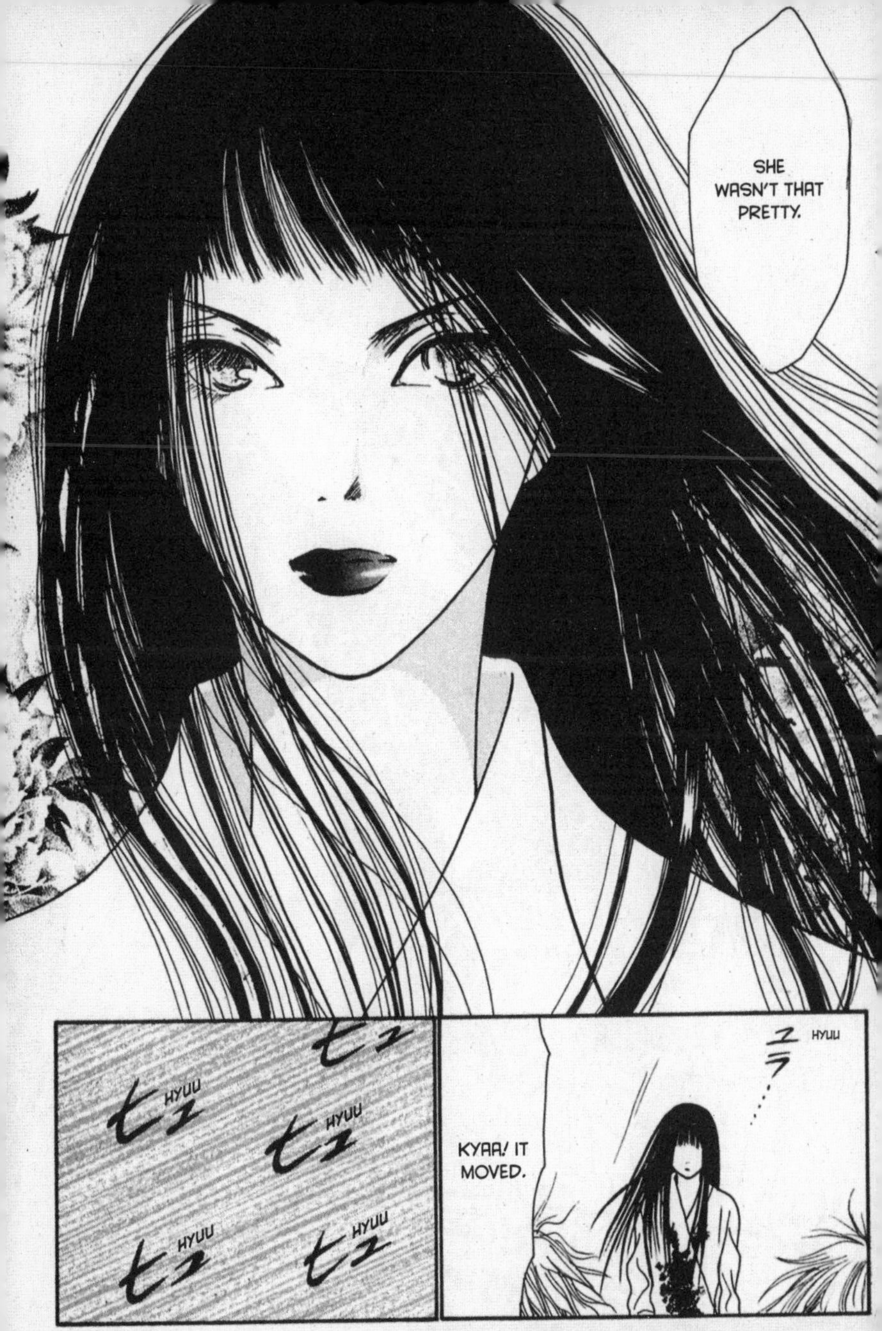
SHE WASN'T THAT PRETTY.
HYUU
KYAA! IT MOVED.
HYUU
HYUU
HYUU
HYUU

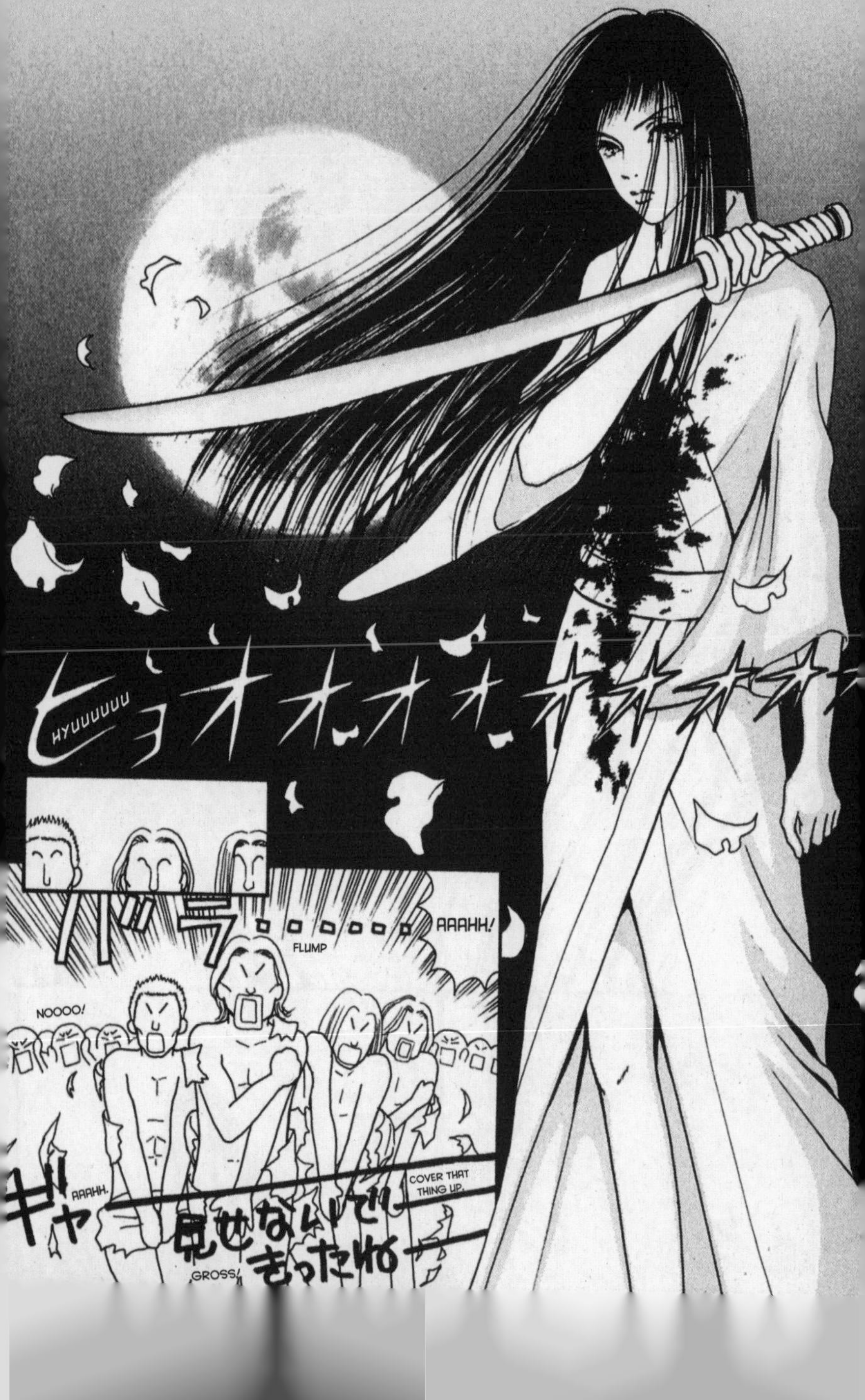

HYUUUUUUU
AAAHH!
FLUMP
NOOOO!
COVER THAT THING UP.
AAAHH.
GROSS!

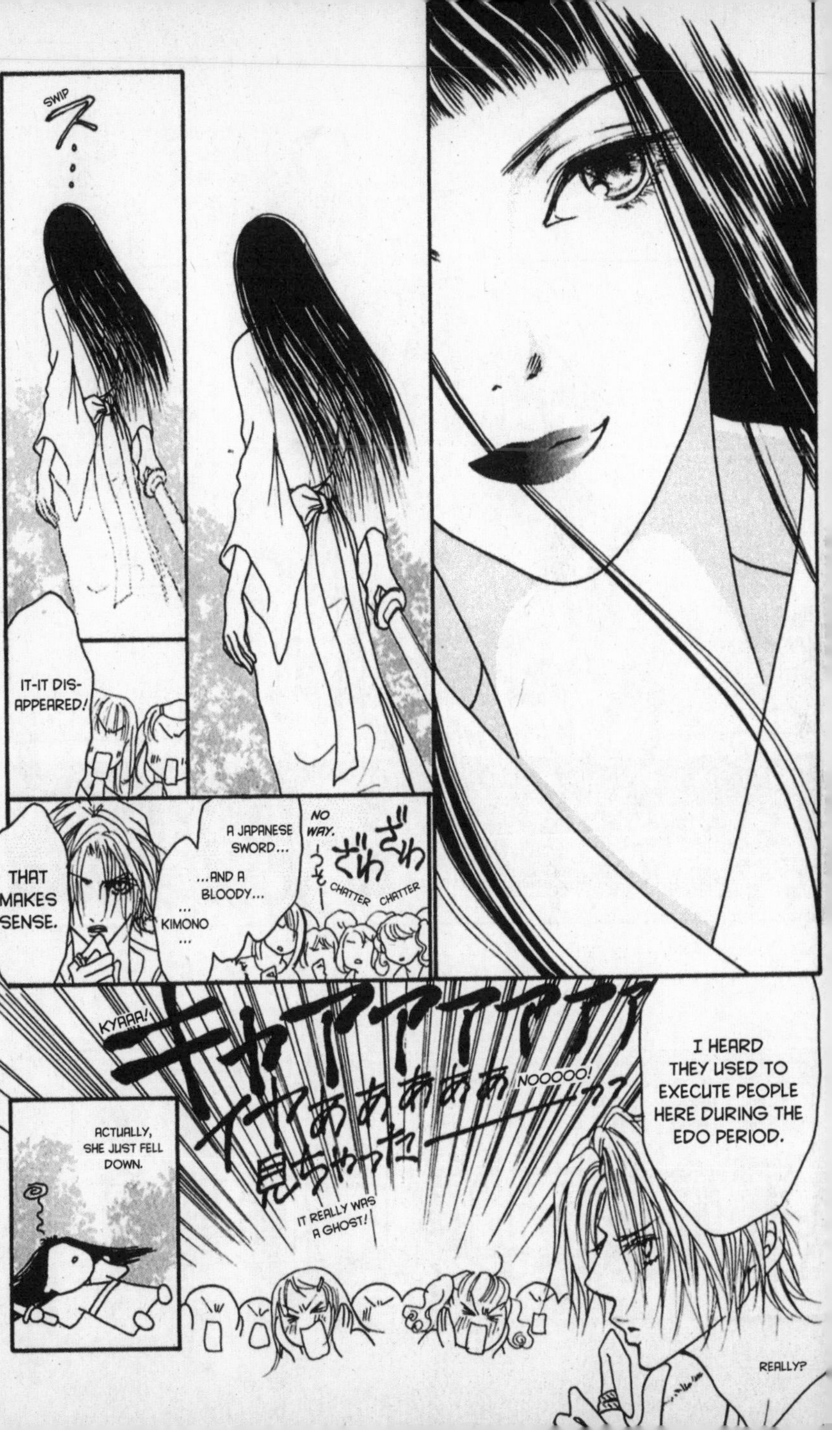
SWIP
ス…
IT-IT DIS-APPEARED!
NO WAY.
うそー
ざわざわ
CHATTER CHATTER
A JAPANESE SWORD...
...AND A BLOODY...
...KIMONO...
THAT MAKES SENSE.
I HEARD THEY USED TO EXECUTE PEOPLE HERE DURING THE EDO PERIOD.
キャアアアアア
KYAAA!
イヤあああああ
NOOOOO!
見ちゃったー
IT REALLY WAS A GHOST!
ACTUALLY, SHE JUST FELL DOWN.
REALLY?

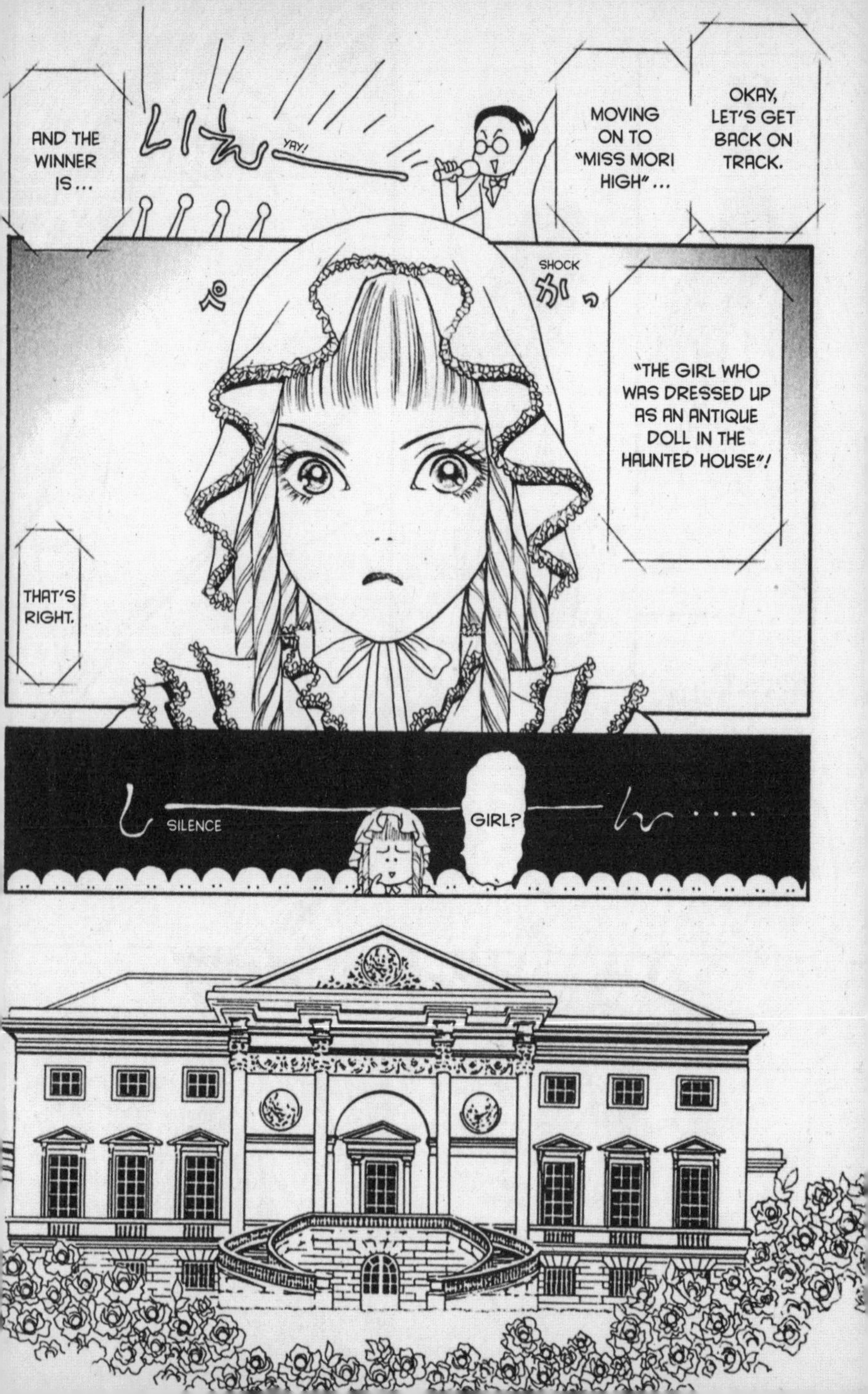
OKAY, LET'S GET BACK ON TRACK.
MOVING ON TO "MISS MORI HIGH"...
YAY!
AND THE WINNER IS...
SHOCK
"THE GIRL WHO WAS DRESSED UP AS AN ANTIQUE DOLL IN THE HAUNTED HOUSE"!
THAT'S RIGHT.
GIRL?
SILENCE

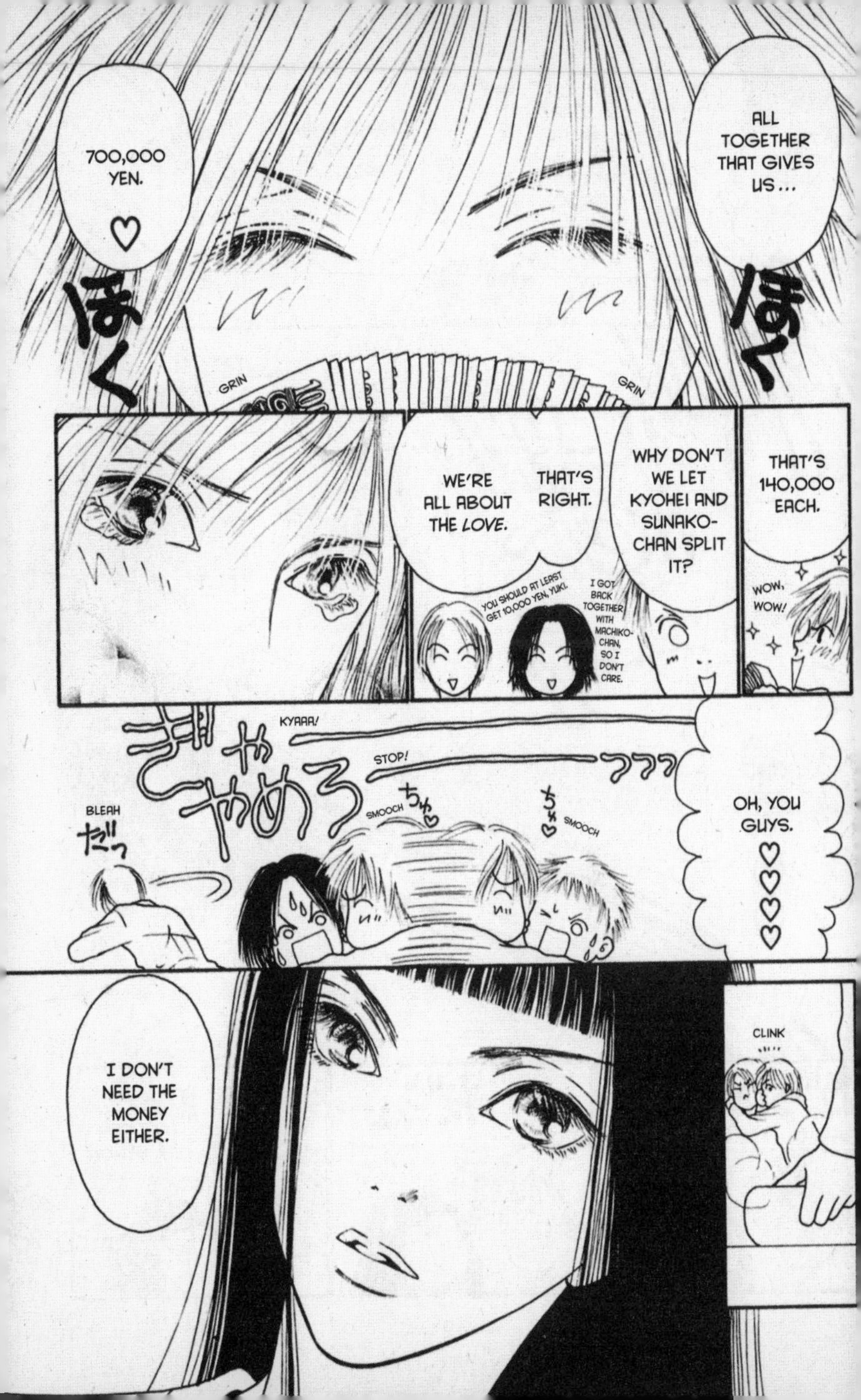
ALL TOGETHER THAT GIVES US...
700,000 YEN. ♡
ほく
ほく
GRIN
GRIN
THAT'S 140,000 EACH.
WOW, WOW!
WHY DON'T WE LET KYOHEI AND SUNAKO-CHAN SPLIT IT?
I GOT BACK TOGETHER WITH MACHIKO-CHAN, SO I DON'T CARE.
THAT'S RIGHT.
WE'RE ALL ABOUT THE *LOVE.*
YOU SHOULD AT LEAST GET 10,000 YEN, YUKI.
OH, YOU GUYS. ♡♡♡♡
SMOOCH
SMOOCH
STOP!
KYAAA!
BLEAH
CLINK
I DON'T NEED THE MONEY EITHER.

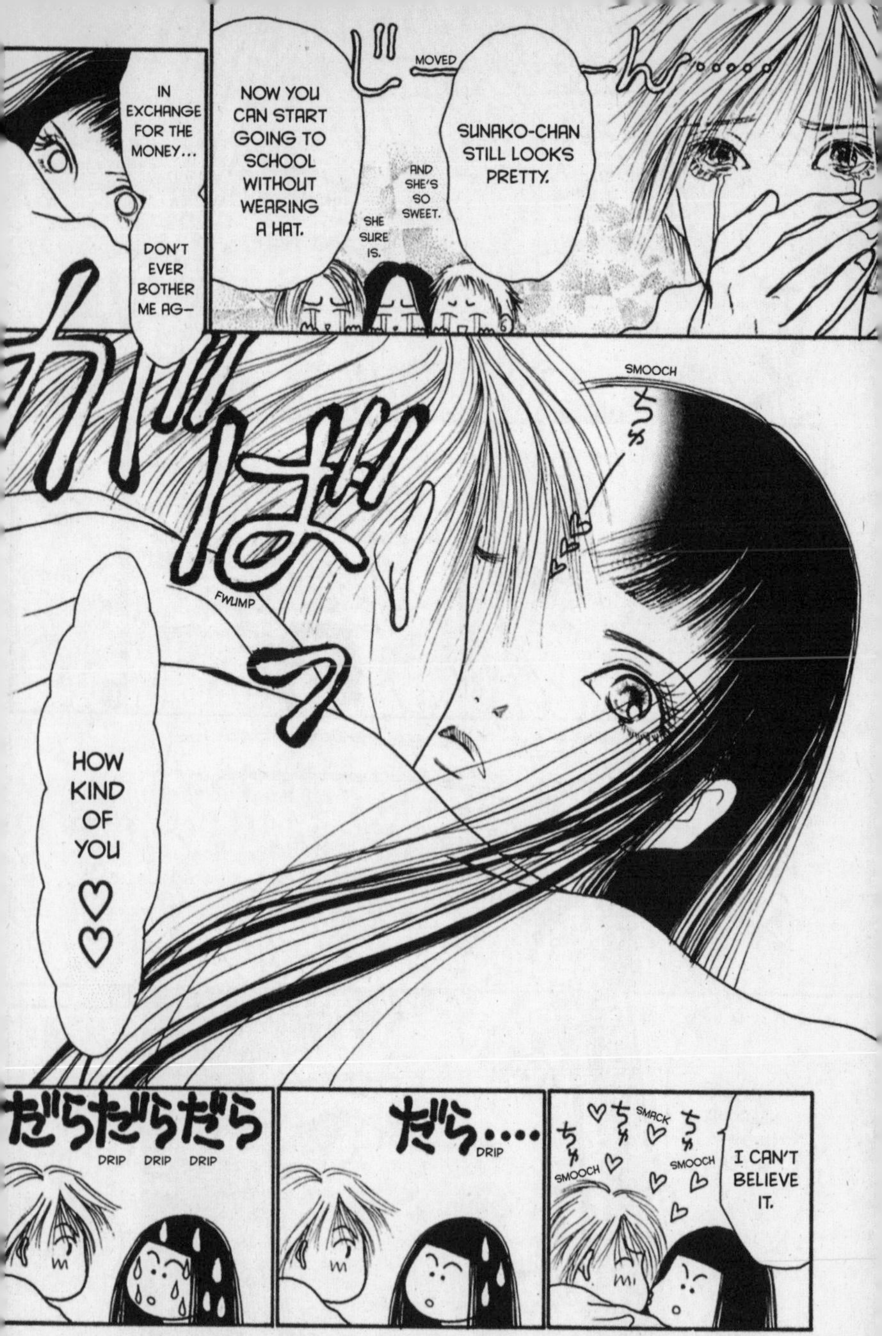

MOVED
SUNAKO-CHAN STILL LOOKS PRETTY.
AND SHE'S SO SWEET.
SHE SURE IS.
NOW YOU CAN START GOING TO SCHOOL WITHOUT WEARING A HAT.
IN EXCHANGE FOR THE MONEY...
DON'T EVER BOTHER ME AG—
SMOOCH
FWUMP
HOW KIND OF YOU ♡ ♡
I CAN'T BELIEVE IT.
SMACK
SMOOCH
SMOOCH
DRIP
DRIP DRIP DRIP

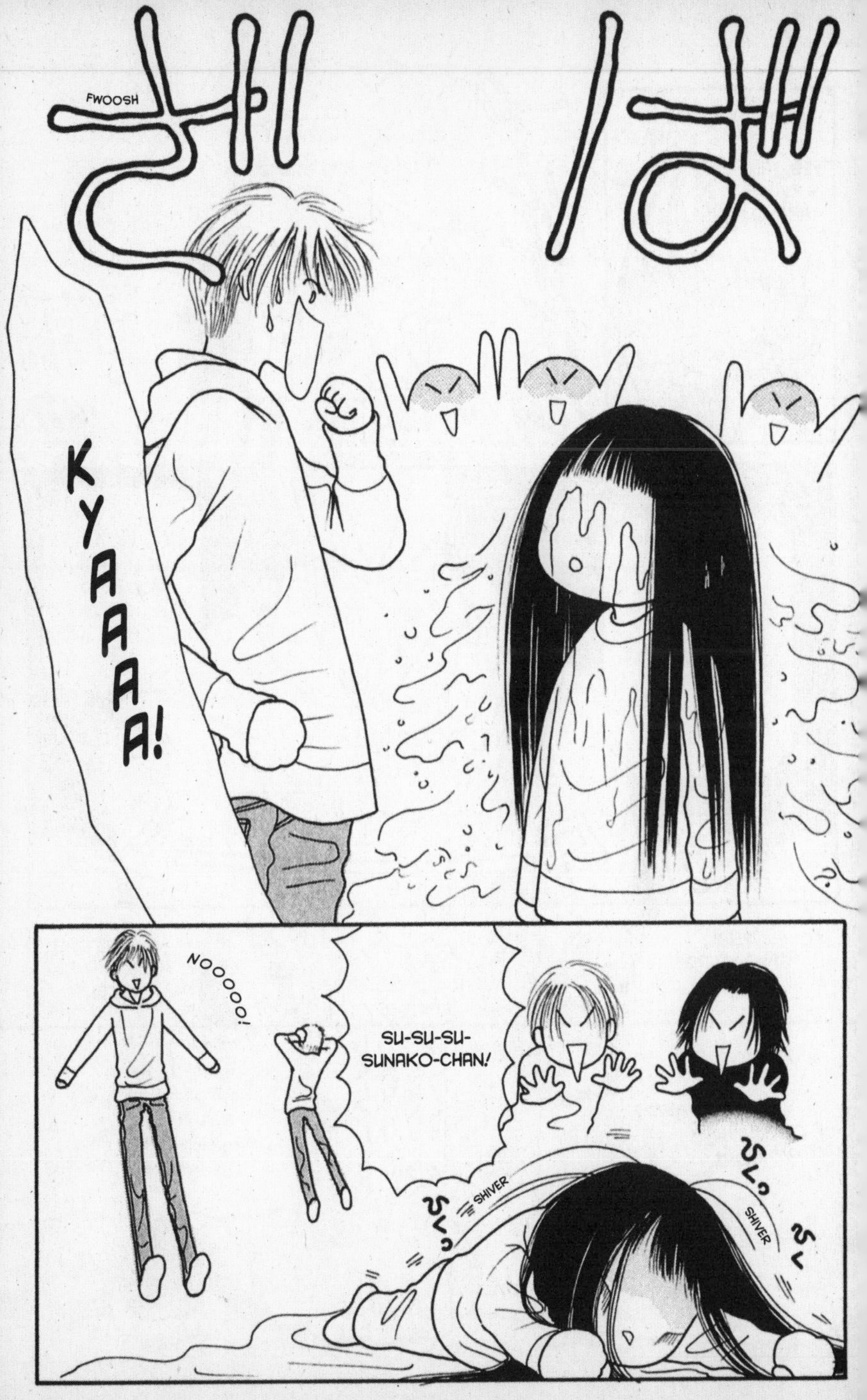
FWOOSH
KYAAAAA!
SHIVER
SHIVER
SU-SU-SU-SUNAKO-CHAN!
NOOOOO!

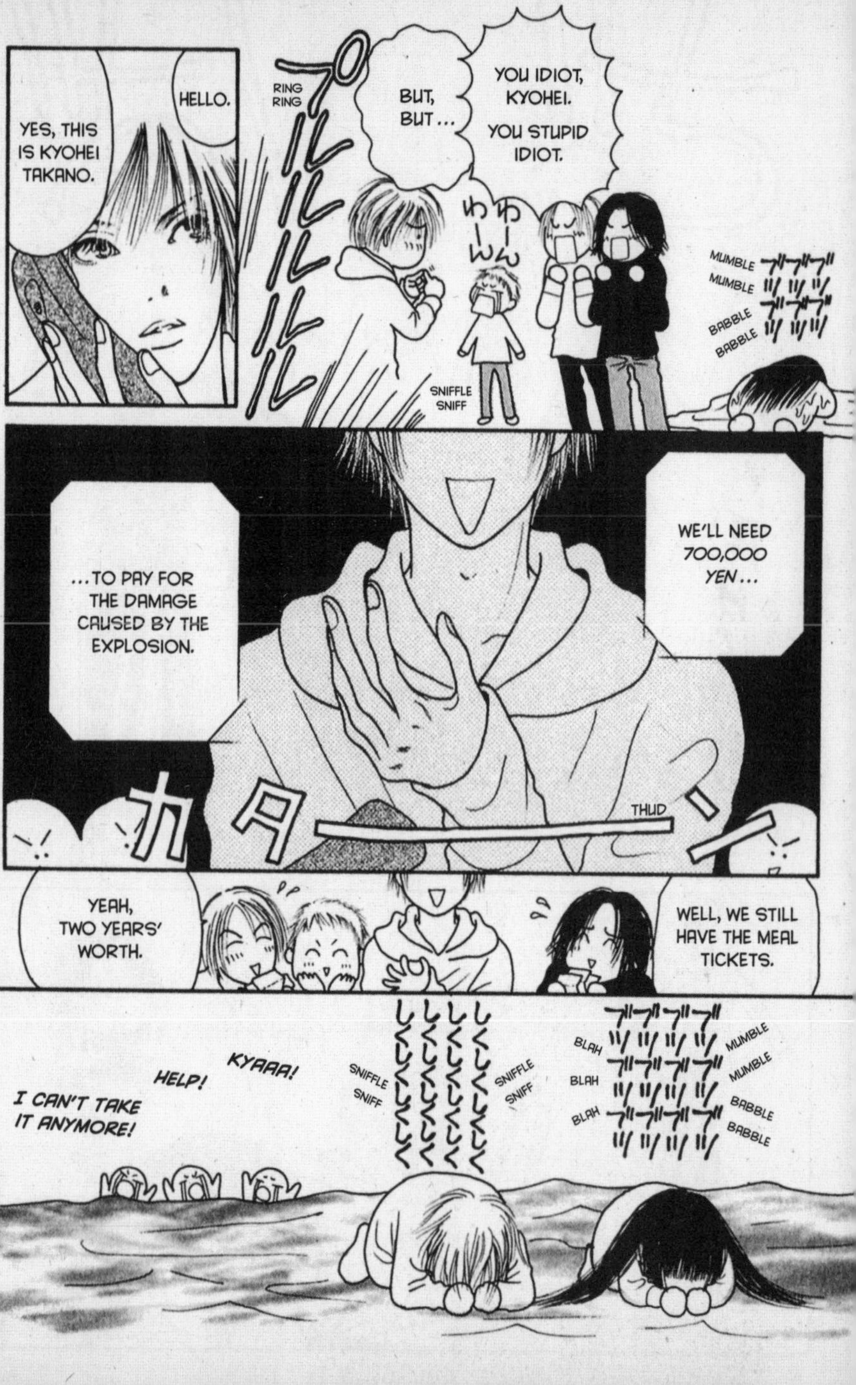
YOU IDIOT, KYOHEI.
YOU STUPID IDIOT.
MUMBLE MUMBLE
BABBLE BABBLE
BUT, BUT...
SNIFFLE SNIFF
RING RING
HELLO.
YES, THIS IS KYOHEI TAKANO.
WE'LL NEED 700,000 YEN...
...TO PAY FOR THE DAMAGE CAUSED BY THE EXPLOSION.
THUD
WELL, WE STILL HAVE THE MEAL TICKETS.
YEAH, TWO YEARS' WORTH.
MUMBLE MUMBLE
BABBLE BABBLE
BLAH
BLAH
BLAH
SNIFFLE SNIFF
SNIFFLE SNIFF
KYAAA!
HELP!
I CAN'T TAKE IT ANYMORE!

Chapter 7
Merry Scary Christmas!

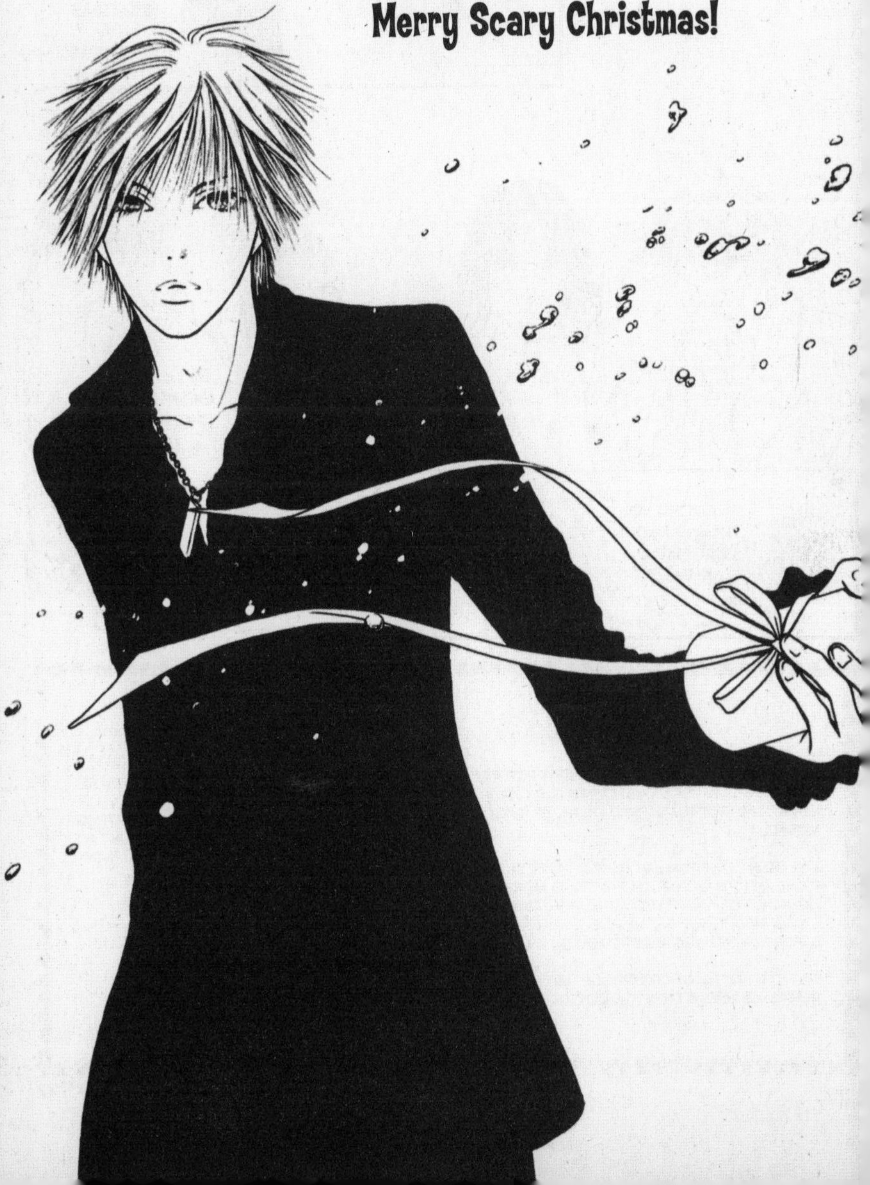

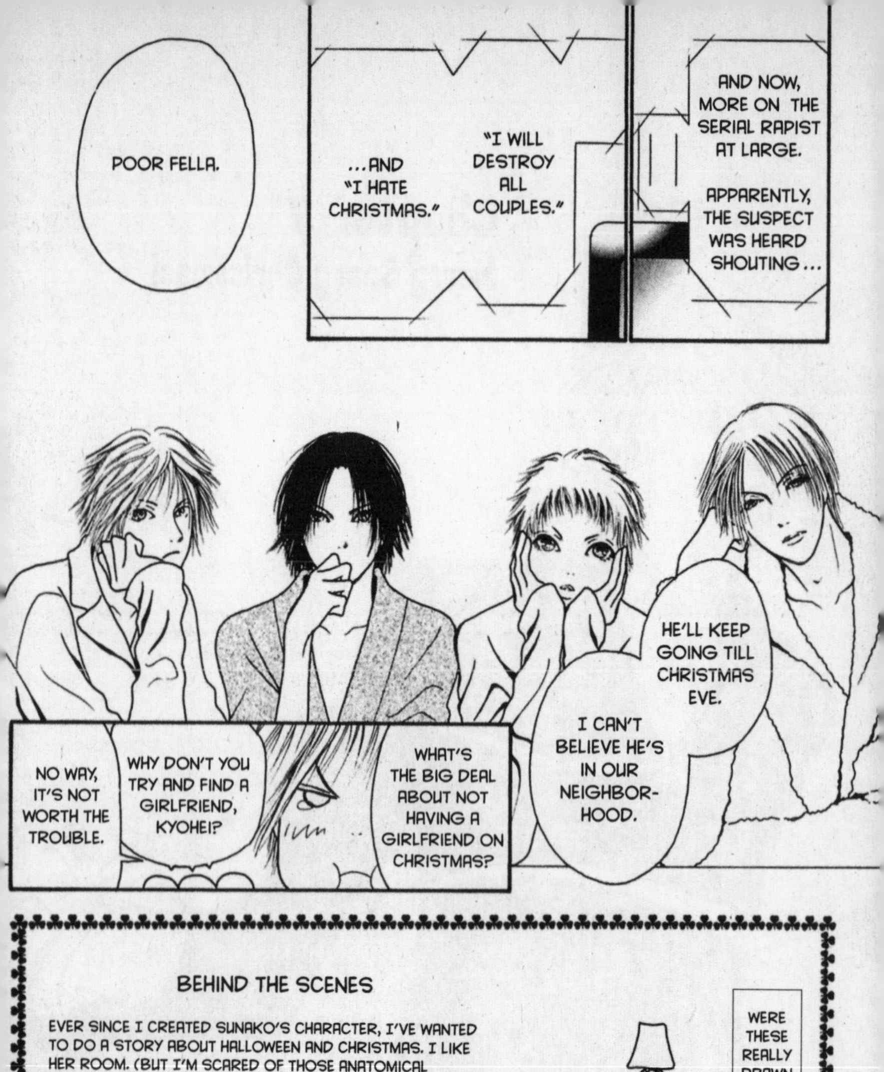
AND NOW, MORE ON THE SERIAL RAPIST AT LARGE.
APPARENTLY, THE SUSPECT WAS HEARD SHOUTING...
"I WILL DESTROY ALL COUPLES."
...AND "I HATE CHRISTMAS."
POOR FELLA.
HE'LL KEEP GOING TILL CHRISTMAS EVE.
I CAN'T BELIEVE HE'S IN OUR NEIGHBOR-HOOD.
WHAT'S THE BIG DEAL ABOUT NOT HAVING A GIRLFRIEND ON CHRISTMAS?
WHY DON'T YOU TRY AND FIND A GIRLFRIEND, KYOHEI?
NO WAY, IT'S NOT WORTH THE TROUBLE.

BEHIND THE SCENES

EVER SINCE I CREATED SUNAKO'S CHARACTER, I'VE WANTED TO DO A STORY ABOUT HALLOWEEN AND CHRISTMAS. I LIKE HER ROOM. (BUT I'M SCARED OF THOSE ANATOMICAL MODELS.)

I'VE BEEN COLLECTING MORE AND MORE SKULL AND SKELETON STUFF. AND I'M GONNA KEEP GETTING MORE. I WANT MORE FIGURINES OF "JACK" FROM *THE NIGHTMARE BEFORE CHRISTMAS.* ♥ EVEN AT MY AGE, I STILL HAVE A *NIGHTMARE BEFORE CHRISTMAS* ADDRESS BOOK AND CELL PHONE STRAP.

I USED A BOTTLE OF CHAMPAGNE THAT A FRIEND GAVE ME AS REFERENCE WHEN I DREW THE BOTTLE. ♥

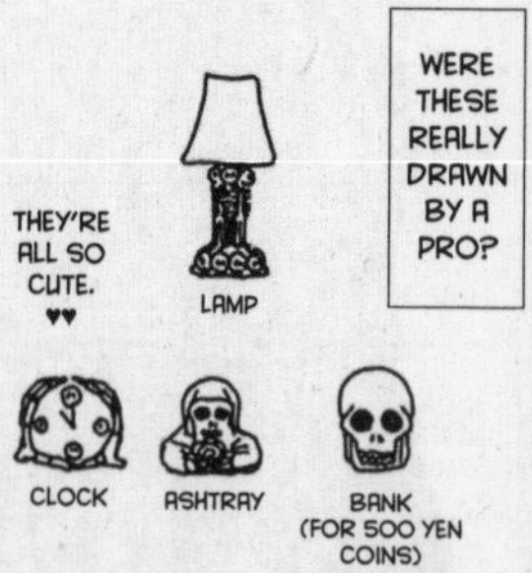
WERE THESE REALLY DRAWN BY A PRO?
THEY'RE ALL SO CUTE. ♥♥
LAMP
CLOCK
ASHTRAY
BANK (FOR 500 YEN COINS)

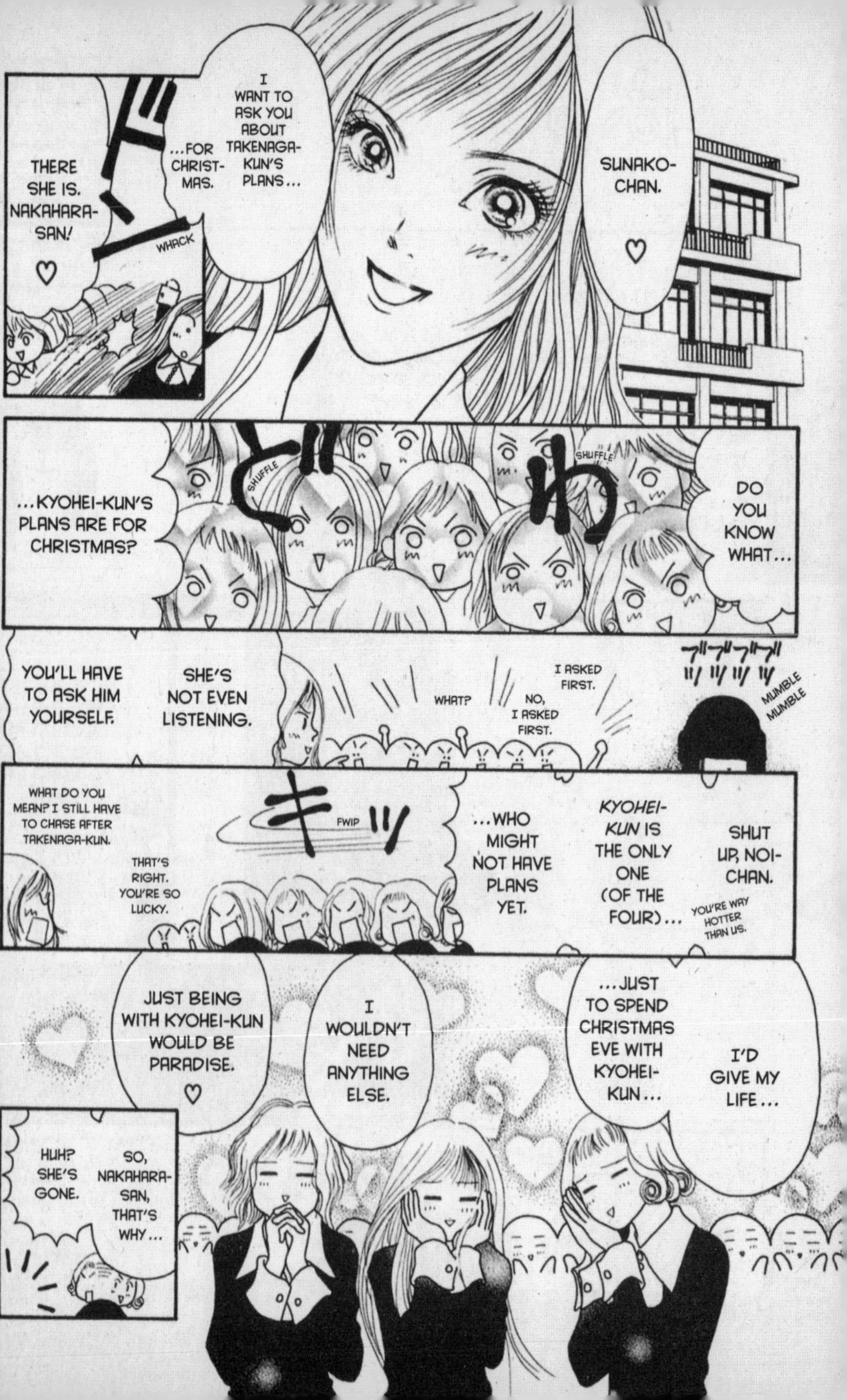
SUNAKO-CHAN. ♡
I WANT TO ASK YOU ABOUT TAKENAGA-KUN'S PLANS...
...FOR CHRISTMAS.
THERE SHE IS. NAKAHARA-SAN! ♡
WHACK
DO YOU KNOW WHAT...
SHUFFLE
SHUFFLE
...KYOHEI-KUN'S PLANS ARE FOR CHRISTMAS?
MUMBLE MUMBLE
I ASKED FIRST.
NO, I ASKED FIRST.
WHAT?
SHE'S NOT EVEN LISTENING.
YOU'LL HAVE TO ASK HIM YOURSELF.
SHUT UP, NOI-CHAN.
YOU'RE WAY HOTTER THAN US.
KYOHEI-KUN IS THE ONLY ONE (OF THE FOUR)...
...WHO MIGHT NOT HAVE PLANS YET.
FWIP
WHAT DO YOU MEAN? I STILL HAVE TO CHASE AFTER TAKENAGA-KUN.
THAT'S RIGHT. YOU'RE SO LUCKY.
I'D GIVE MY LIFE...
...JUST TO SPEND CHRISTMAS EVE WITH KYOHEI-KUN...
I WOULDN'T NEED ANYTHING ELSE.
JUST BEING WITH KYOHEI-KUN WOULD BE PARADISE. ♡
SO, NAKAHARA-SAN, THAT'S WHY...
HUH? SHE'S GONE.

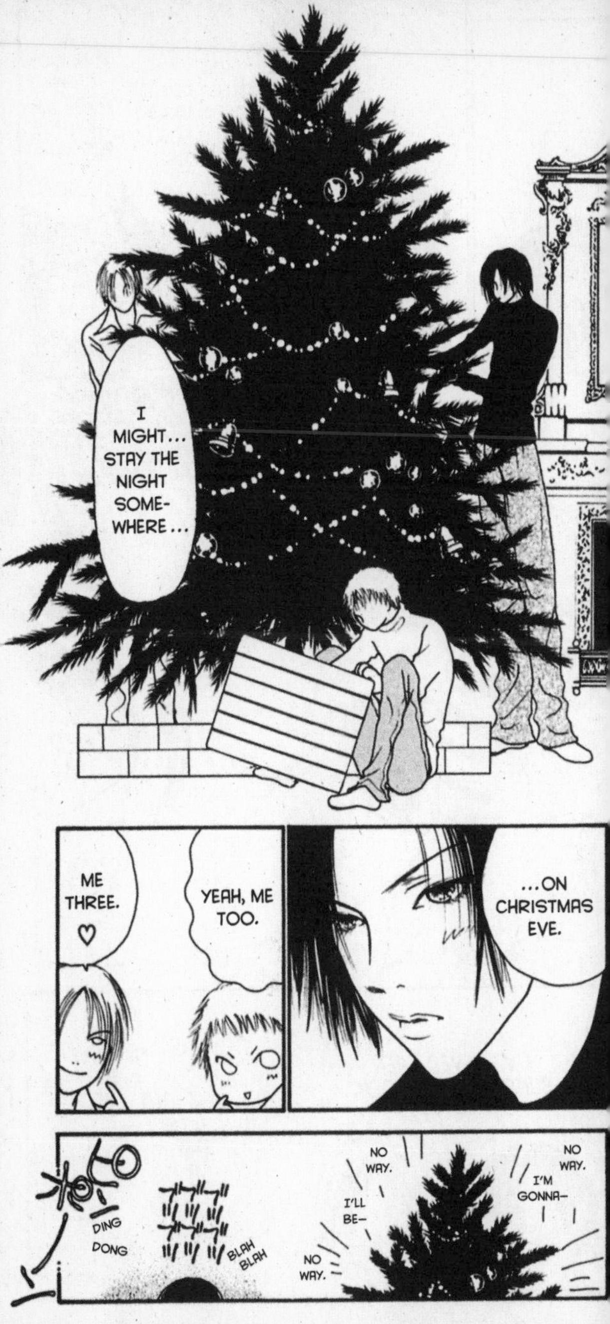
I MIGHT... STAY THE NIGHT SOME-WHERE...
...ON CHRISTMAS EVE.
YEAH, ME TOO.
ME THREE. ♡
NO WAY.
I'M GONNA—
NO WAY.
I'LL BE—
NO WAY.
BLAH BLAH
DING DONG

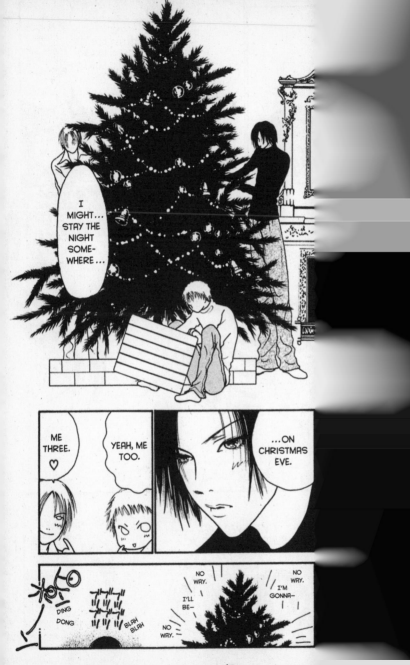

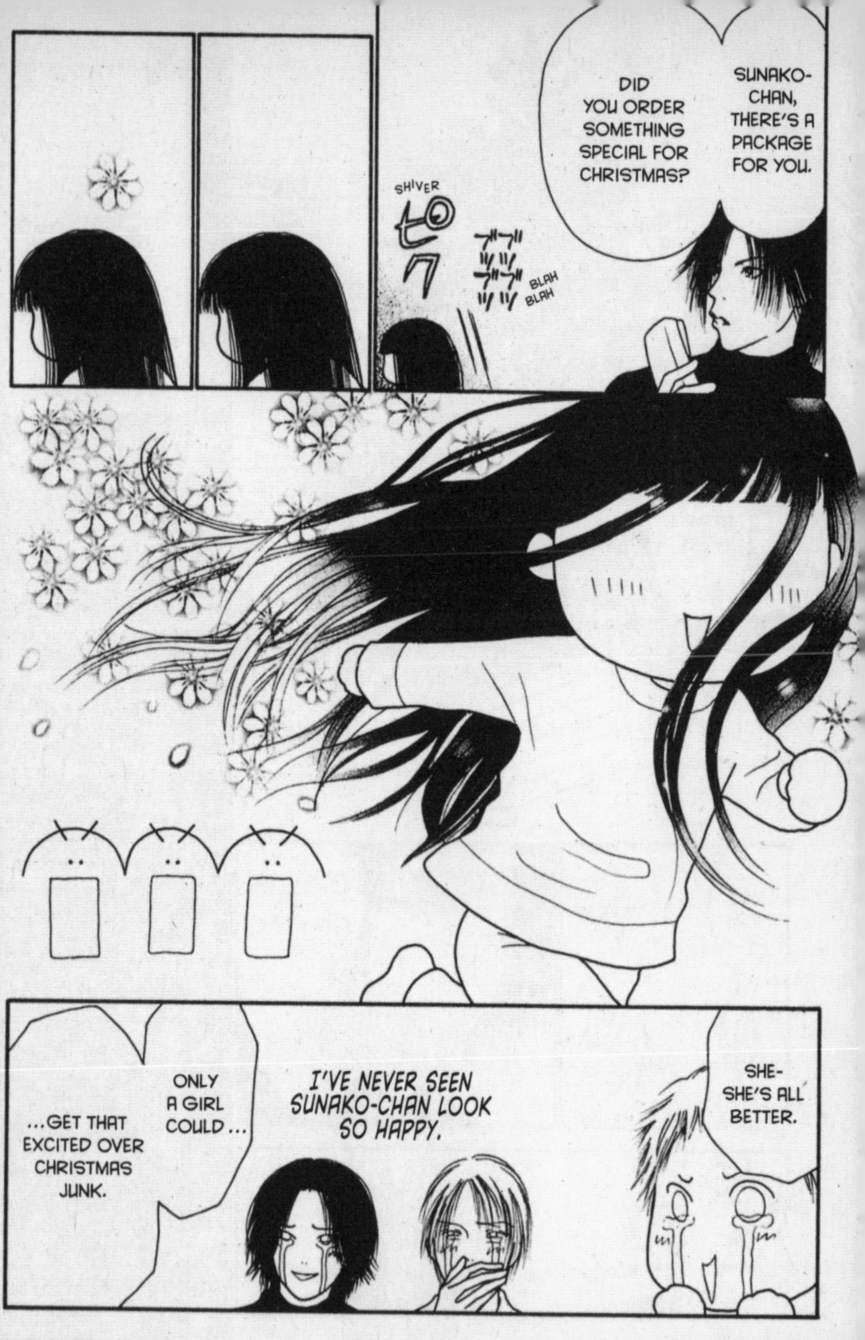
SUNAKO-CHAN, THERE'S A PACKAGE FOR YOU.
DID YOU ORDER SOMETHING SPECIAL FOR CHRISTMAS?
SHIVER
BLAH BLAH
SHE-SHE'S ALL BETTER.
I'VE NEVER SEEN SUNAKO-CHAN LOOK SO HAPPY.
ONLY A GIRL COULD...
...GET THAT EXCITED OVER CHRISTMAS JUNK.

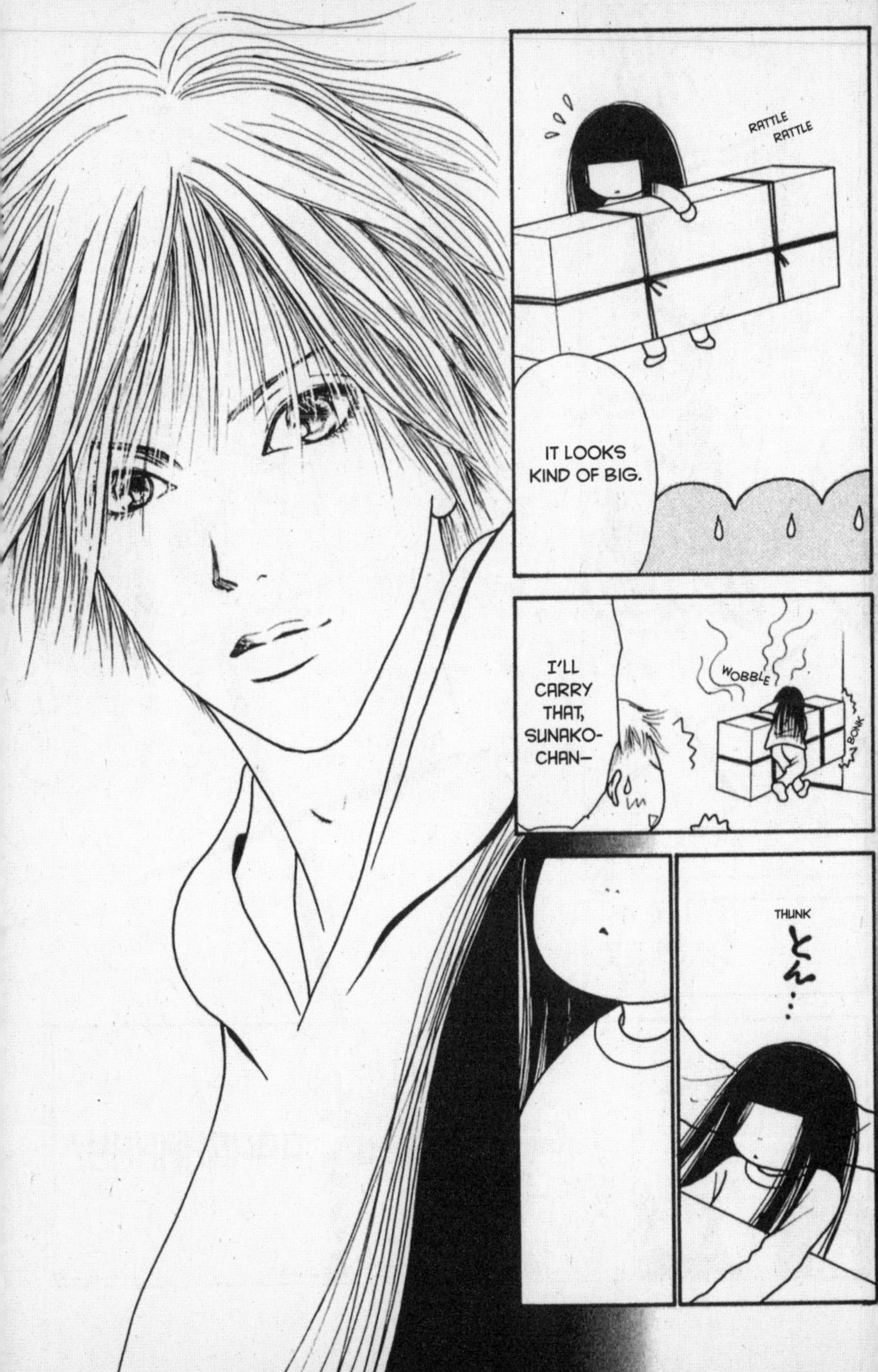
RATTLE RATTLE
IT LOOKS KIND OF BIG.
I'LL CARRY THAT, SUNAKO-CHAN—
WOBBLE
BONK
THUNK
とん…

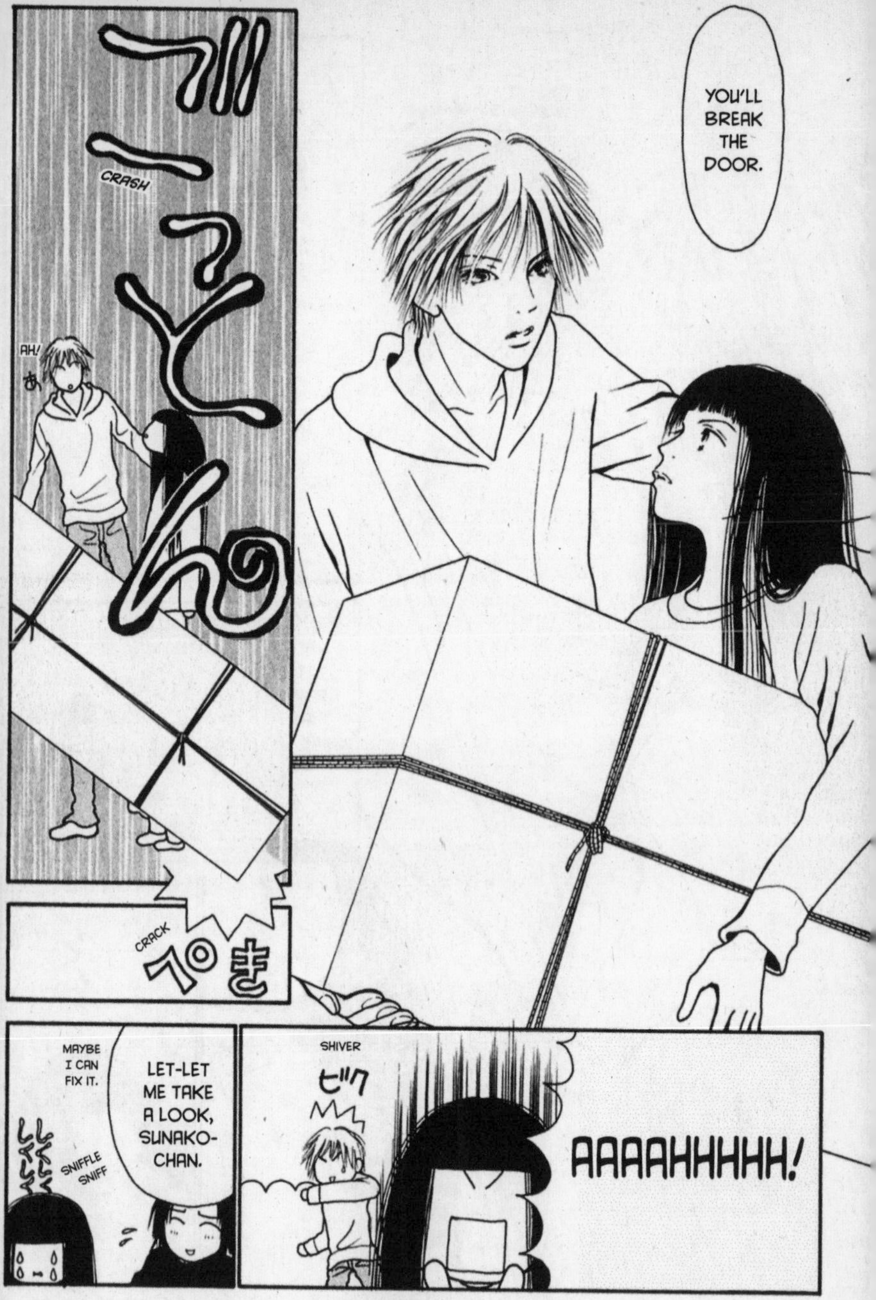
YOU'LL BREAK THE DOOR.
ガーっとん
CRASH
AH!
あ
ぺき
CRACK
ビク
SHIVER
AAAAHHHHH!
LET-LET ME TAKE A LOOK, SUNAKO-CHAN.
MAYBE I CAN FIX IT.
しくしく
SNIFFLE SNIFF

CASKET

NOW, NOW. YOU TWO HAD BETTER MAKE UP...

WHAT'S WITH THAT FACE?

GRR

SNIFFLE SNIFF

SHIVER

WHAT'RE YOU GONNA DO WITH THAT THING?

...SINCE YOU'LL BE SPENDING CHRISTMAS EVE TOGETHER.

SHIVER

NOOOOO!

AFTER ALL, WE'RE ALL GONNA BE—

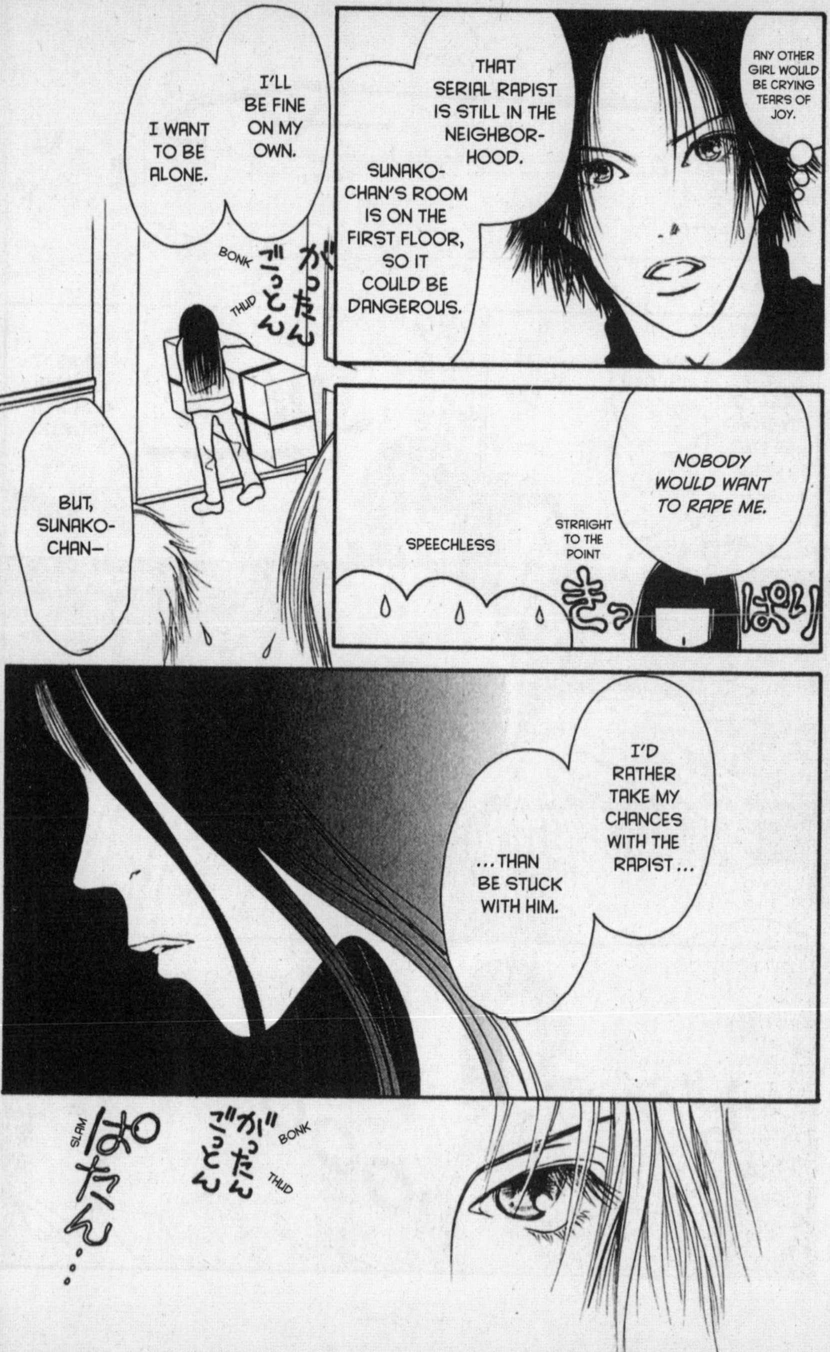
ANY OTHER GIRL WOULD BE CRYING TEARS OF JOY.
THAT SERIAL RAPIST IS STILL IN THE NEIGHBOR-HOOD.
SUNAKO-CHAN'S ROOM IS ON THE FIRST FLOOR, SO IT COULD BE DANGEROUS.
NOBODY WOULD WANT TO RAPE ME.
きっぱり
STRAIGHT TO THE POINT
SPEECHLESS
I'LL BE FINE ON MY OWN.
I WANT TO BE ALONE.
がったん ごっとん
BONK
THUD
BUT, SUNAKO-CHAN—
I'D RATHER TAKE MY CHANCES WITH THE RAPIST...
...THAN BE STUCK WITH HIM.
がったん ごっとん
BONK
THUD
ぱたん...
SLAM

— 55 —

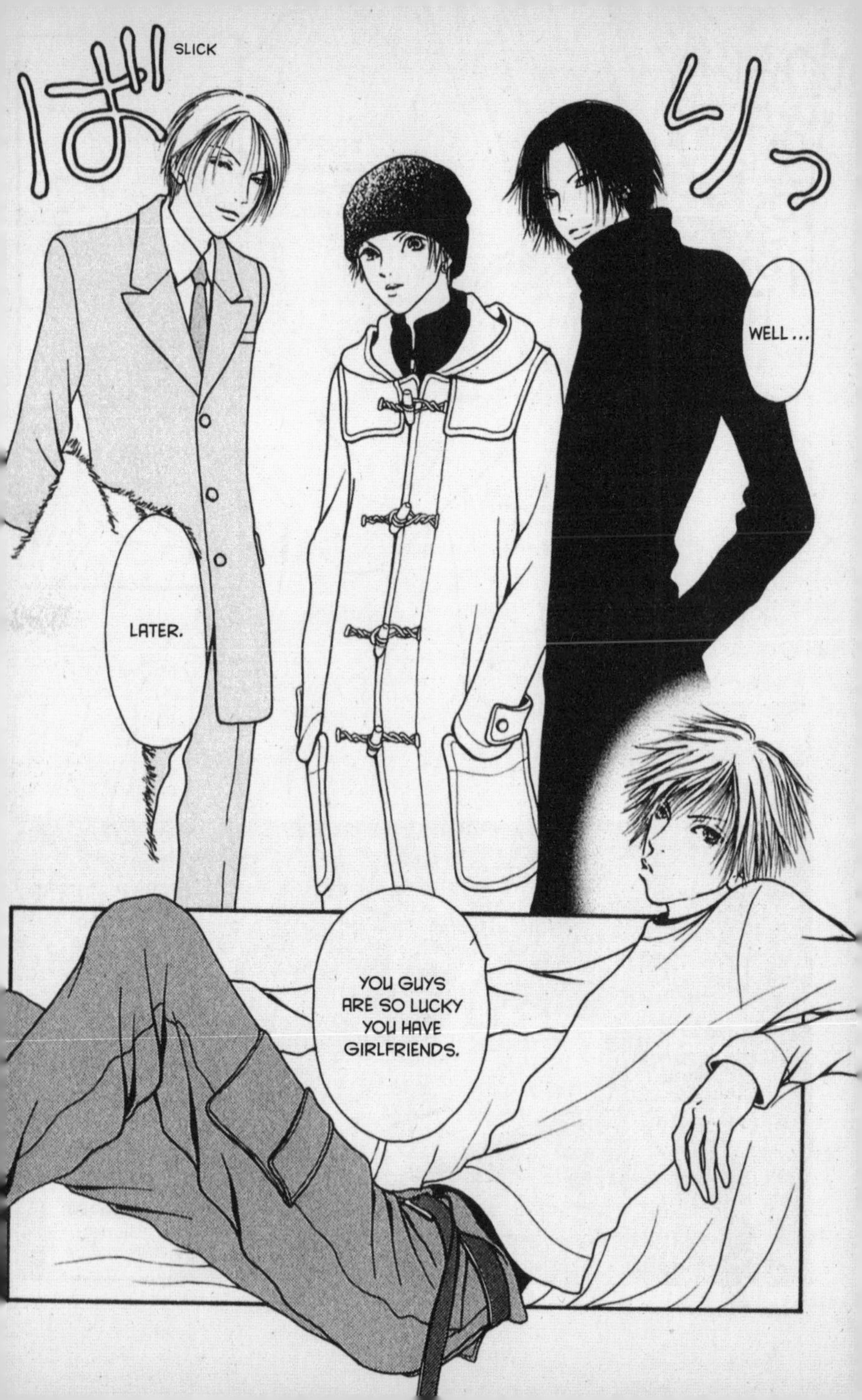
SLICK
WELL...
LATER.
YOU GUYS ARE SO LUCKY YOU HAVE GIRLFRIENDS.

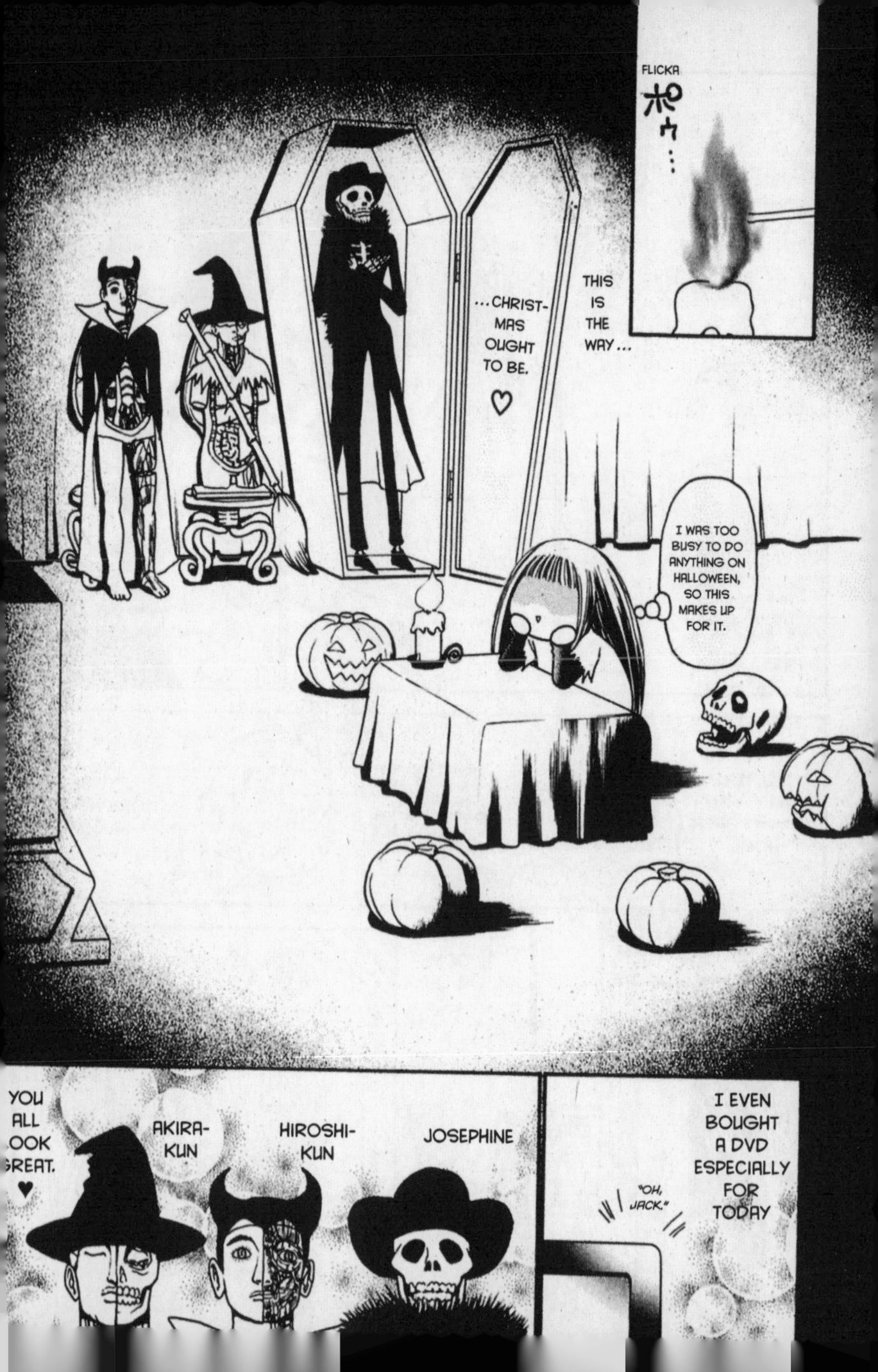
FLICKA
ポウ…
THIS IS THE WAY…
…CHRISTMAS OUGHT TO BE. ♡
I WAS TOO BUSY TO DO ANYTHING ON HALLOWEEN, SO THIS MAKES UP FOR IT.
I EVEN BOUGHT A DVD ESPECIALLY FOR TODAY
"OH, JACK."
YOU ALL OOK REAT. ♥
AKIRA-KUN
HIROSHI-KUN
JOSEPHINE

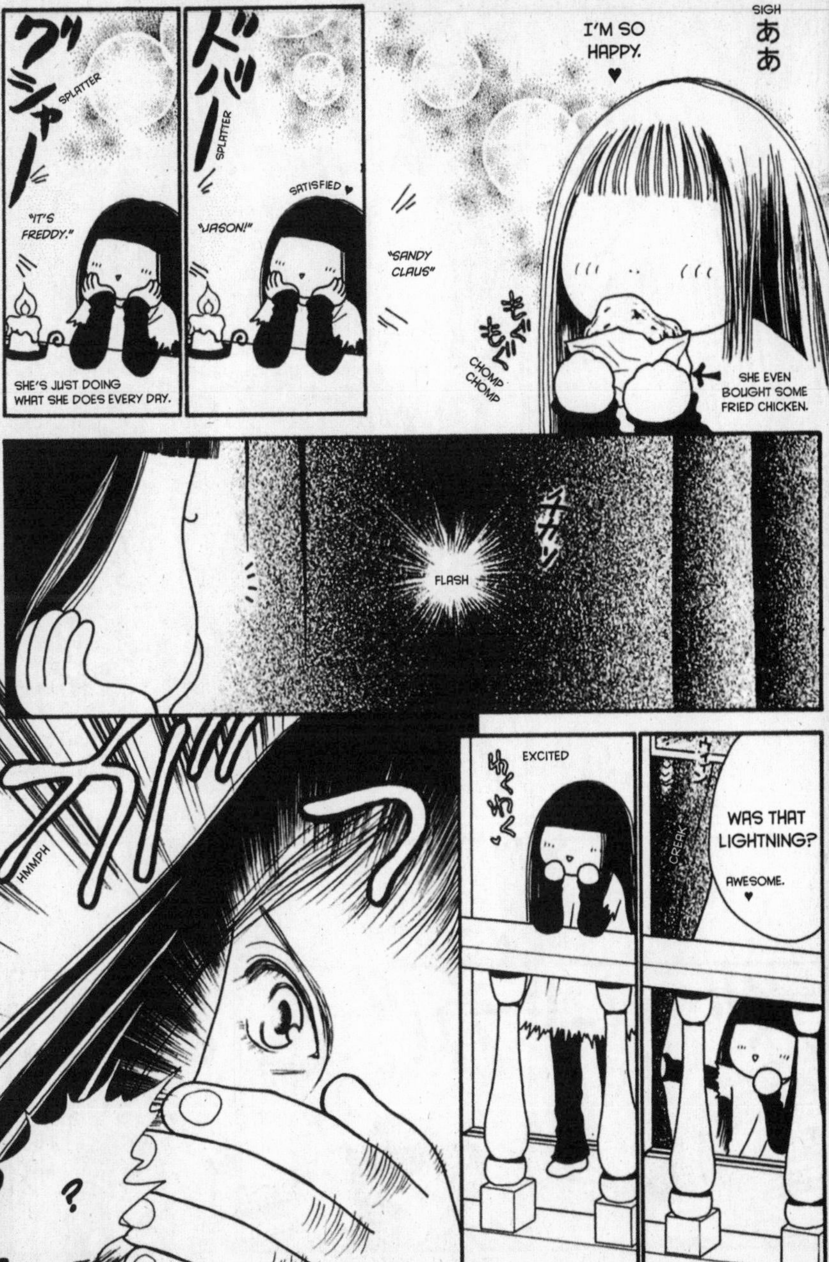
SIGH
ああ
I'M SO HAPPY. ♥
CHOMP CHOMP
SHE EVEN BOUGHT SOME FRIED CHICKEN.
"SANDY CLAUS"
SPLATTER
SATISFIED ♥
"JASON!"
SPLATTER
"IT'S FREDDY."
SHE'S JUST DOING WHAT SHE DOES EVERY DAY.
FLASH
WAS THAT LIGHTNING?
AWESOME. ♥
CREAK
EXCITED
HMMPH
?

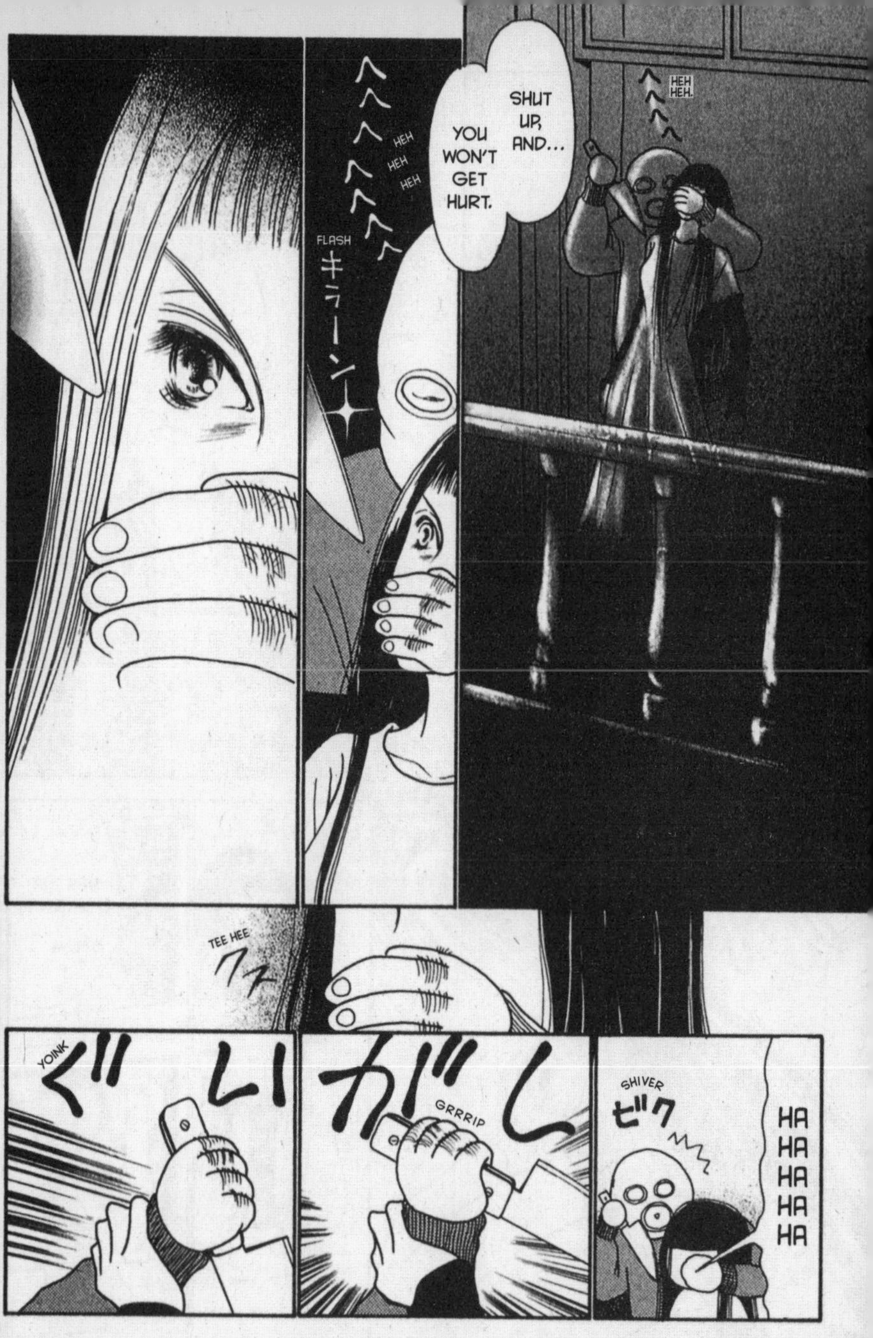

へへへへ
HEH HEH.
SHUT UP, AND...
YOU WON'T GET HURT.
へへへへへへへへ
HEH HEH HEH
FLASH
キラーン
TEE HEE
クク
SHIVER
ビク
HA HA HA HA HA
GRRRIP
がし
YOINK
ぐい

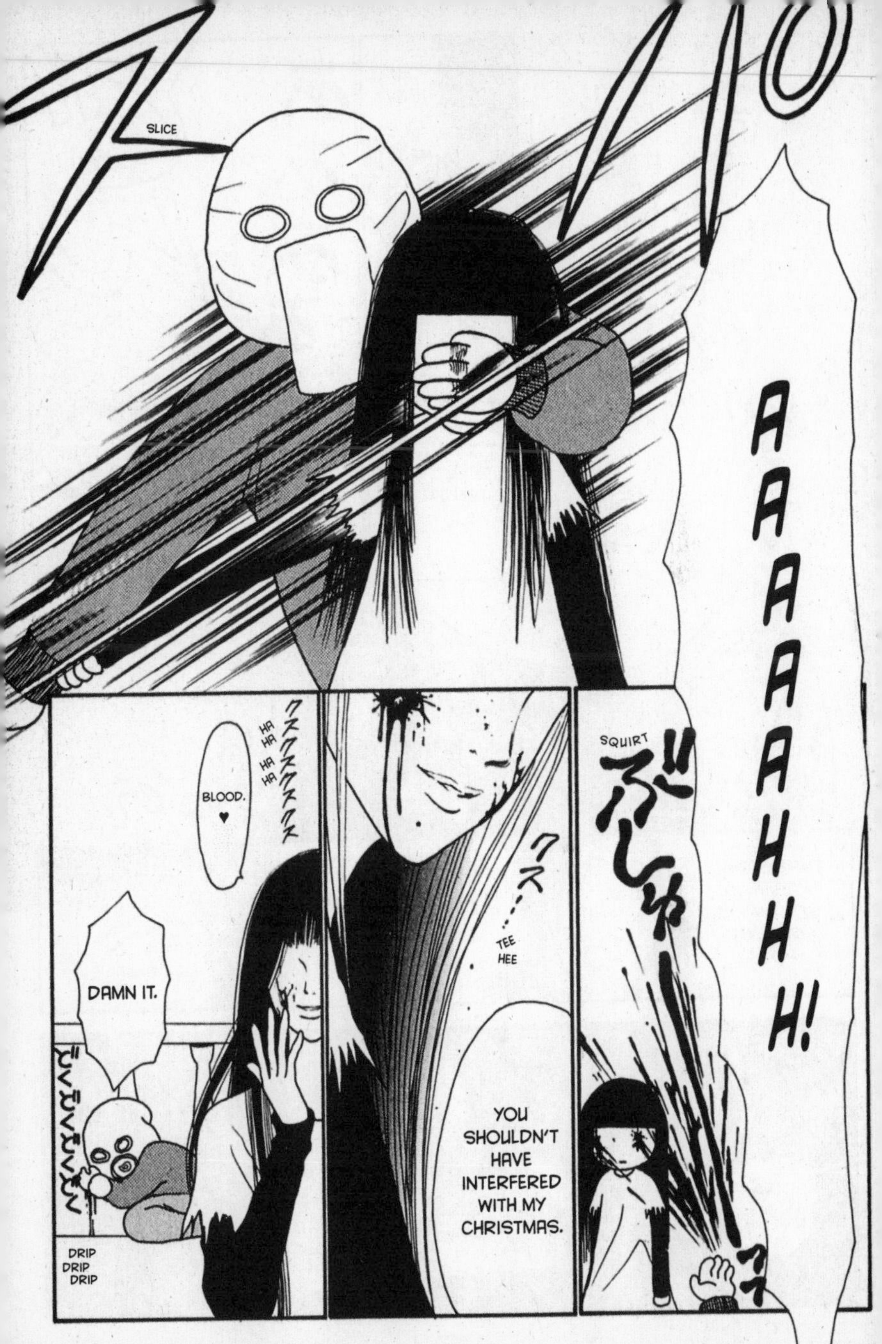
SLICE
AAAAAHHH!
SQUIRT
ぶしゅー
クス…
TEE HEE
YOU SHOULDN'T HAVE INTERFERED WITH MY CHRISTMAS.
クスクスクスクス
HA HA HA HA
BLOOD. ♥
DAMN IT.
DRIP DRIP DRIP

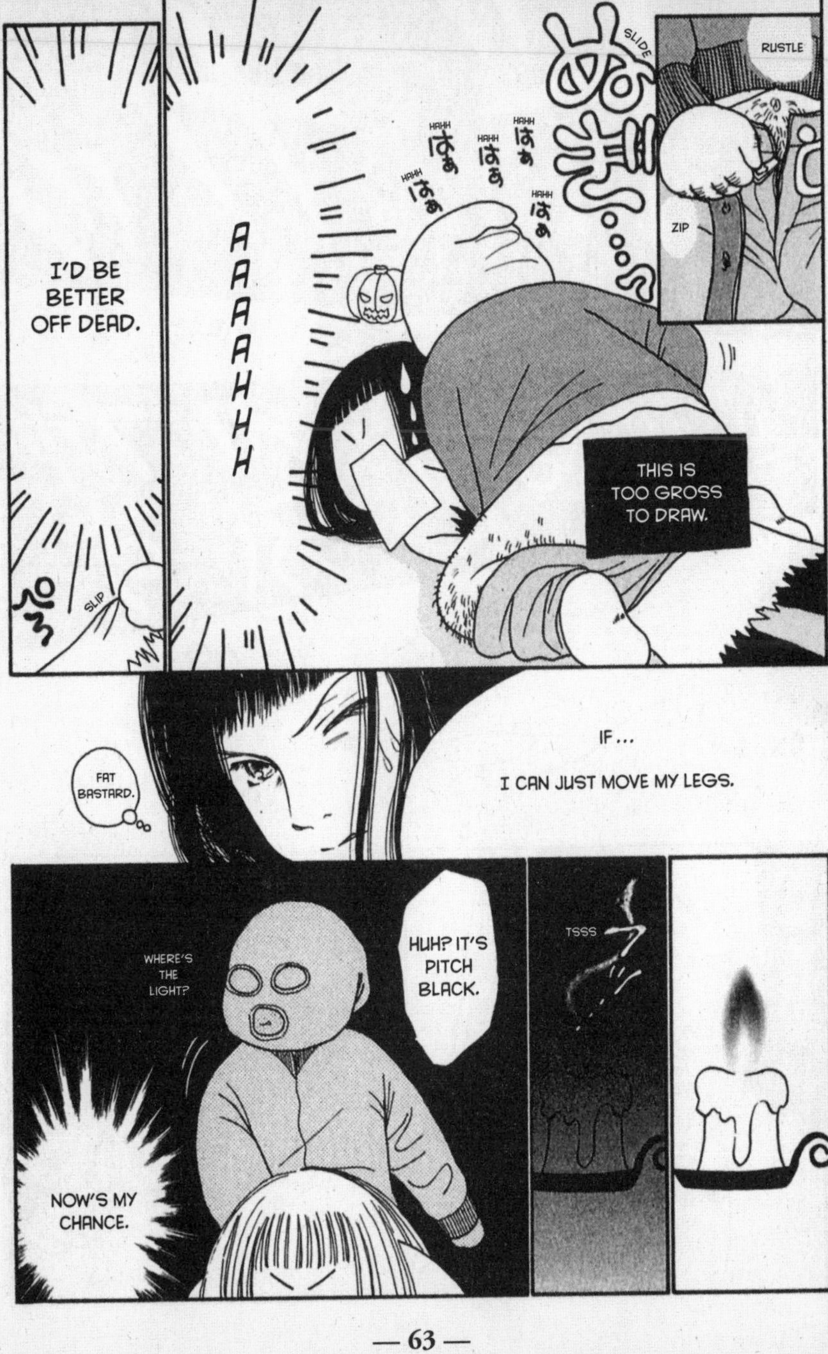
RUSTLE
ZIP
SLIDE
ぬき〜
HAHH はぁ
HAHH はぁ
HAHH はぁ
HAHH はぁ
AAAAAHHHH
THIS IS TOO GROSS TO DRAW.
I'D BE BETTER OFF DEAD.
SLIP
IF...
I CAN JUST MOVE MY LEGS.
FAT BASTARD.
TSSS
HUH? IT'S PITCH BLACK.
WHERE'S THE LIGHT?
NOW'S MY CHANCE.

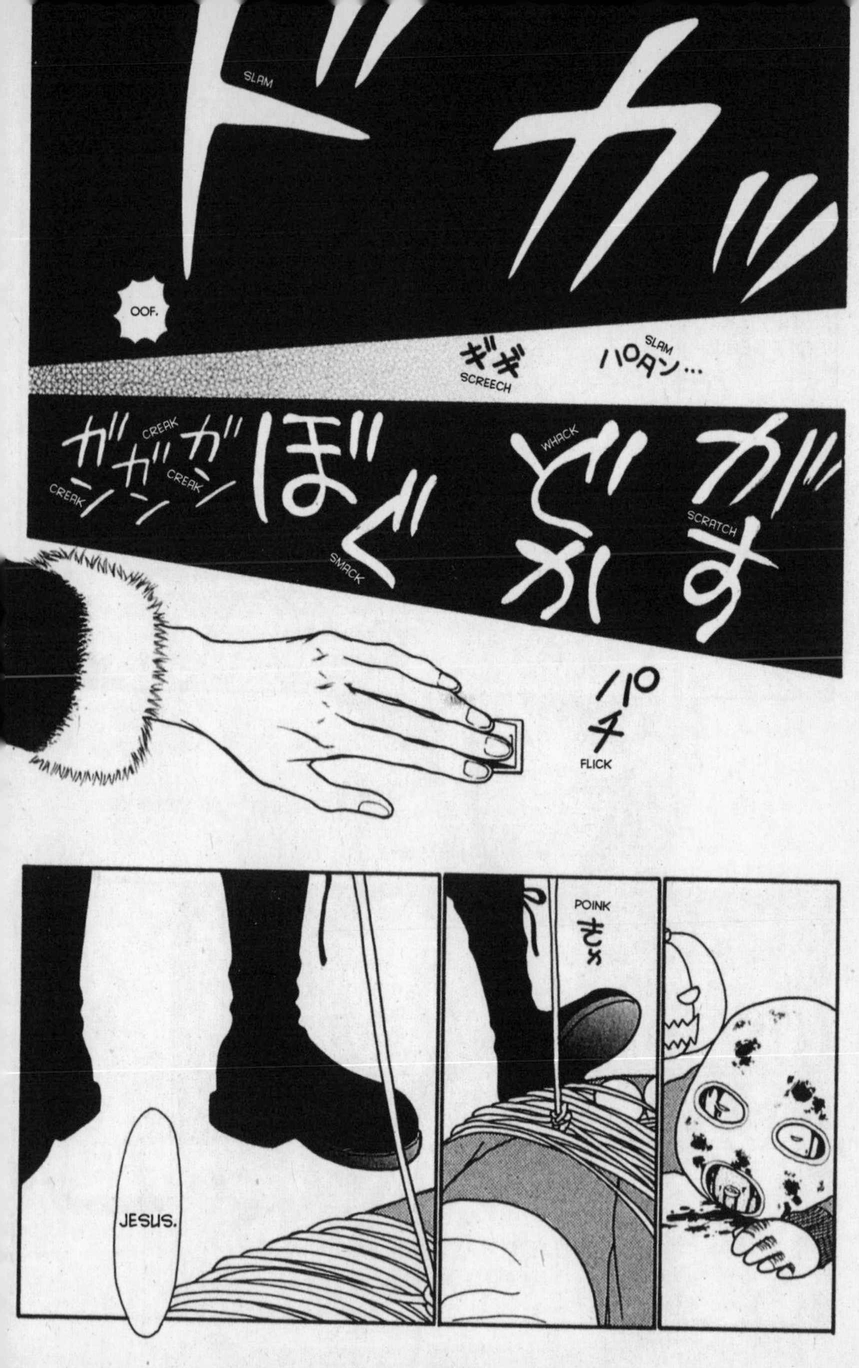
ドカッ
SLAM
OOF.
バタン…
SLAM
ギギ
SCREECH
がす
SCRATCH
どか
WHACK
ぼぐ
SMACK
ガガガン
CREAK
CREAK
CREAK
パチ
FLICK
POINK
JESUS.

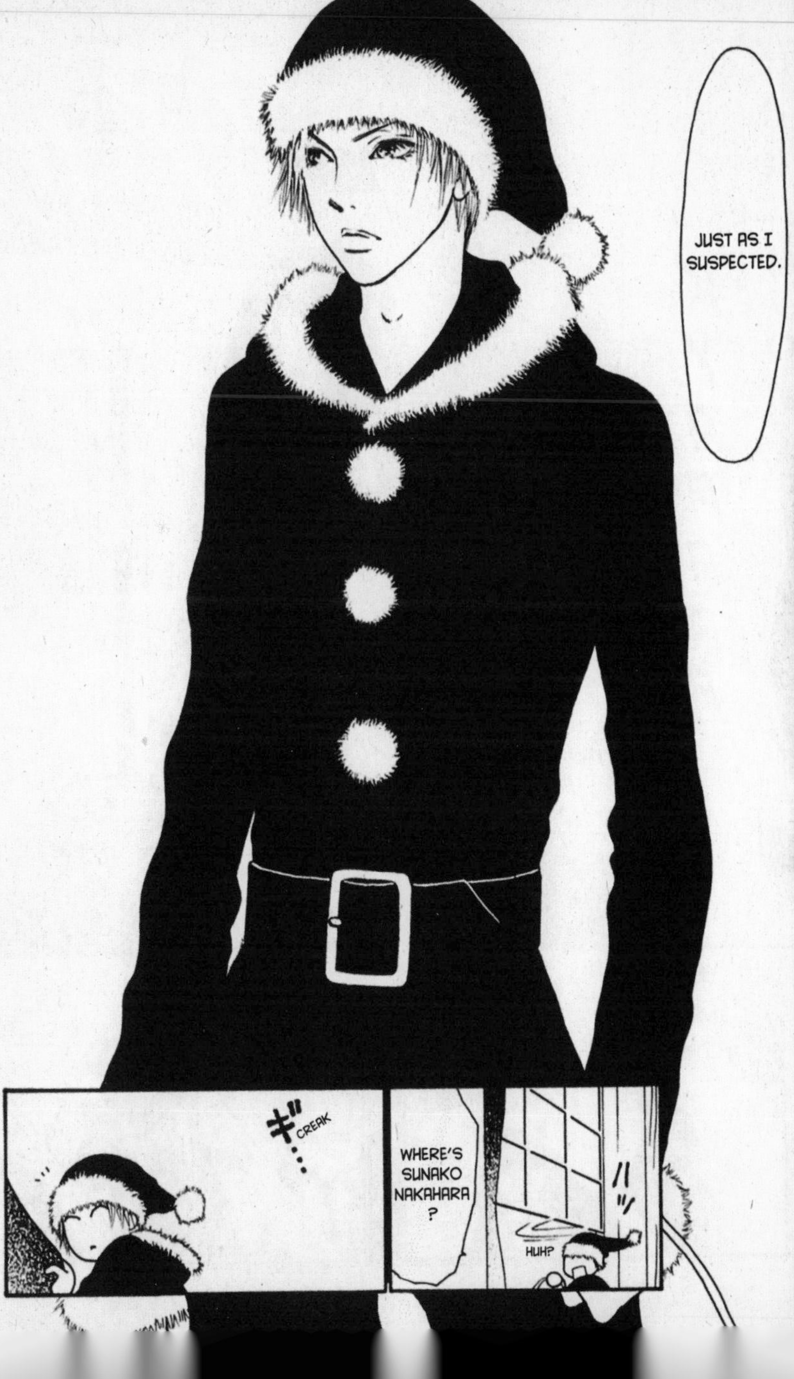
JUST AS I SUSPECTED.
ハッ
HUH?
WHERE'S SUNAKO NAKAHARA ?
ギ
CREAK

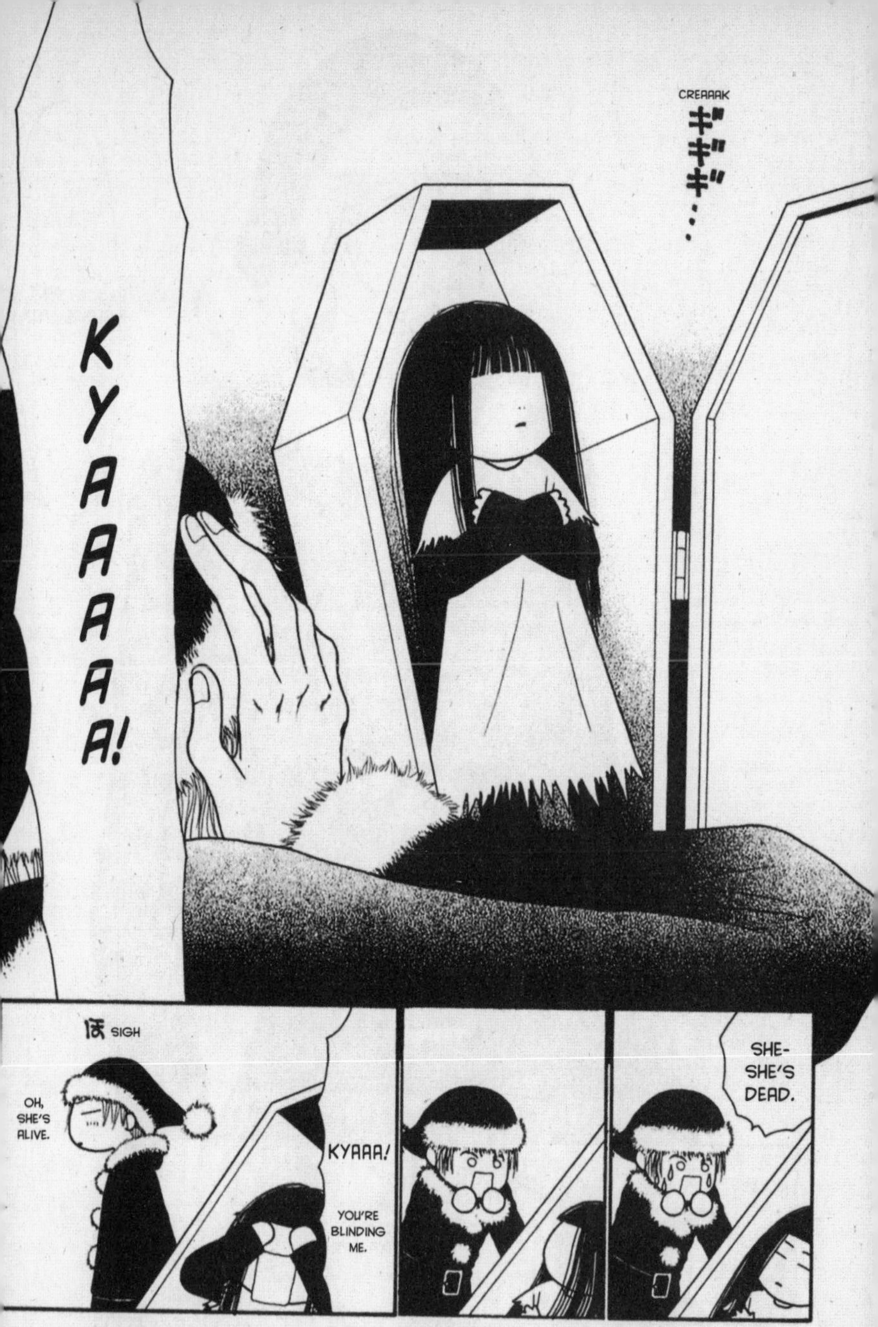
CREAAAK
ギギギ…
KYAAAAAAA!
SHE-SHE'S DEAD.
KYAAA!
YOU'RE BLINDING ME.
ほ SIGH
OH, SHE'S ALIVE.

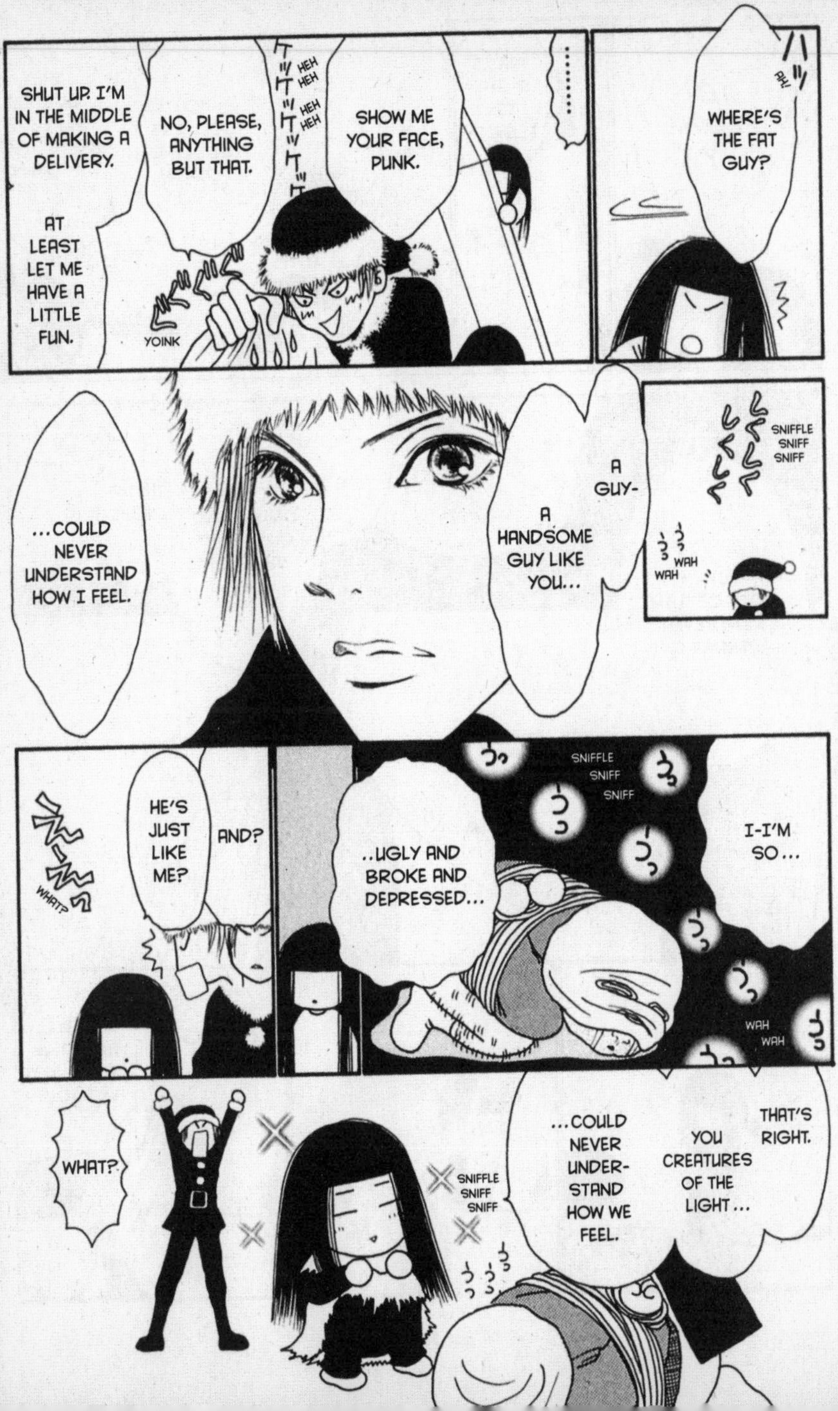
AH!
WHERE'S THE FAT GUY?
......
SHOW ME YOUR FACE, PUNK.
HEH HEH HEH HEH
NO, PLEASE, ANYTHING BUT THAT.
SHUT UP. I'M IN THE MIDDLE OF MAKING A DELIVERY.
AT LEAST LET ME HAVE A LITTLE FUN.
YOINK
SNIFFLE SNIFF SNIFF
WAH WAH
A GUY-
A HANDSOME GUY LIKE YOU...
...COULD NEVER UNDERSTAND HOW I FEEL.
I-I'M SO...
SNIFFLE SNIFF SNIFF
..UGLY AND BROKE AND DEPRESSED...
WAH WAH
AND?
HE'S JUST LIKE ME?
WHAT?
THAT'S RIGHT.
YOU CREATURES OF THE LIGHT...
...COULD NEVER UNDER-STAND HOW WE FEEL.
SNIFFLE SNIFF SNIFF
WHAT?

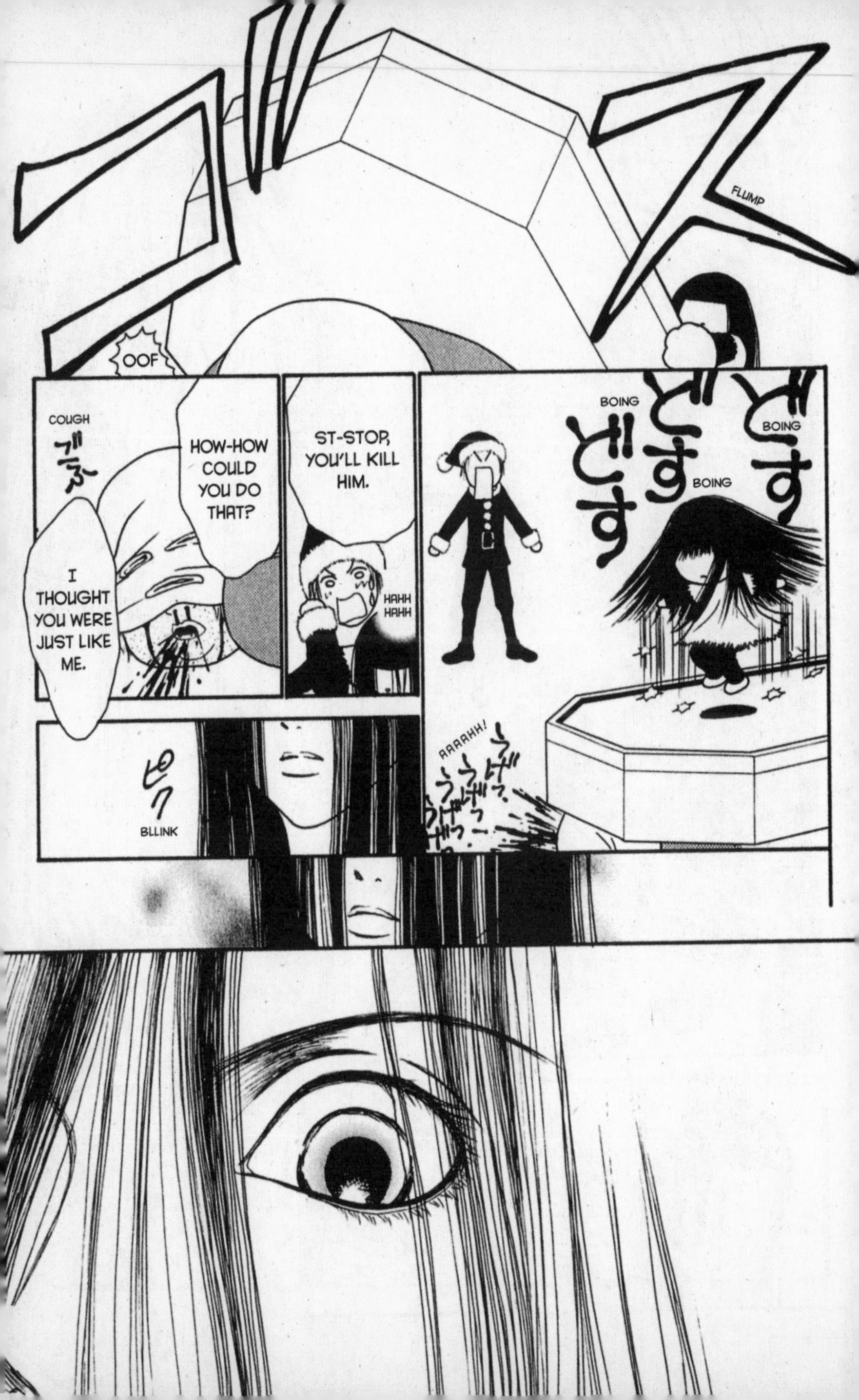
FLUMP
OOF
どす
BOING
どす
BOING
どす
BOING
AAAAHH!
ST-STOP, YOU'LL KILL HIM.
HAHH HAHH
HOW-HOW COULD YOU DO THAT?
COUGH
I THOUGHT YOU WERE JUST LIKE ME.
BLLINK

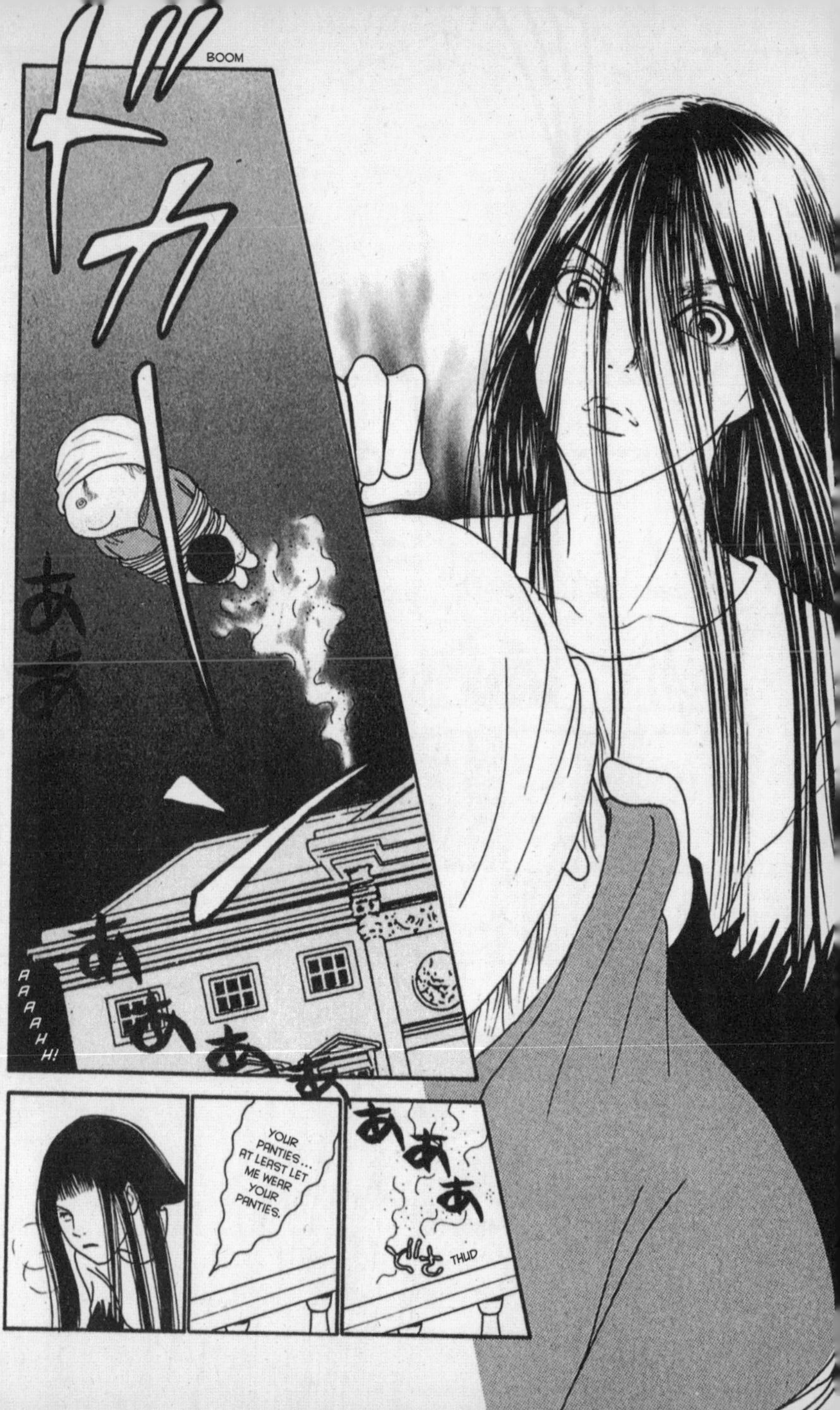
BOOM
AAAAAH!
THUD
YOUR PANTIES... AT LEAST LET ME WEAR YOUR PANTIES.

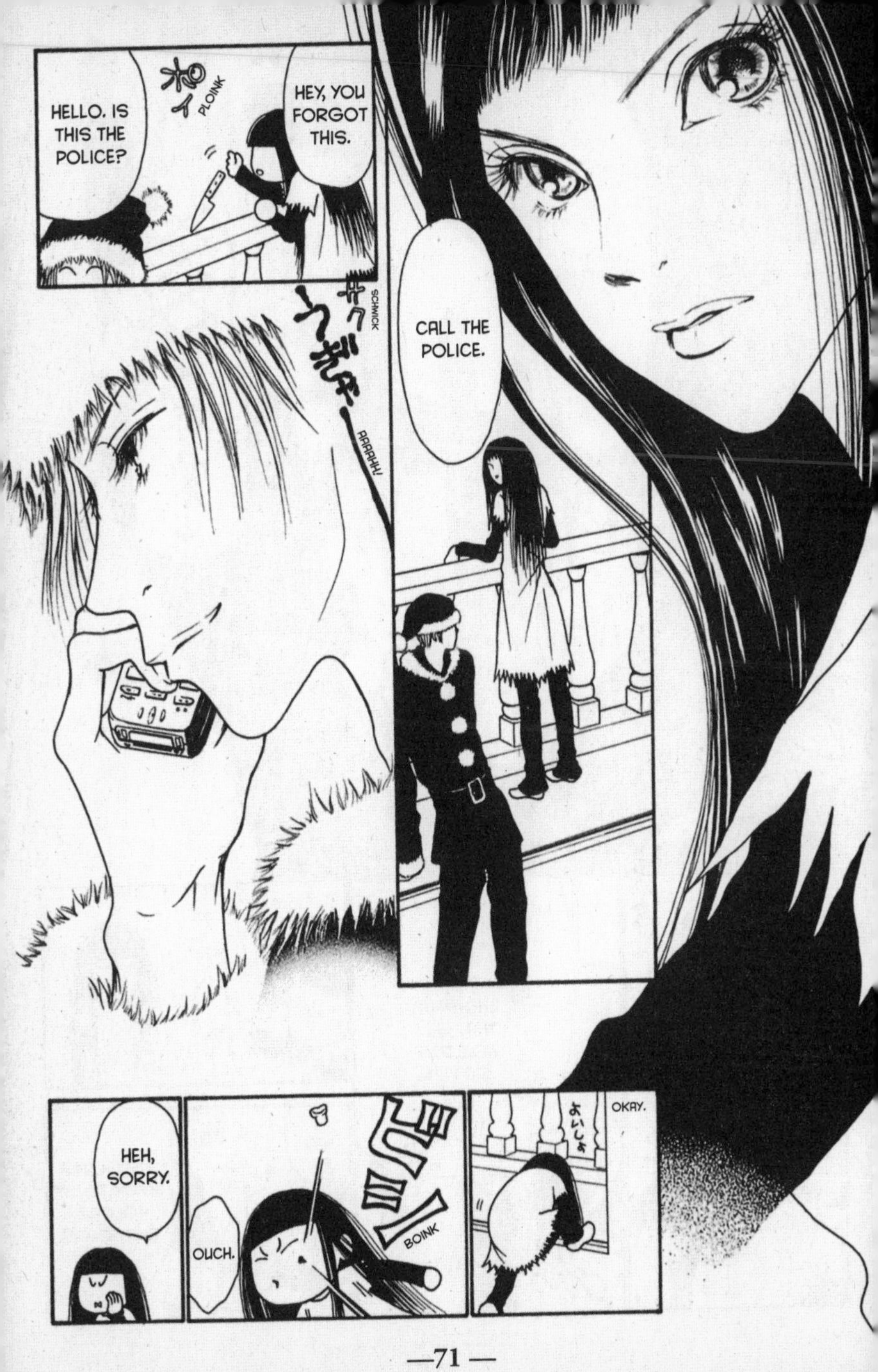
CALL THE POLICE.
HEY, YOU FORGOT THIS.
PLOINK
HELLO. IS THIS THE POLICE?
SCHWICK
AAAAHH!
OKAY.
よいしょ
BOINK
OUCH.
HEH, SORRY.

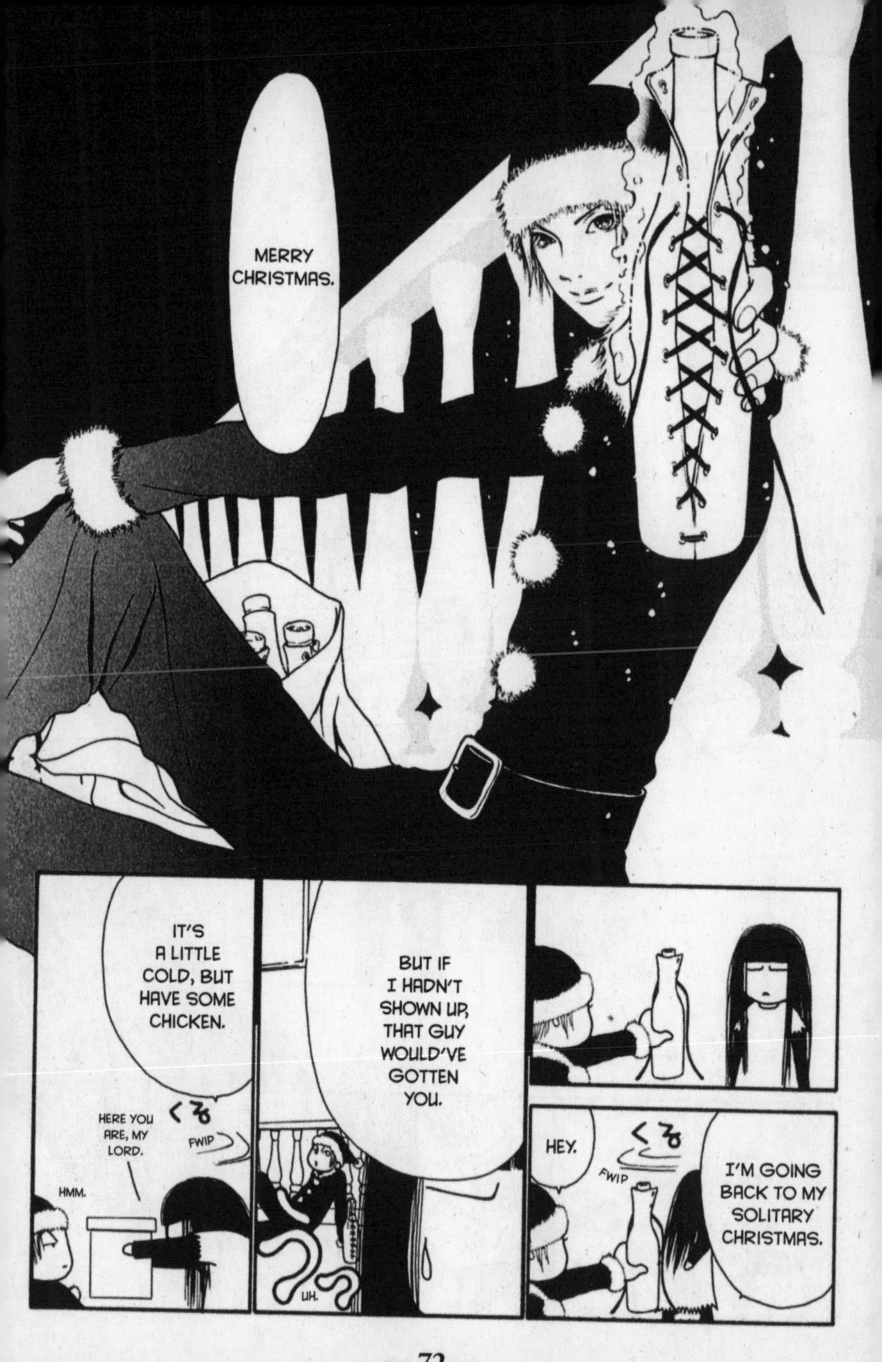
MERRY CHRISTMAS.
I'M GOING BACK TO MY SOLITARY CHRISTMAS.
くる
FWIP
HEY.
BUT IF I HADN'T SHOWN UP, THAT GUY WOULD'VE GOTTEN YOU.
UH.
IT'S A LITTLE COLD, BUT HAVE SOME CHICKEN.
くる
FWIP
HERE YOU ARE, MY LORD.
HMM.

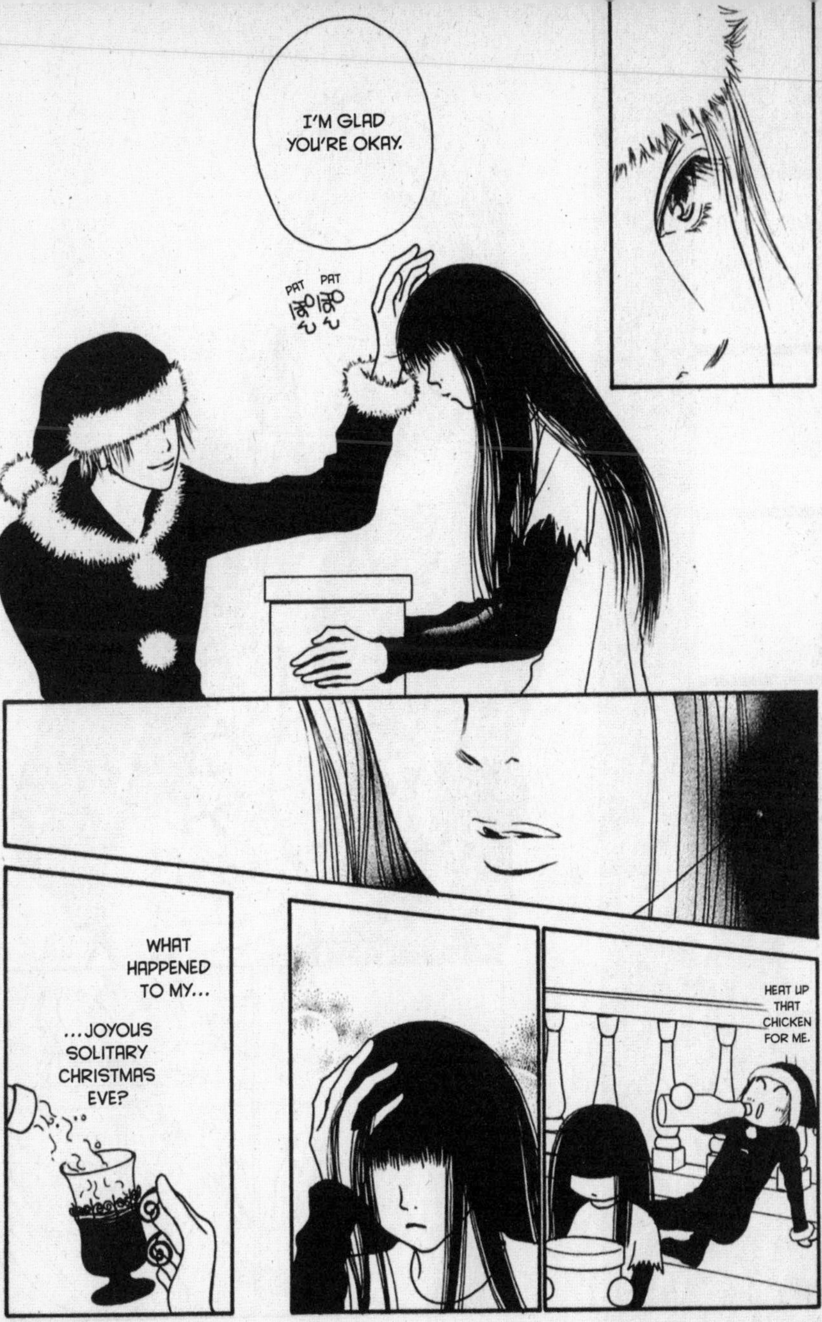
I'M GLAD YOU'RE OKAY.
PAT PAT
HEAT UP THAT CHICKEN FOR ME.
WHAT HAPPENED TO MY...
...JOYOUS SOLITARY CHRISTMAS EVE?

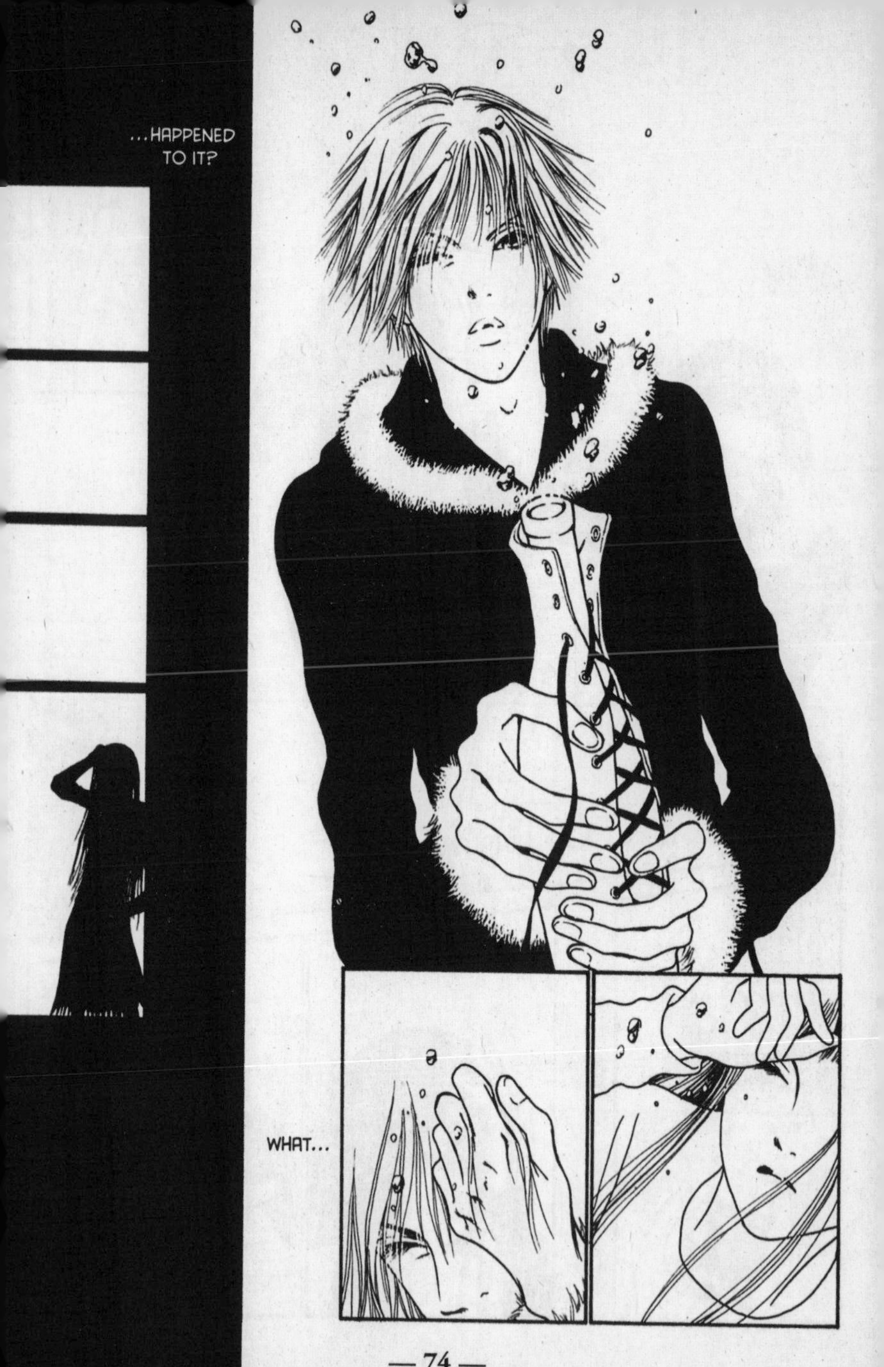
WHAT...
...HAPPENED
TO IT?

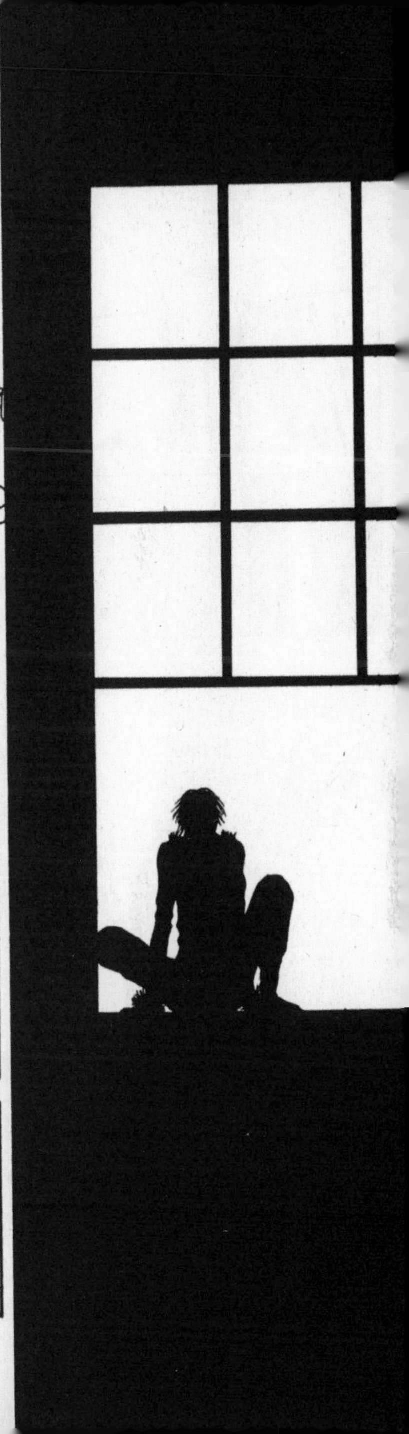
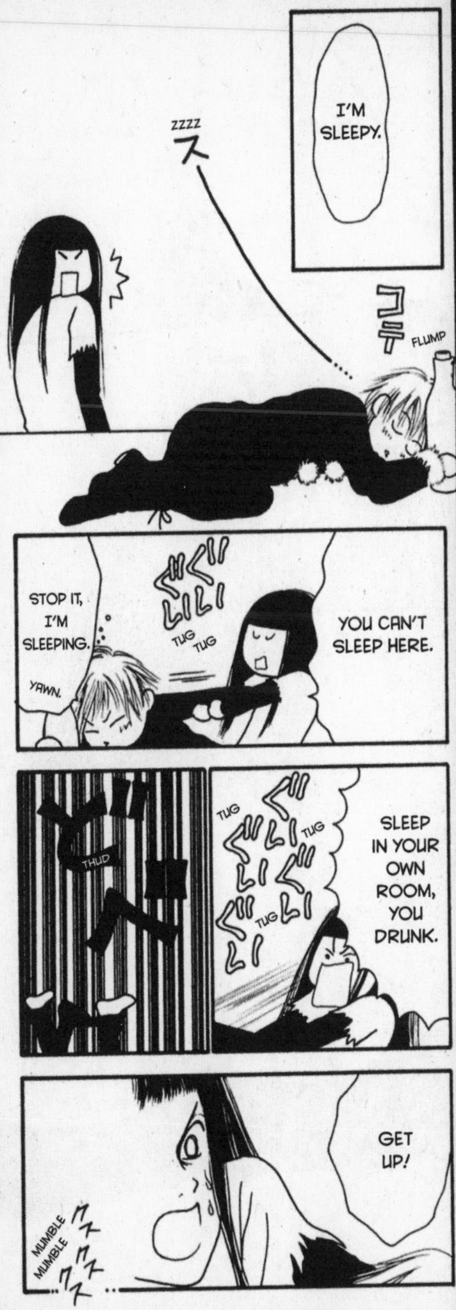
I'M SLEEPY.
ZZZZ
FLUMP
YOU CAN'T SLEEP HERE.
TUG TUG
STOP IT, I'M SLEEPING.
YAWN.
SLEEP IN YOUR OWN ROOM, YOU DRUNK.
TUG TUG TUG
THUD
GET UP!
MUMBLE MUMBLE

クスクス MUMBLE
MUMBLE... I'M FULL... MUMBLE.
クスクス MUMBLE
ZZZ ス

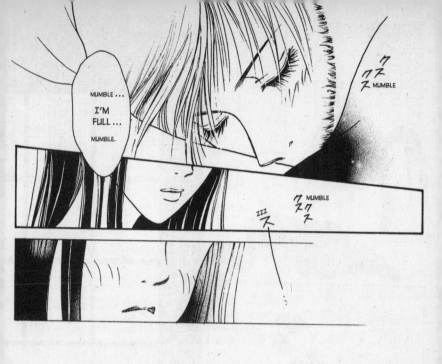

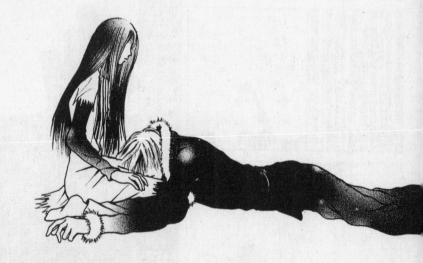

OH, S-SORRY.

NO, IT'S NOT WHAT YOU THINK.

HELP ME CARRY KYOHEI TO HIS ROOM.

バターン

SLAM

LISTEN TO WHAT HAPPENED TO ME, SUNAKO-CHAN.

ばん？

SLAM

DON'T YOU THINK THAT'S AWFUL?

JUST HELP ME CARRY KYOHEI.

SHE TOLD ME THAT HER HUSBAND MIGHT COME HOME SUDDENLY.

LISTEN TO WHAT HAPPENED.

HELP ME CARRY HIM—

LET'S ALL GET DRUNK TOGETHER, DAMN IT!

GO GET US SOME BOOZE.

ばん

SLAM

OH, HI EVERYBODY.

LISTEN TO WHAT HAPPENED TO ME, SUNAKO-CHAN.

ばん

SLAM

OH, HI KYOHEI, HI RANMARU.

LISTEN TO WHAT HAPPENED TO ME, SUNAKO-CHAN.

— 77 —

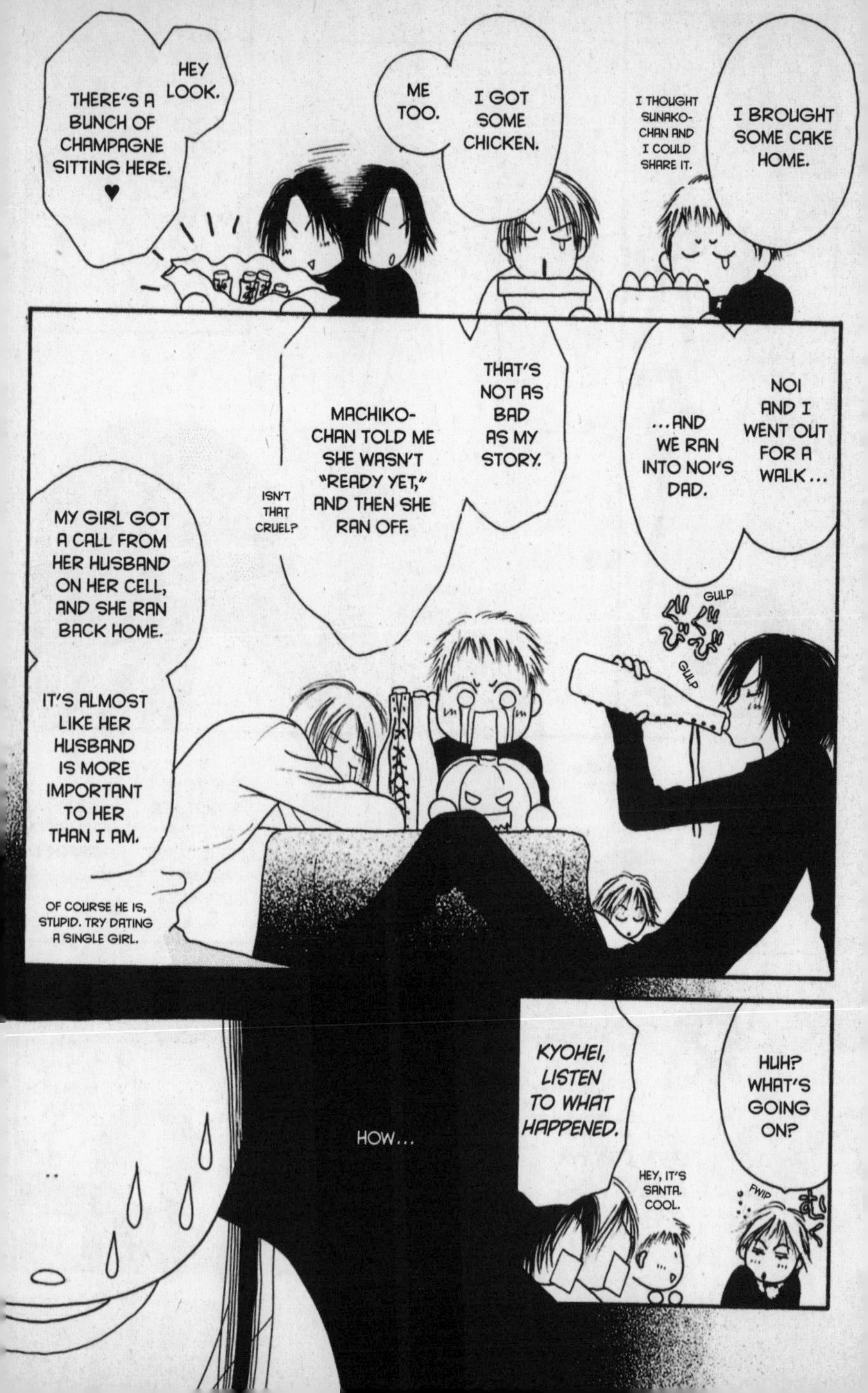
I BROUGHT SOME CAKE HOME.
I THOUGHT SUNAKO-CHAN AND I COULD SHARE IT.
I GOT SOME CHICKEN.
ME TOO.
HEY LOOK.
THERE'S A BUNCH OF CHAMPAGNE SITTING HERE. ♥
NOI AND I WENT OUT FOR A WALK...
...AND WE RAN INTO NOI'S DAD.
THAT'S NOT AS BAD AS MY STORY.
MACHIKO-CHAN TOLD ME SHE WASN'T "READY YET," AND THEN SHE RAN OFF.
ISN'T THAT CRUEL?
GULP
GULP
MY GIRL GOT A CALL FROM HER HUSBAND ON HER CELL, AND SHE RAN BACK HOME.
IT'S ALMOST LIKE HER HUSBAND IS MORE IMPORTANT TO HER THAN I AM.
OF COURSE HE IS, STUPID. TRY DATING A SINGLE GIRL.
HUH? WHAT'S GOING ON?
FWIP
HEY, IT'S SANTA. COOL.
KYOHEI, LISTEN TO WHAT HAPPENED.
HOW...
..

...COULD
THIS
HAPPEN...

...TO MY
LOVELY
CHRISTMAS?

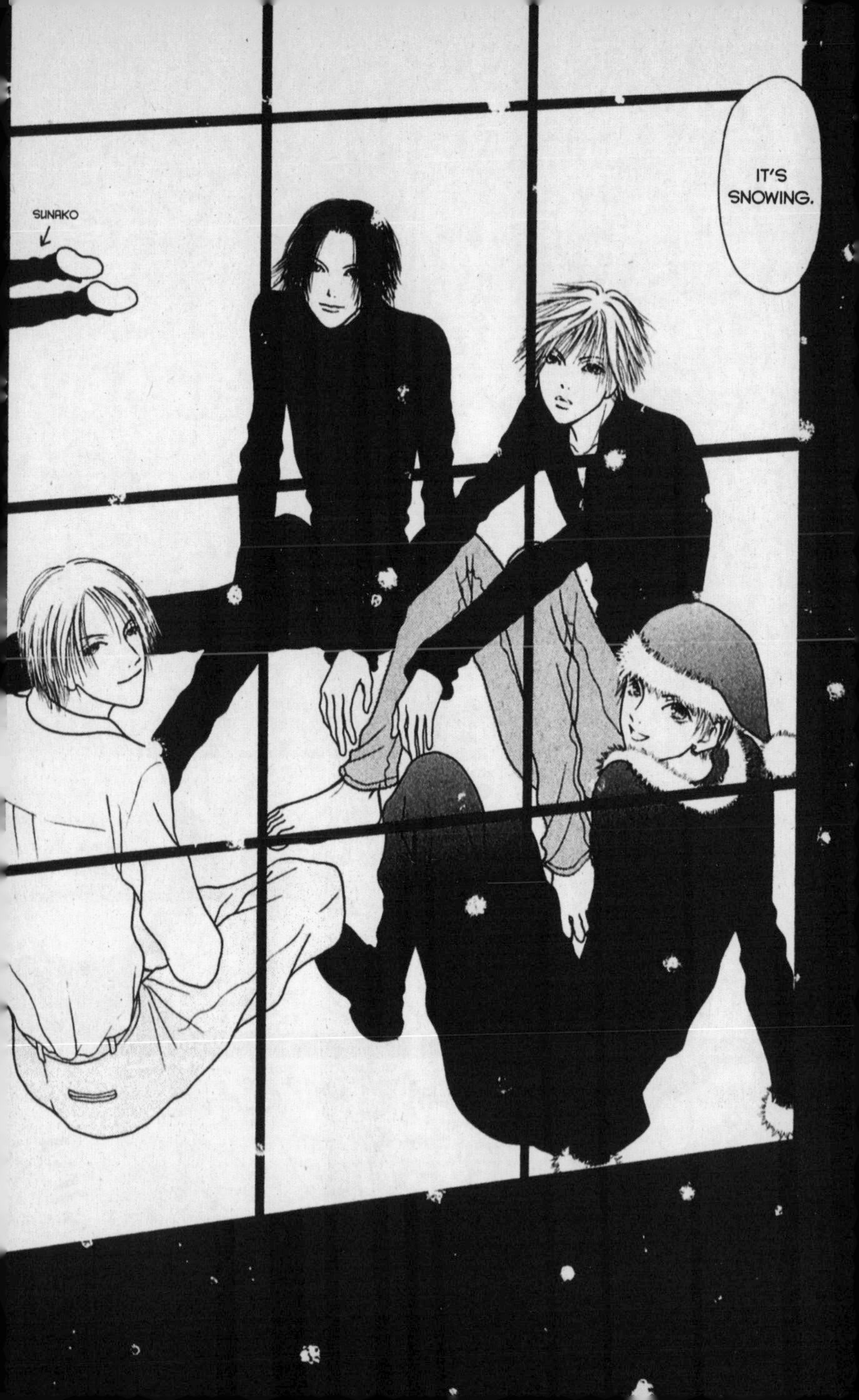
IT'S SNOWING.
SUNAKO

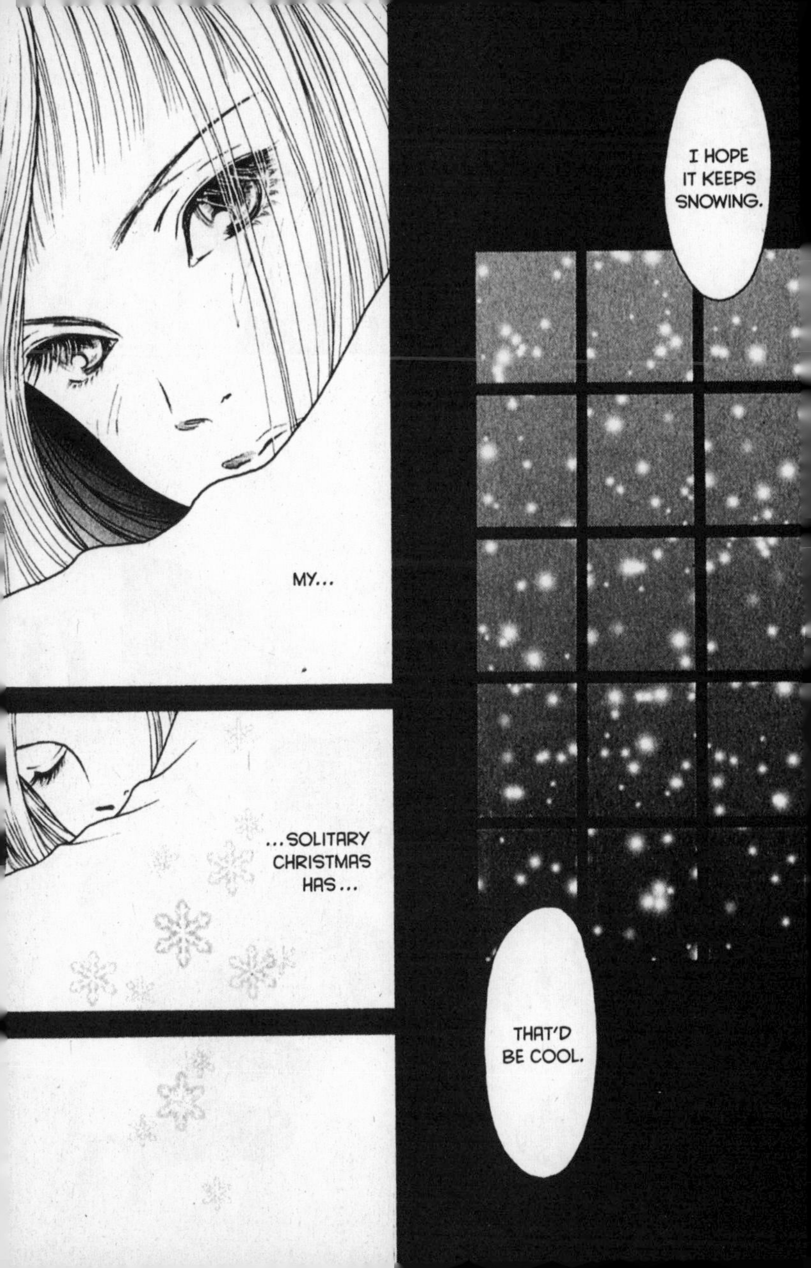
I HOPE IT KEEPS SNOWING.
THAT'D BE COOL.
MY...
...SOLITARY CHRISTMAS HAS...

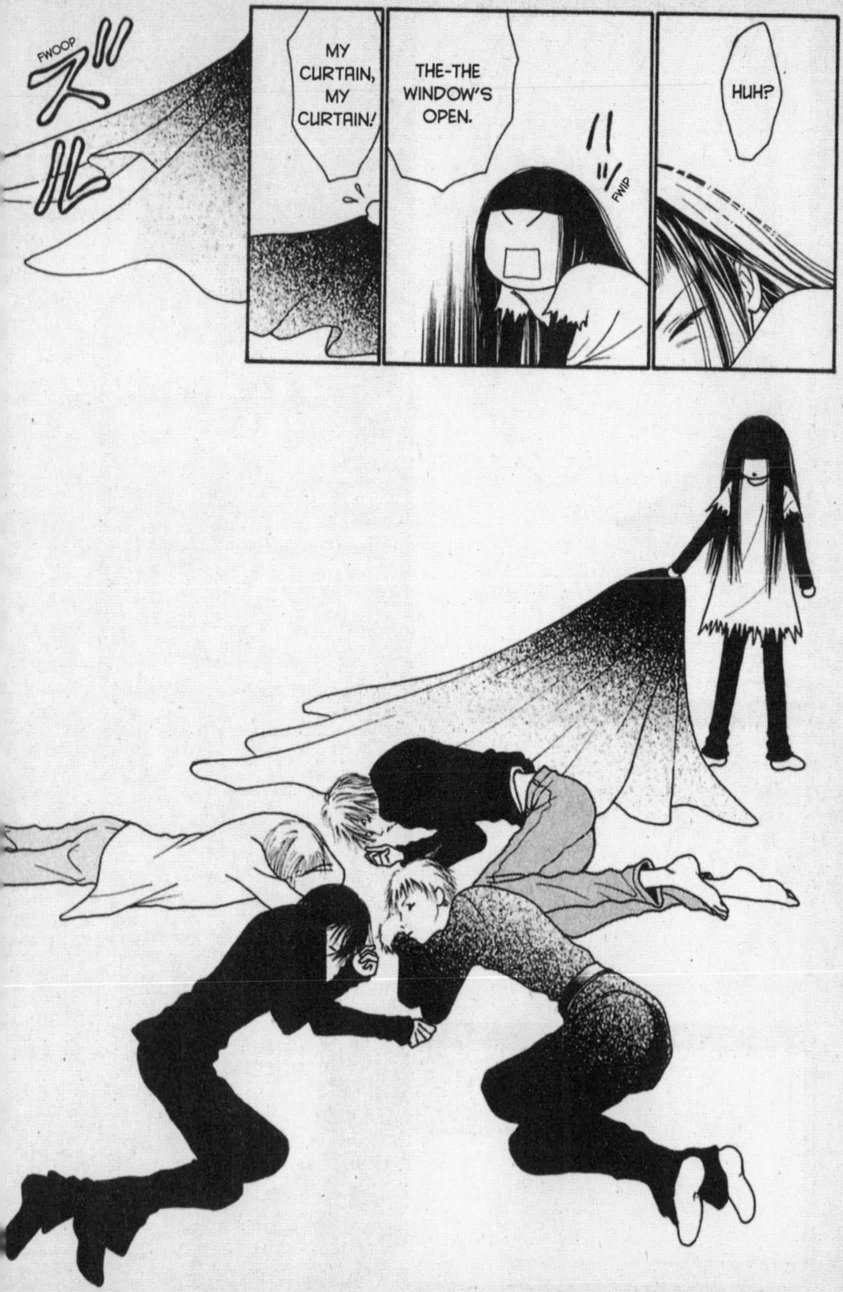
HUH?
THE-THE WINDOW'S OPEN.
FWIP
MY CURTAIN, MY CURTAIN!
FWOOP

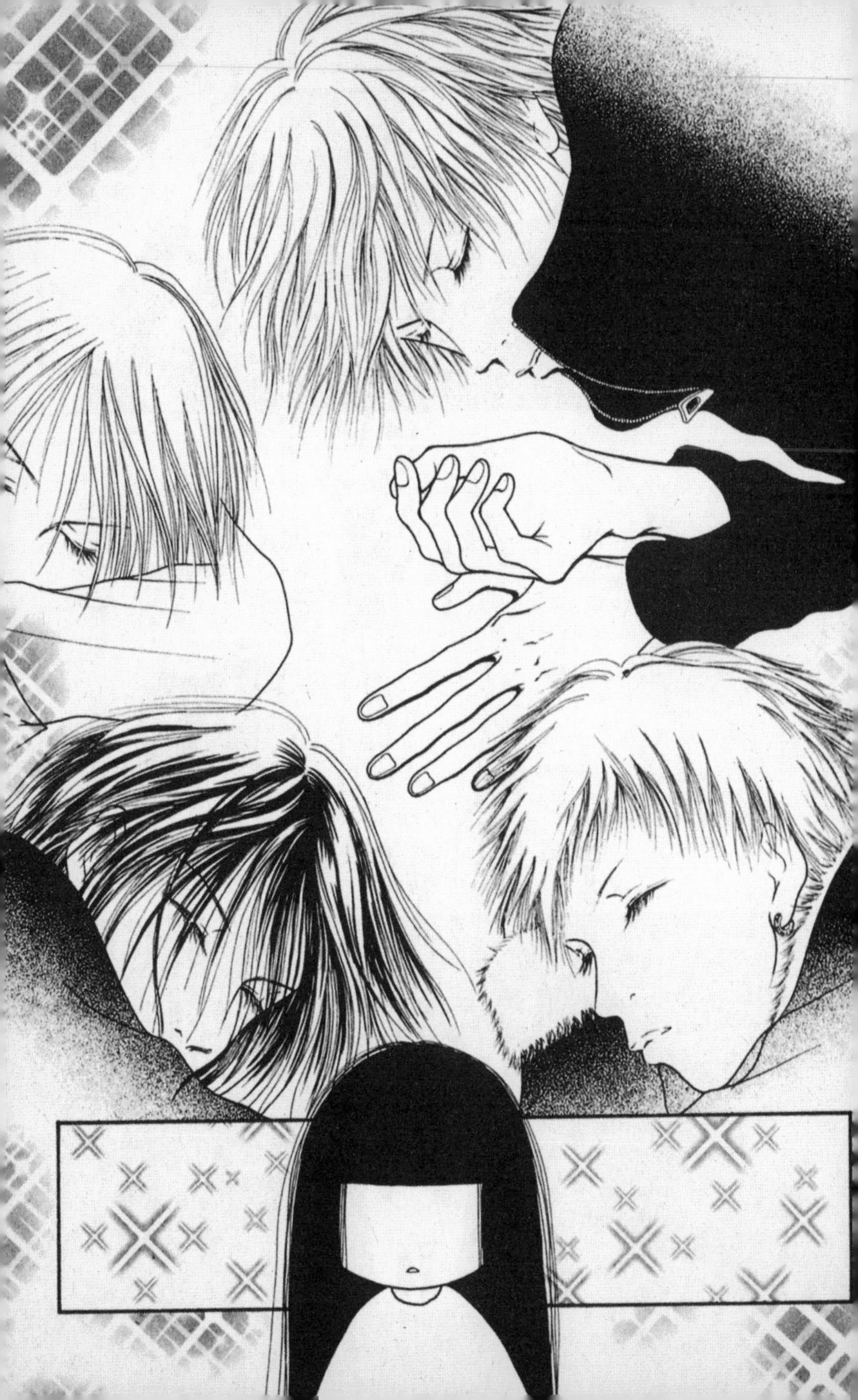

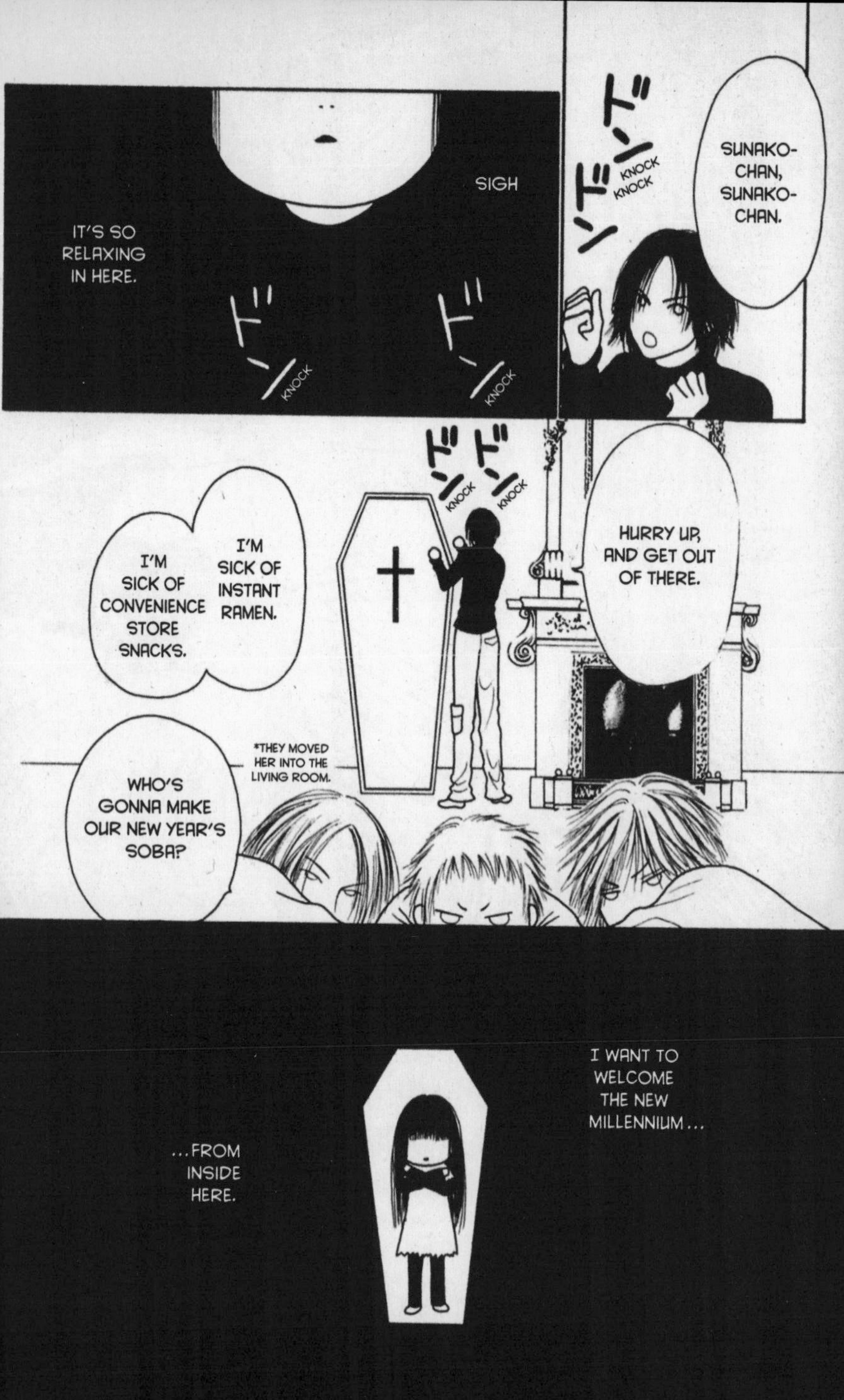
KNOCK KNOCK
SUNAKO-CHAN, SUNAKO-CHAN.
SIGH
IT'S SO RELAXING IN HERE.
KNOCK
KNOCK
HURRY UP, AND GET OUT OF THERE.
KNOCK
KNOCK
I'M SICK OF INSTANT RAMEN.
I'M SICK OF CONVENIENCE STORE SNACKS.
*THEY MOVED HER INTO THE LIVING ROOM.
WHO'S GONNA MAKE OUR NEW YEAR'S SOBA?
I WANT TO WELCOME THE NEW MILLENNIUM...
...FROM INSIDE HERE.

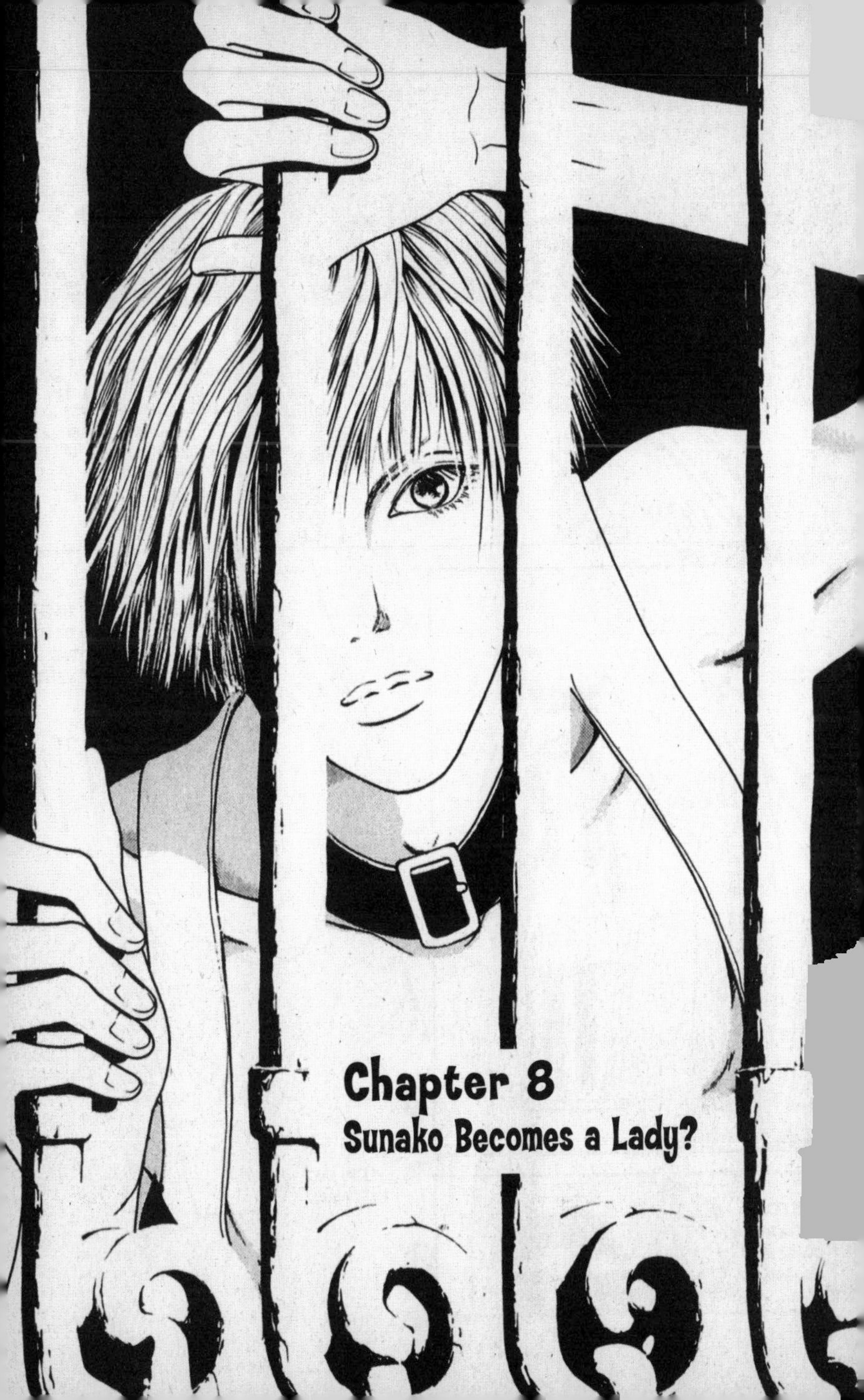
Chapter 8
Sunako Becomes a Lady?

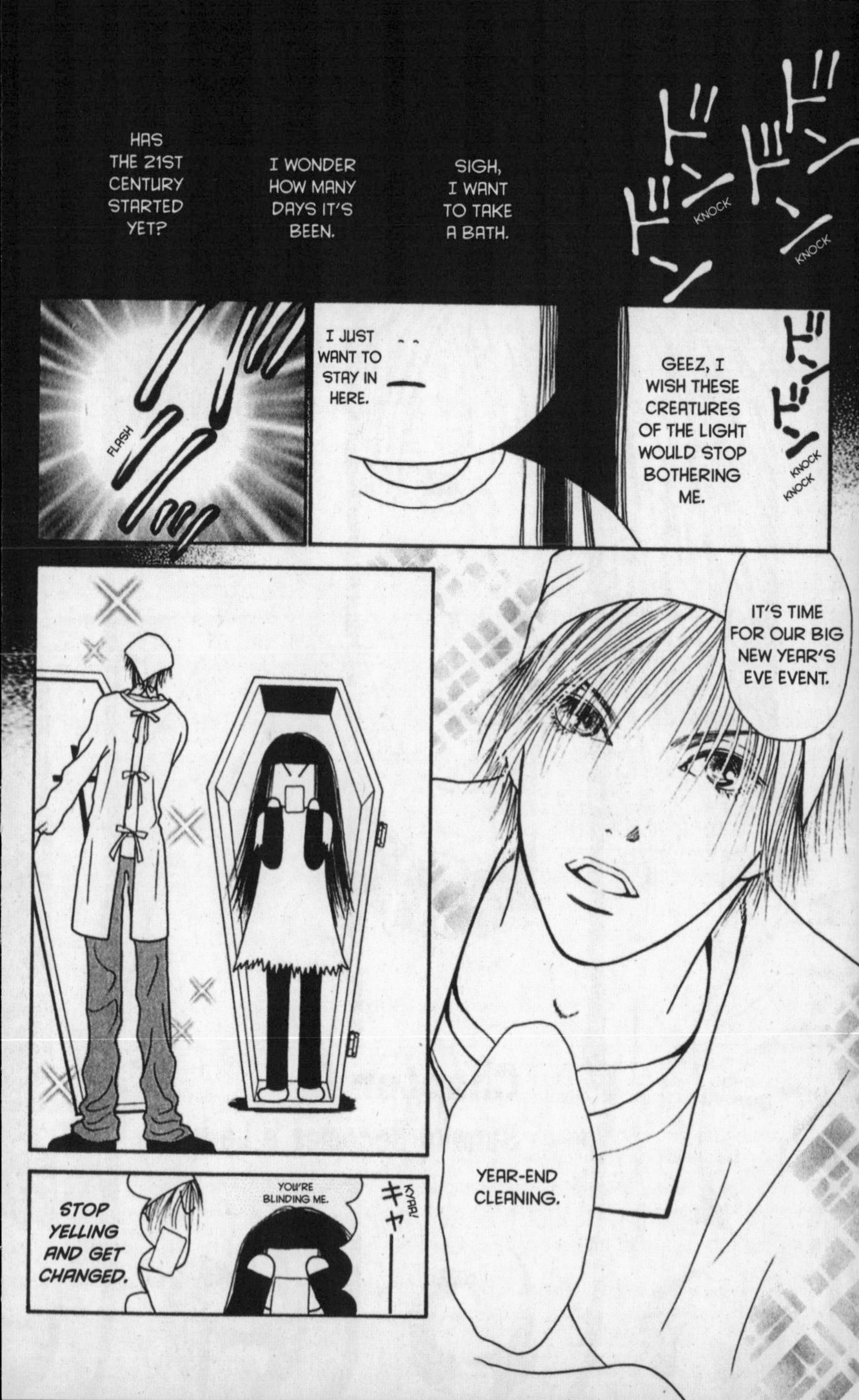
ドンドン
KNOCK KNOCK
SIGH, I WANT TO TAKE A BATH.
I WONDER HOW MANY DAYS IT'S BEEN.
HAS THE 21ST CENTURY STARTED YET?
ドンドン
KNOCK KNOCK
GEEZ, I WISH THESE CREATURES OF THE LIGHT WOULD STOP BOTHERING ME.
I JUST WANT TO STAY IN HERE.
FLASH
IT'S TIME FOR OUR BIG NEW YEAR'S EVE EVENT.
YEAR-END CLEANING.
キャー
KYAA!
YOU'RE BLINDING ME.
STOP YELLING AND GET CHANGED.

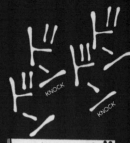

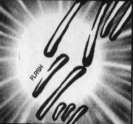

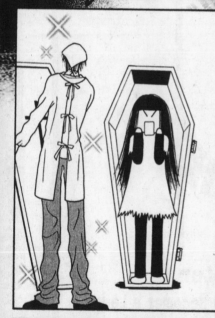

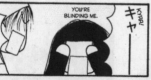

BEHIND THE SCENES

LOOKS LIKE I'VE WRITTEN A MANGA WITH NO MAIN CHARACTER. UH-OH.

IT WAS HARD TO MAKE SUNAKO LOOK SEXY. I WAS LISTENING TO SONGS BY THE BANDS KUROYUME AND SADS WHEN I DREW HER. THAT HELPED ME GET INTO THE MOOD.

KYOHEI IS SINGING THE FAMOUS SONG "PISTOL." IF YOU SEE THE VIDEO FOR THAT SONG, YOU'LL GET IT.

I DIDN'T HAVE ENOUGH ASSISTANTS. I HAD TO BEG AYA WATANABE AT *BEKKAN FRIEND* FOR HELP. THANKS AYA.

HYSTERIA'S SONGS ♪ "LET'S DANCE" ... ♪ "SHOW ME HOW YOU LICK" "JUST LIKE A WHORE" ... AND STUFF LIKE THAT. I ALSO LISTENED ♪ TO THE SONG "STRAWBERRY" AND MANY, MANY OTHERS.

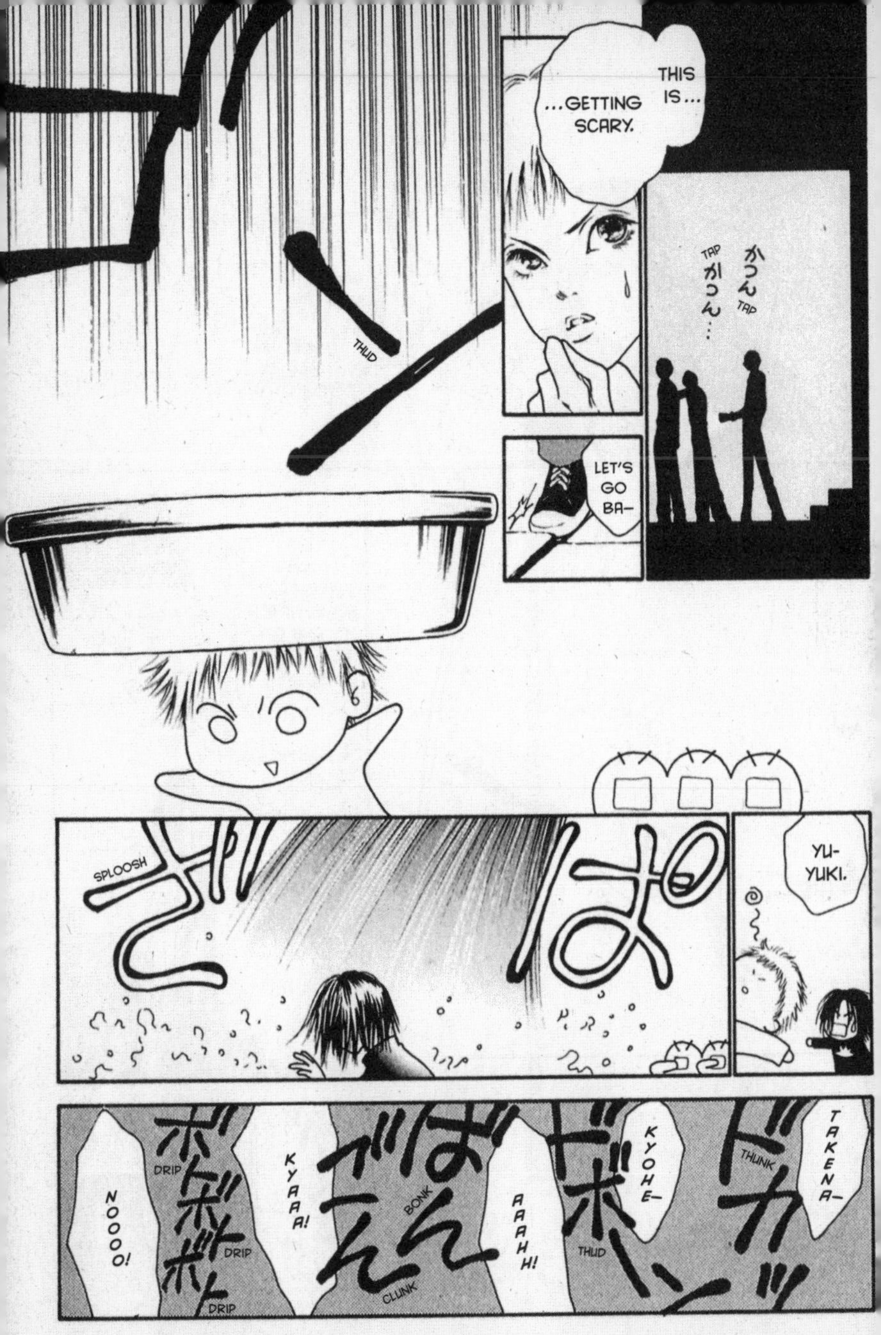
かつん TAP
かつん… TAP
THIS IS…
…GETTING SCARY.
LET'S GO BA–
THUD
YU-YUKI.
SPLOOSH
TAKENA–
THUNK
KYOHE–
THUD
AAAAHH!
KYAAA!
BONK
CLUNK
DRIP
DRIP
DRIP
NOOOO!

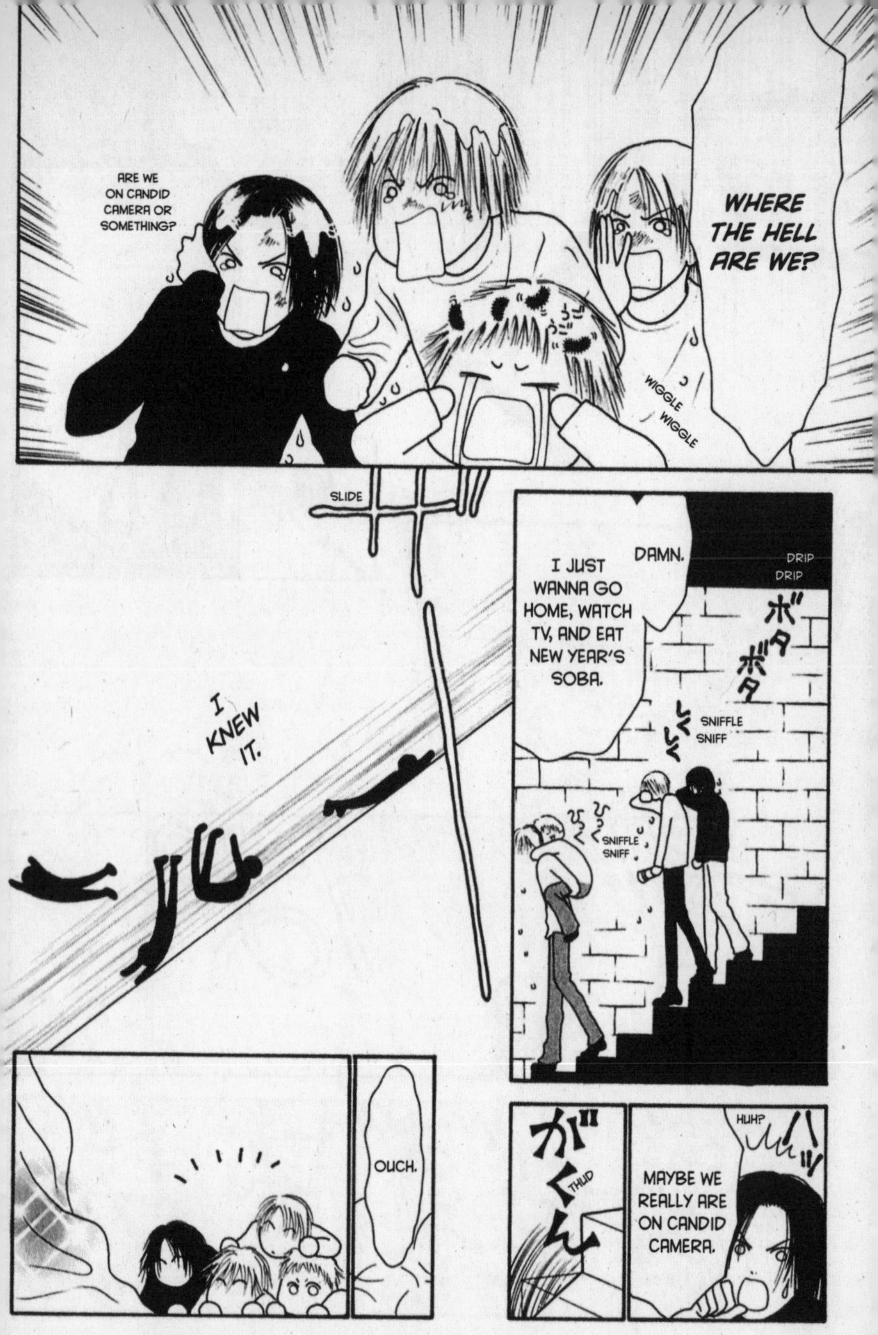
WHERE THE HELL ARE WE?
ARE WE ON CANDID CAMERA OR SOMETHING?
WIGGLE WIGGLE
DAMN.
I JUST WANNA GO HOME, WATCH TV, AND EAT NEW YEAR'S SOBA.
ボタボタ
DRIP DRIP
SNIFFLE SNIFF
SNIFFLE SNIFF
SLIDE
I KNEW IT.
HUH?
ハッ
MAYBE WE REALLY ARE ON CANDID CAMERA.
がくん
THUD
OUCH.

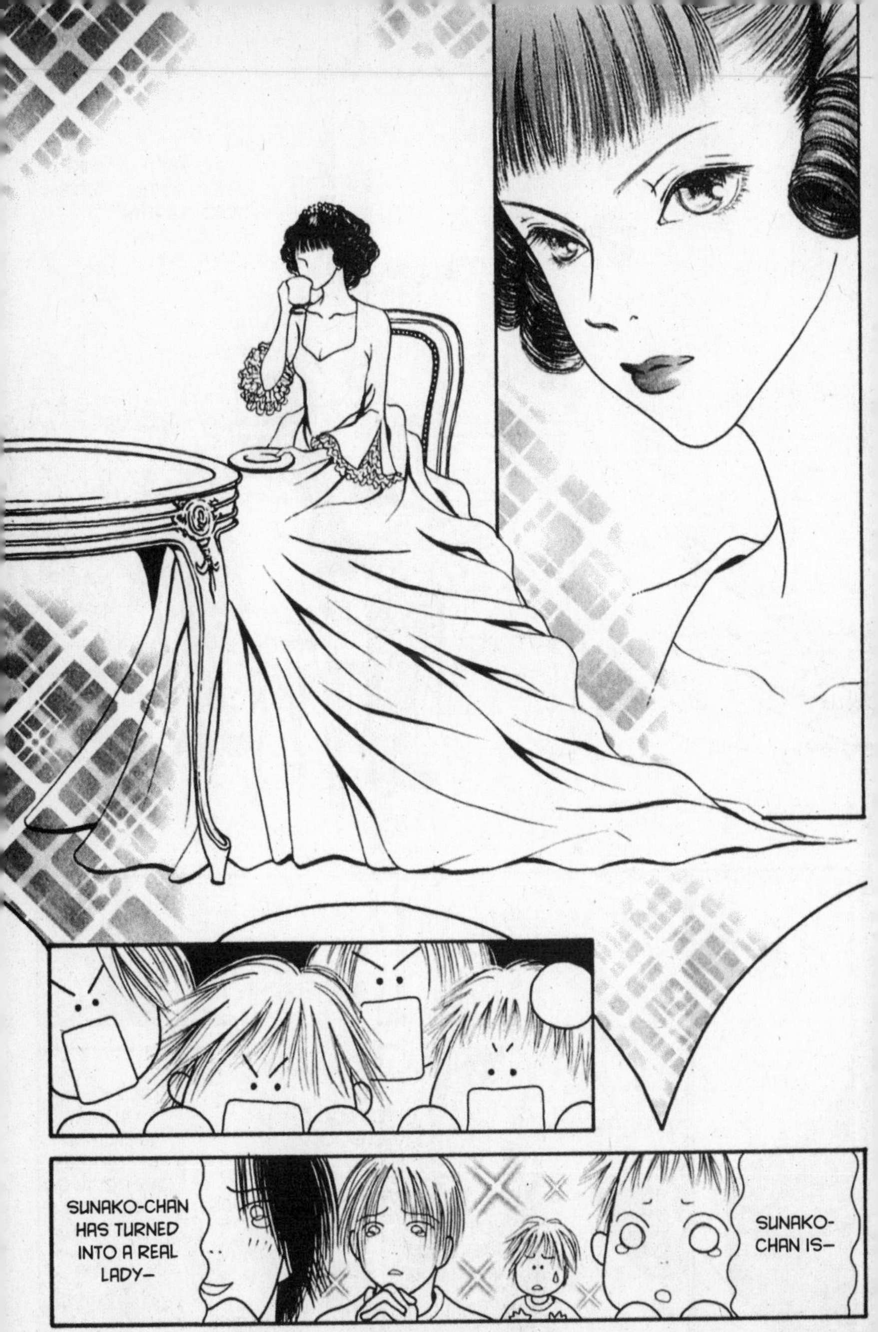
SUNAKO-CHAN IS—
SUNAKO-CHAN HAS TURNED INTO A REAL LADY—

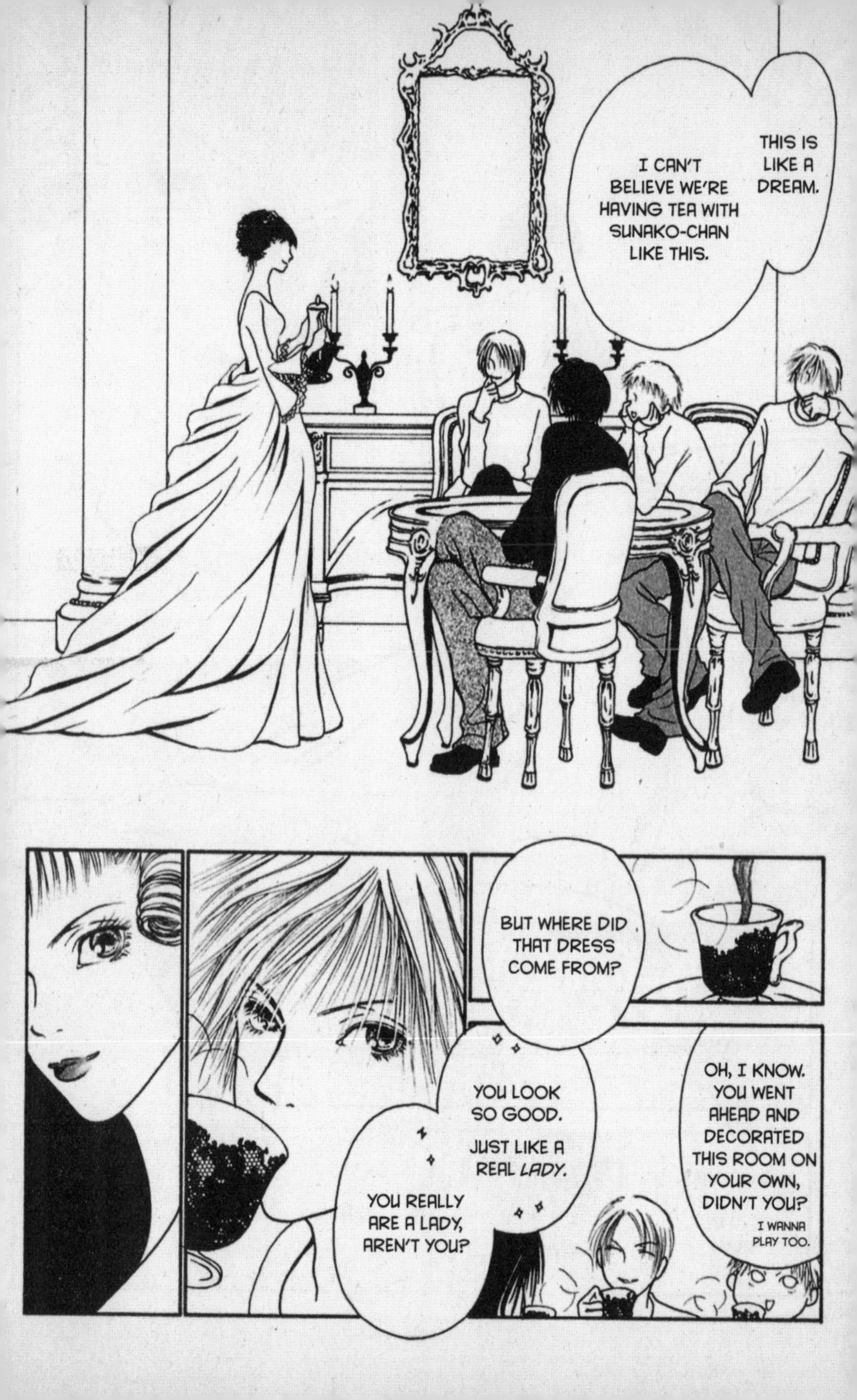
THIS IS LIKE A DREAM.
I CAN'T BELIEVE WE'RE HAVING TEA WITH SUNAKO-CHAN LIKE THIS.
BUT WHERE DID THAT DRESS COME FROM?
OH, I KNOW. YOU WENT AHEAD AND DECORATED THIS ROOM ON YOUR OWN, DIDN'T YOU?
I WANNA PLAY TOO.
YOU LOOK SO GOOD.
JUST LIKE A REAL *LADY*.
YOU REALLY ARE A LADY, AREN'T YOU?

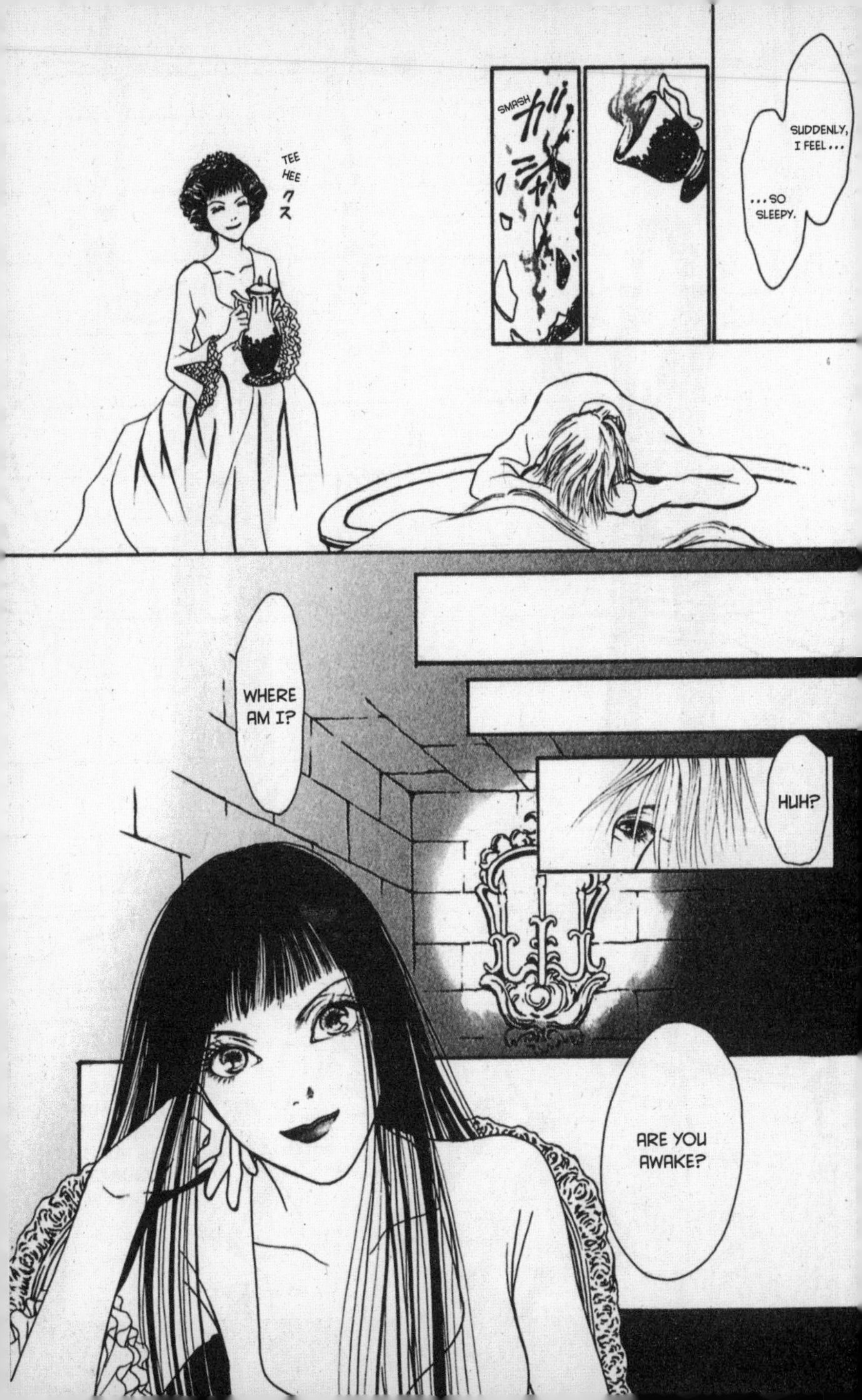
SUDDENLY, I FEEL...
...SO SLEEPY.
SMASH
TEE HEE クス
WHERE AM I?
HUH?
ARE YOU AWAKE?

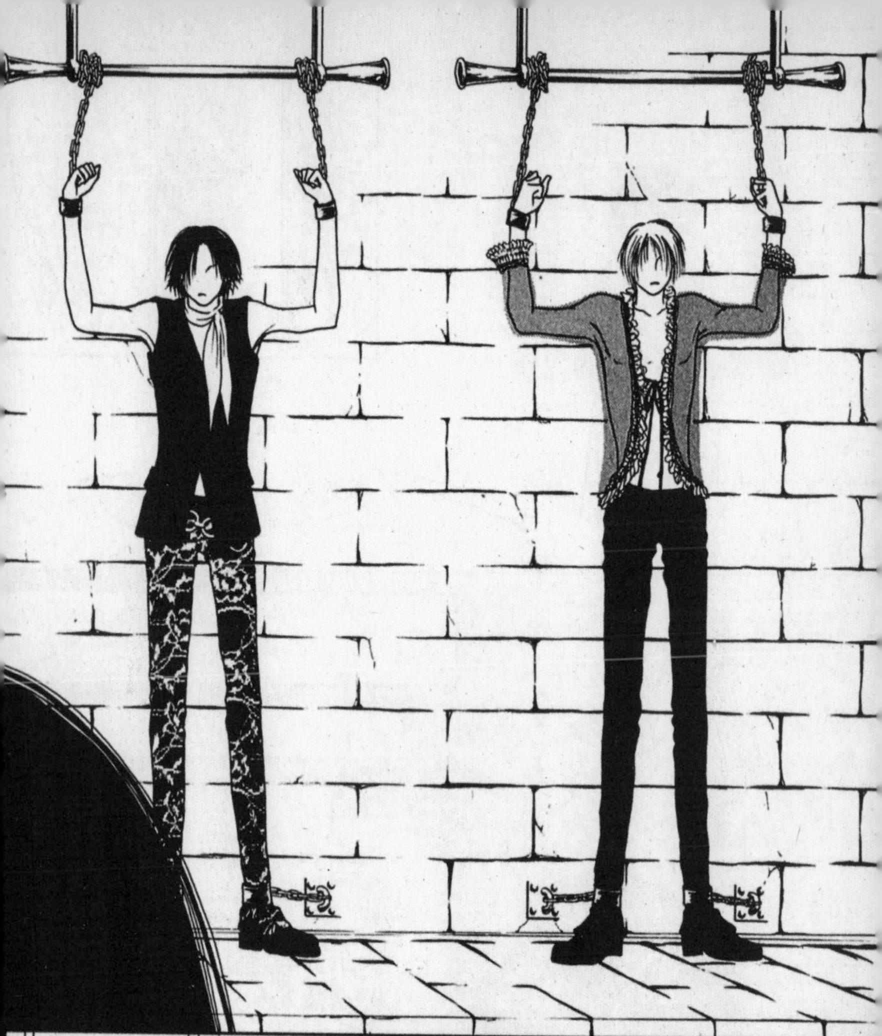

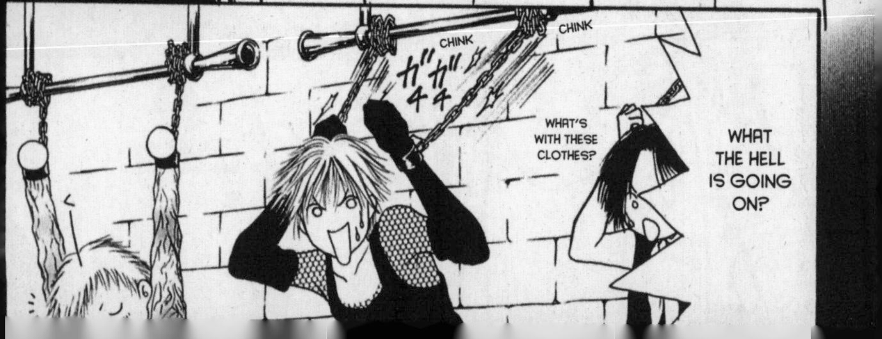
WHAT THE HELL IS GOING ON?
WHAT'S WITH THESE CLOTHES?
CHINK
CHINK
ガチガチ

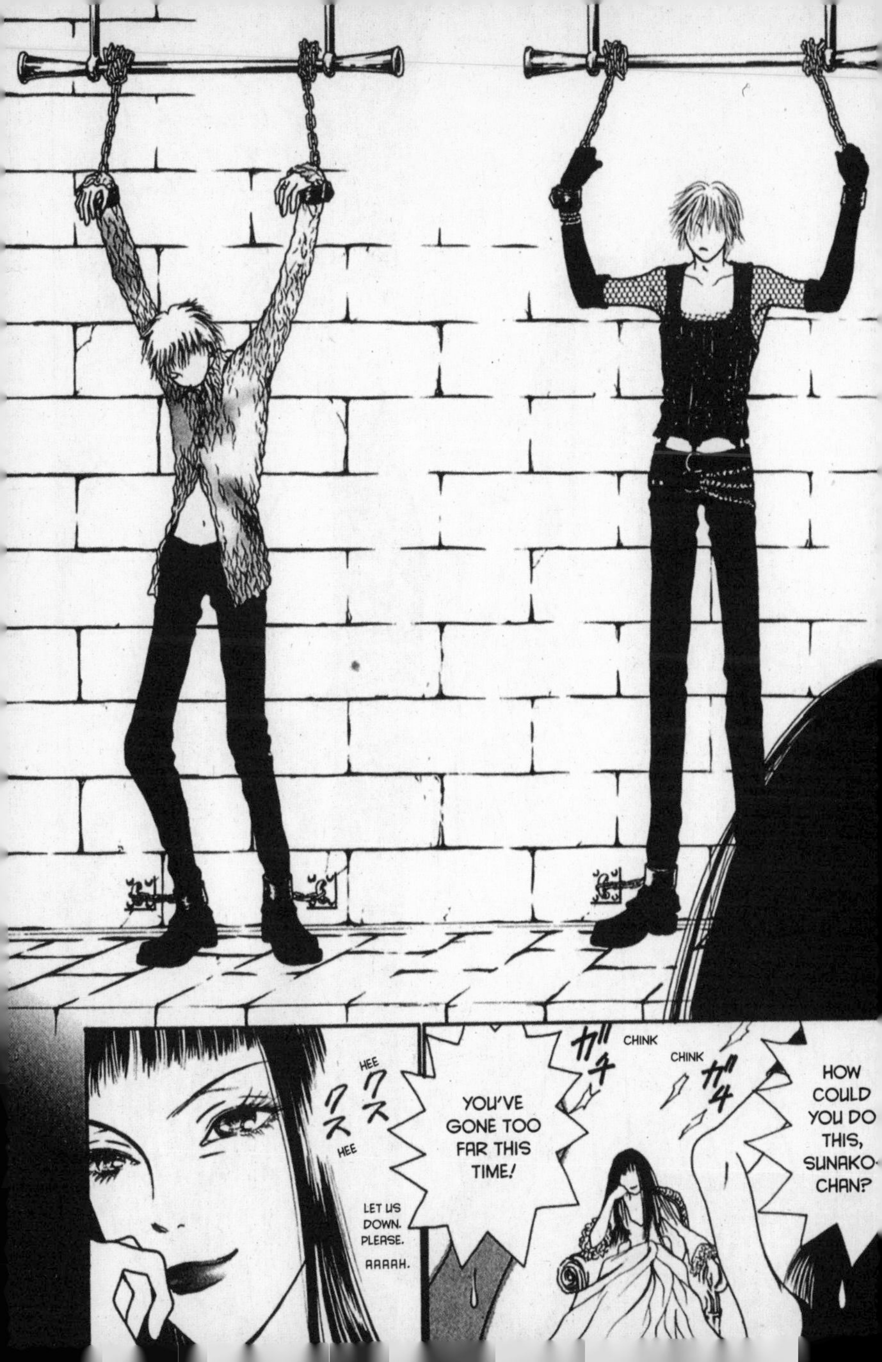
HOW COULD YOU DO THIS, SUNAKO-CHAN?
ガチ CHINK
ガチ CHINK
YOU'VE GONE TOO FAR THIS TIME!
LET US DOWN. PLEASE.
AAAAH.
クスクス HEE HEE

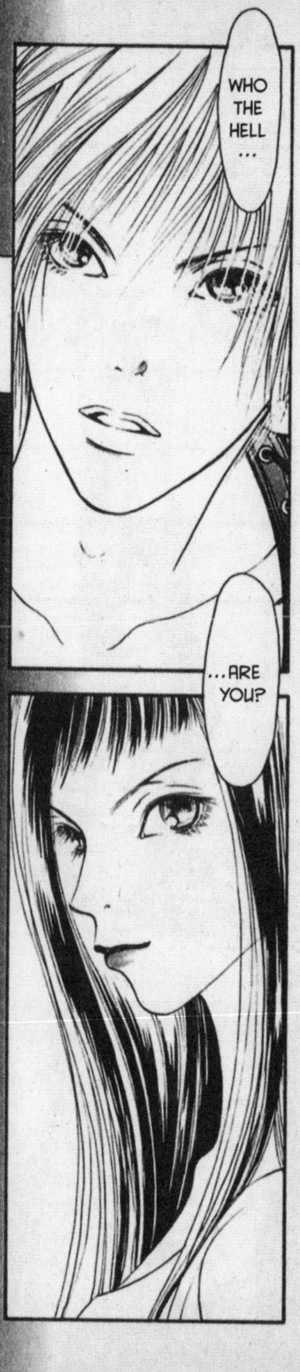
WHO THE HELL ...
...ARE YOU?

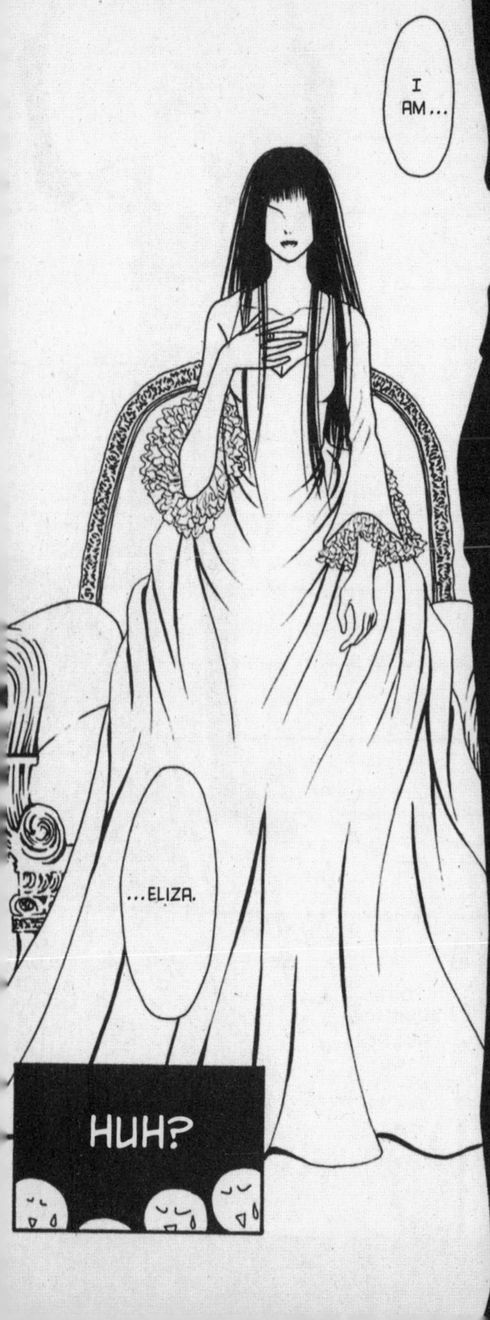
I AM...
...ELIZA.
HUH?

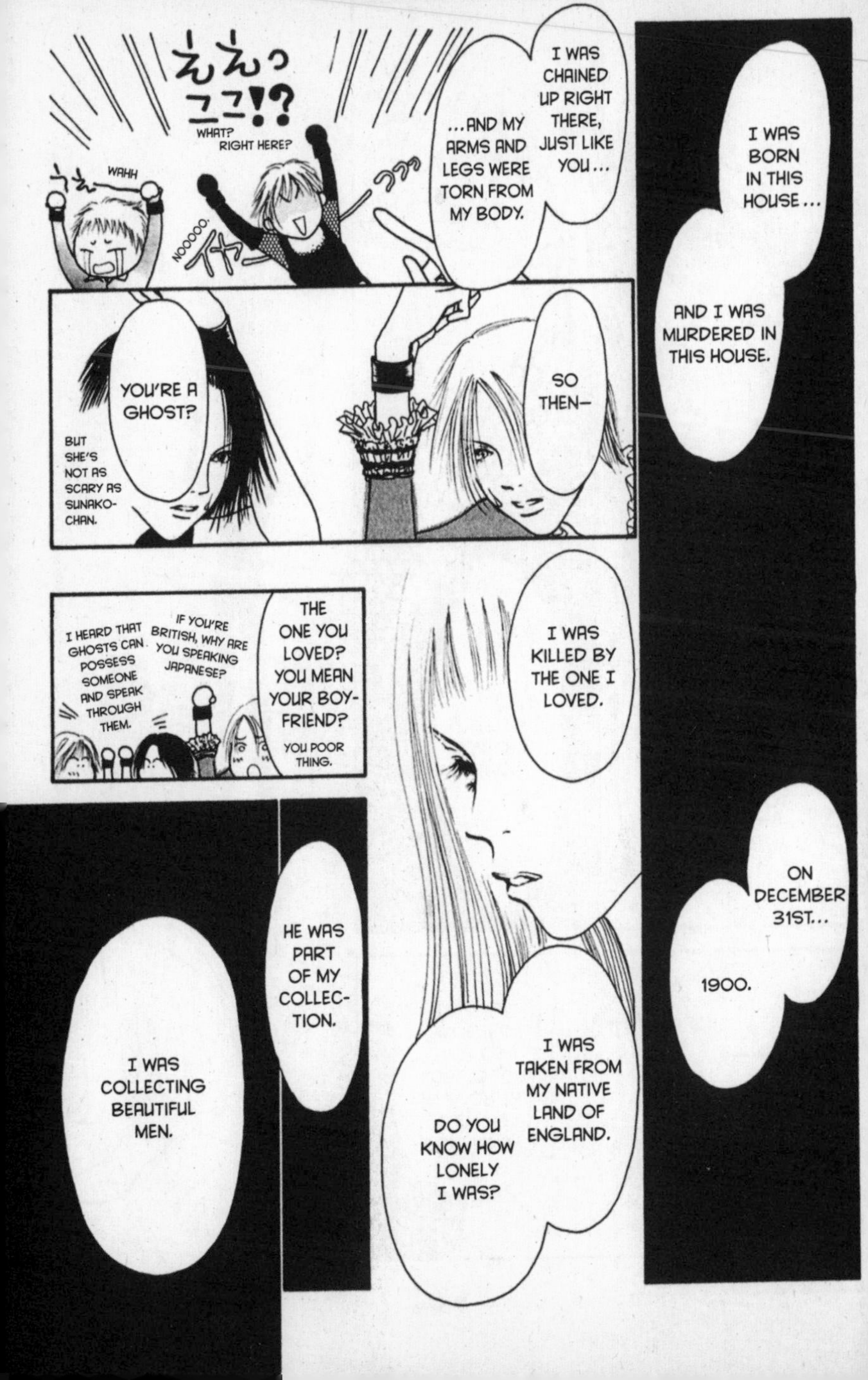

I WAS BORN IN THIS HOUSE...
AND I WAS MURDERED IN THIS HOUSE.
ON DECEMBER 31ST...
1900.
I WAS CHAINED UP RIGHT THERE, JUST LIKE YOU...
...AND MY ARMS AND LEGS WERE TORN FROM MY BODY.
えぇっ ココ!?
WHAT? RIGHT HERE?
イヤー
NOOOOO.
うぇー
WAHH
SO THEN—
YOU'RE A GHOST?
BUT SHE'S NOT AS SCARY AS SUNAKO-CHAN.
I WAS KILLED BY THE ONE I LOVED.
I WAS TAKEN FROM MY NATIVE LAND OF ENGLAND.
DO YOU KNOW HOW LONELY I WAS?
THE ONE YOU LOVED? YOU MEAN YOUR BOY-FRIEND?
YOU POOR THING.
IF YOU'RE BRITISH, WHY ARE YOU SPEAKING JAPANESE?
I HEARD THAT GHOSTS CAN POSSESS SOMEONE AND SPEAK THROUGH THEM.
HE WAS PART OF MY COLLEC-TION.
I WAS COLLECTING BEAUTIFUL MEN.

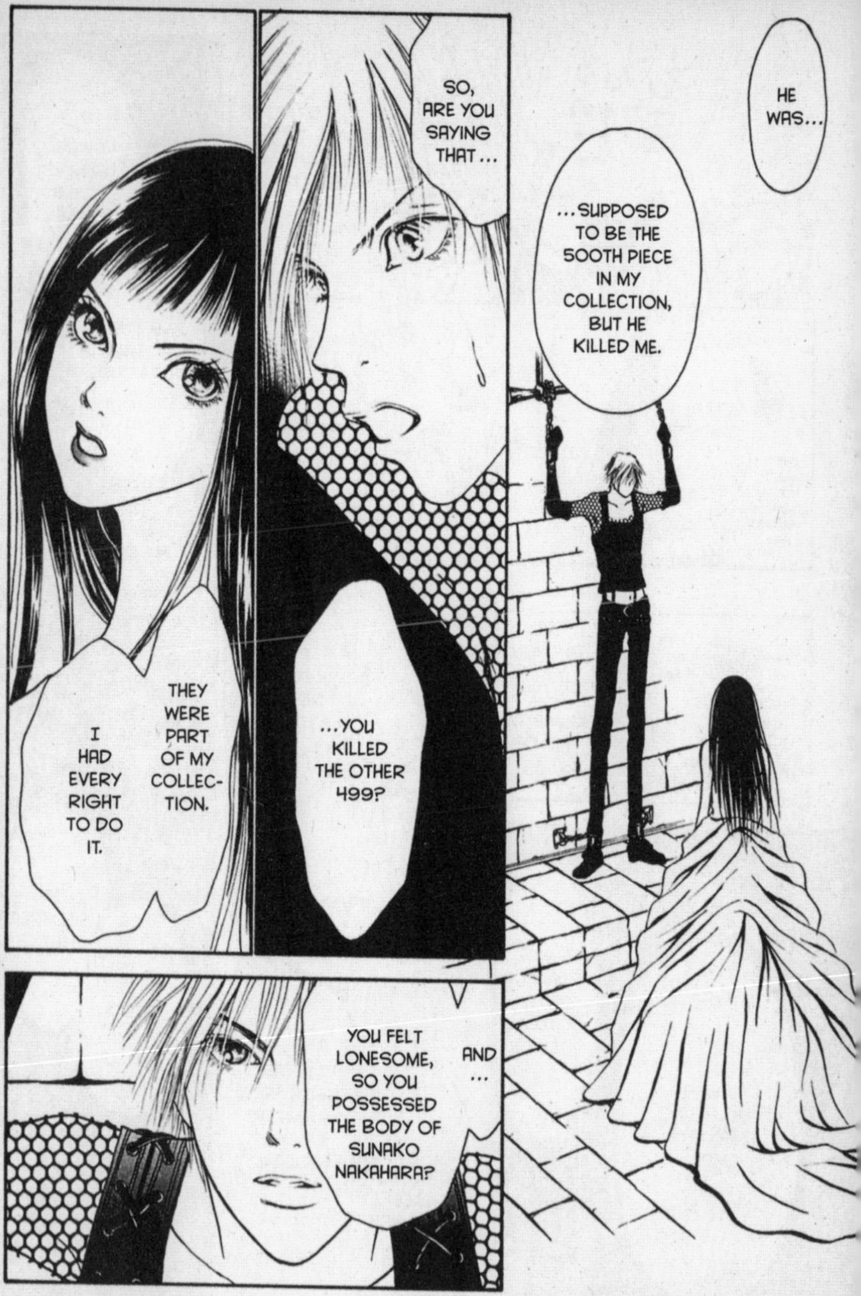
HE WAS...
...SUPPOSED TO BE THE 500TH PIECE IN MY COLLECTION, BUT HE KILLED ME.
SO, ARE YOU SAYING THAT...
...YOU KILLED THE OTHER 499?
THEY WERE PART OF MY COLLECTION.
I HAD EVERY RIGHT TO DO IT.
AND...
YOU FELT LONESOME, SO YOU POSSESSED THE BODY OF SUNAKO NAKAHARA?

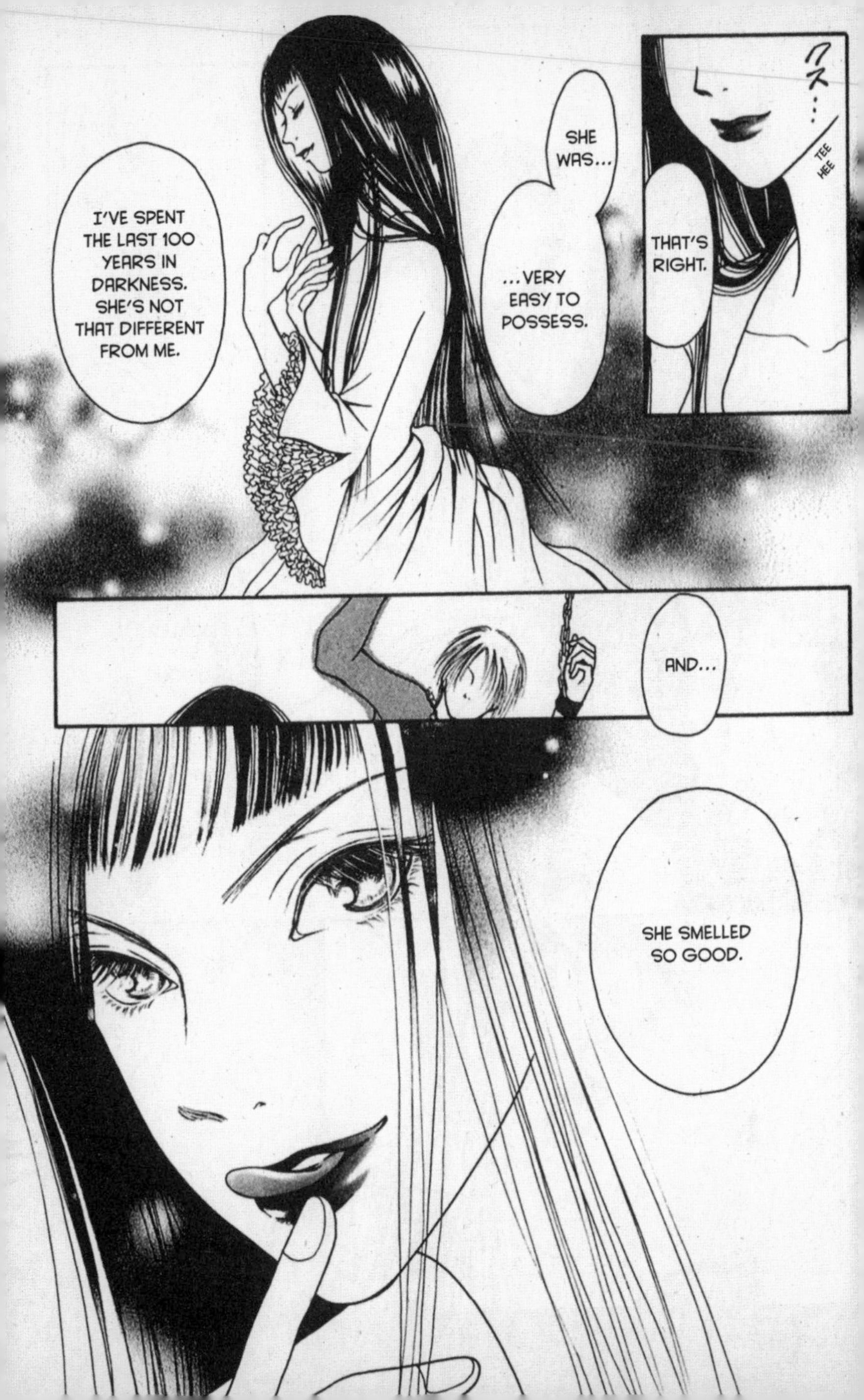
クス…
TEE HEE
THAT'S RIGHT.
SHE WAS...
...VERY EASY TO POSSESS.
I'VE SPENT THE LAST 100 YEARS IN DARKNESS. SHE'S NOT THAT DIFFERENT FROM ME.
AND...
SHE SMELLED SO GOOD.

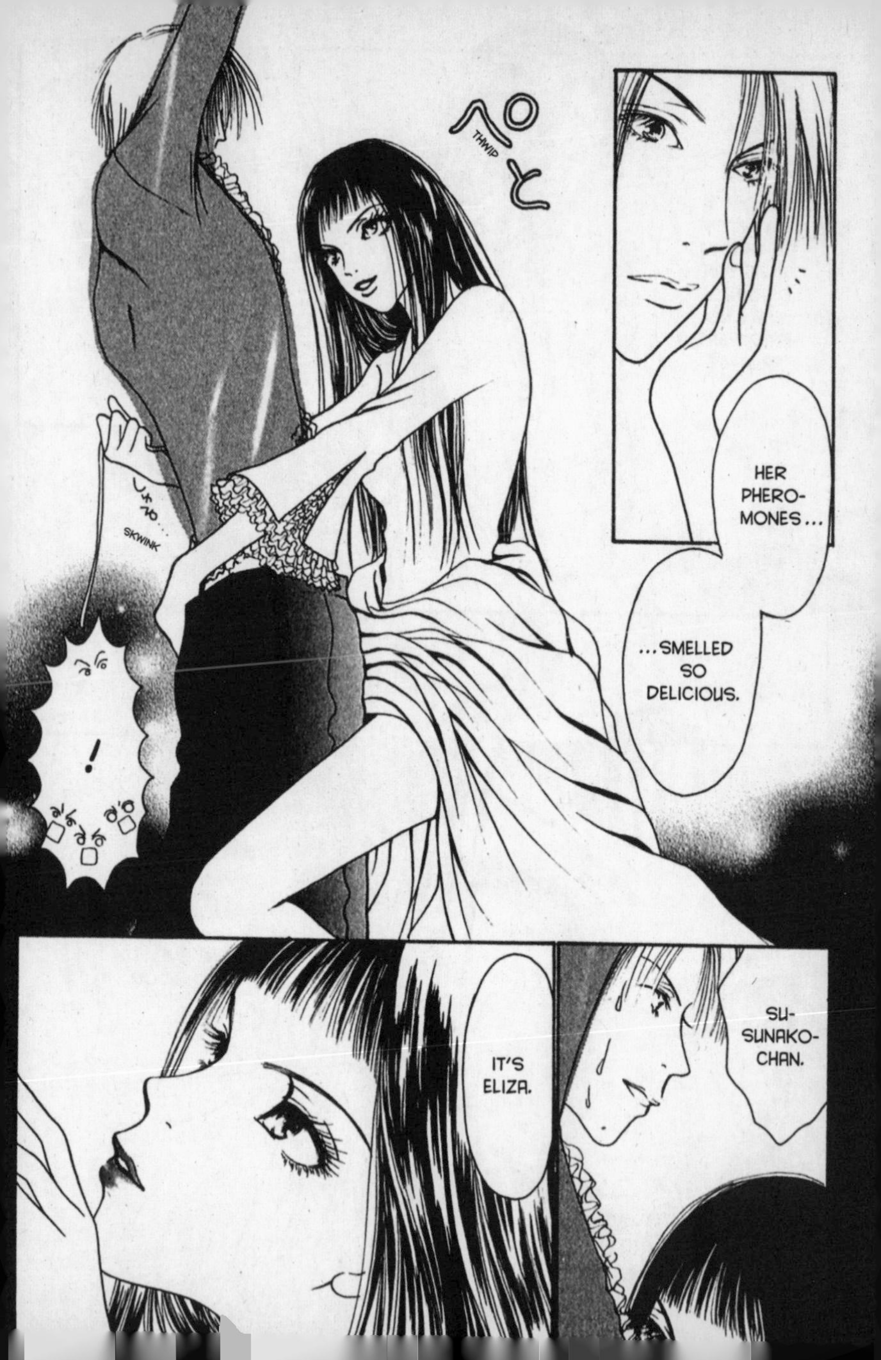
HER PHERO-MONES...
...SMELLED SO DELICIOUS.
THWIP
SKWINK
!
SU-SUNAKO-CHAN.
IT'S ELIZA.

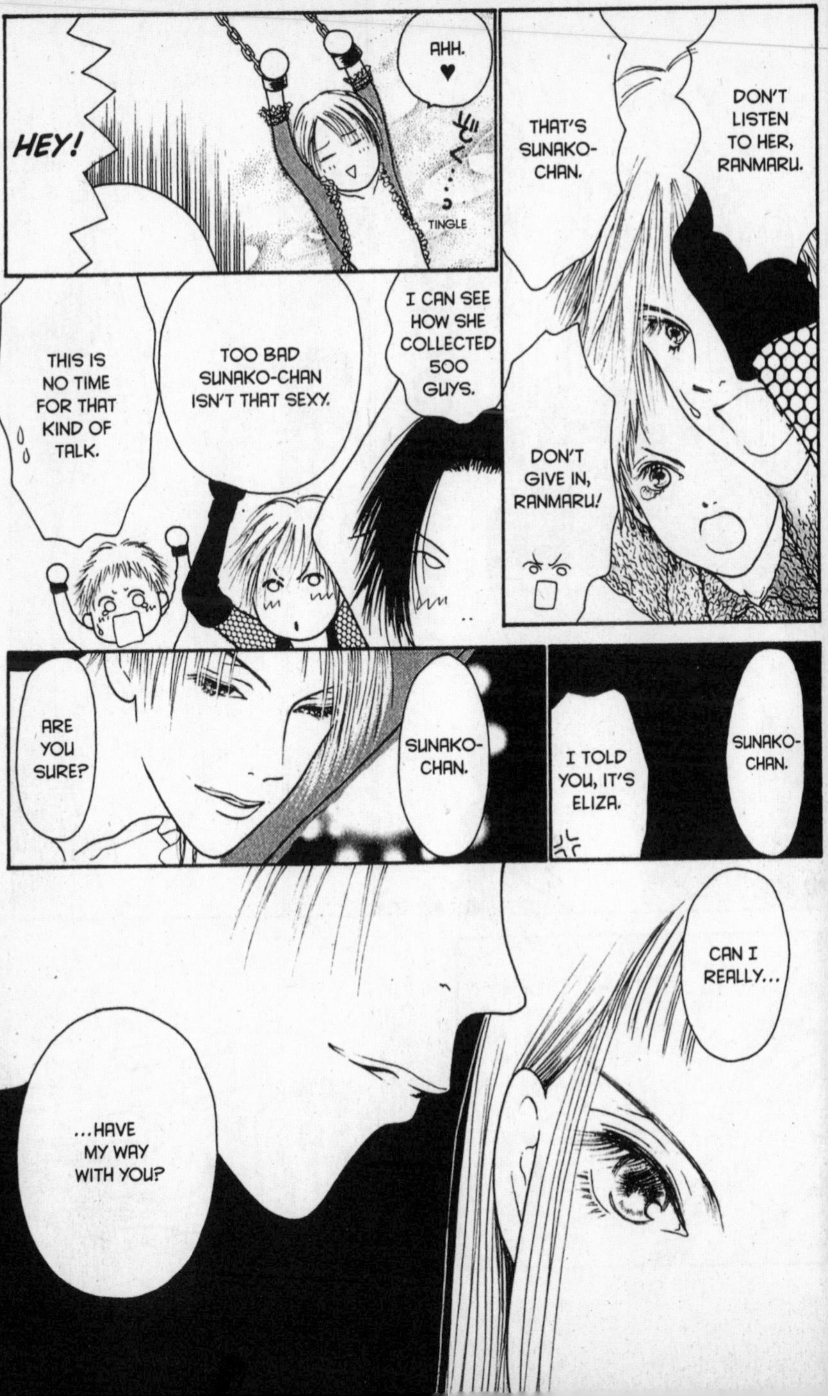
DON'T LISTEN TO HER, RANMARU.
THAT'S SUNAKO-CHAN.
DON'T GIVE IN, RANMARU!
AHH. ♥
ぞく…っ
TINGLE
HEY!
I CAN SEE HOW SHE COLLECTED 500 GUYS.
TOO BAD SUNAKO-CHAN ISN'T THAT SEXY.
THIS IS NO TIME FOR THAT KIND OF TALK.
SUNAKO-CHAN.
I TOLD YOU, IT'S ELIZA.
SUNAKO-CHAN.
ARE YOU SURE?
CAN I REALLY...
...HAVE MY WAY WITH YOU?

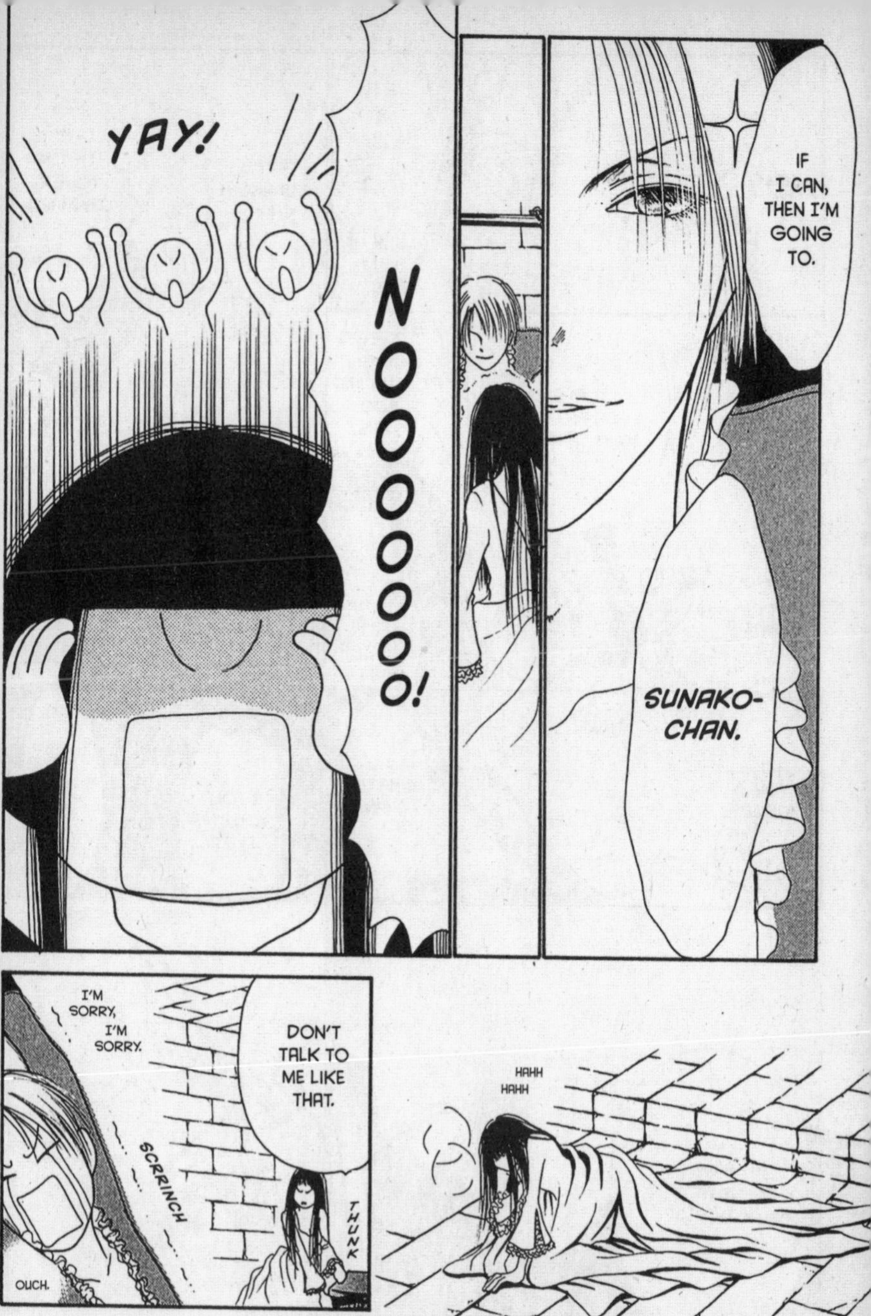
IF I CAN, THEN I'M GOING TO.
SUNAKO-CHAN.
YAY!
NOOOOOOOO!
HAHH HAHH
DON'T TALK TO ME LIKE THAT.
THUNK
I'M SORRY, I'M SORRY.
SCRRINCH
OUCH.

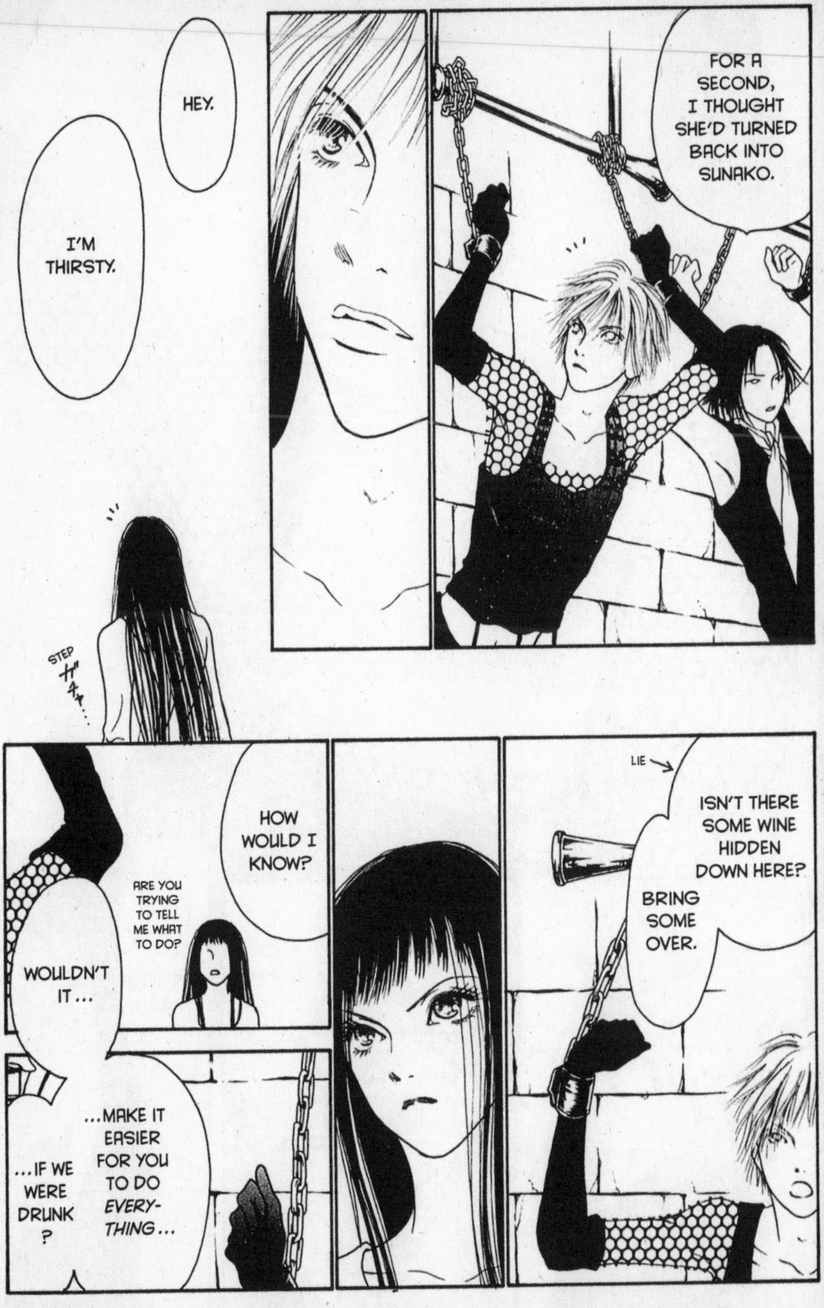
FOR A SECOND, I THOUGHT SHE'D TURNED BACK INTO SUNAKO.
HEY.
I'M THIRSTY.
STEP
LIE
ISN'T THERE SOME WINE HIDDEN DOWN HERE?
BRING SOME OVER.
HOW WOULD I KNOW?
ARE YOU TRYING TO TELL ME WHAT TO DO?
WOULDN'T IT...
...MAKE IT EASIER FOR YOU TO DO *EVERYTHING*...
...IF WE WERE DRUNK?

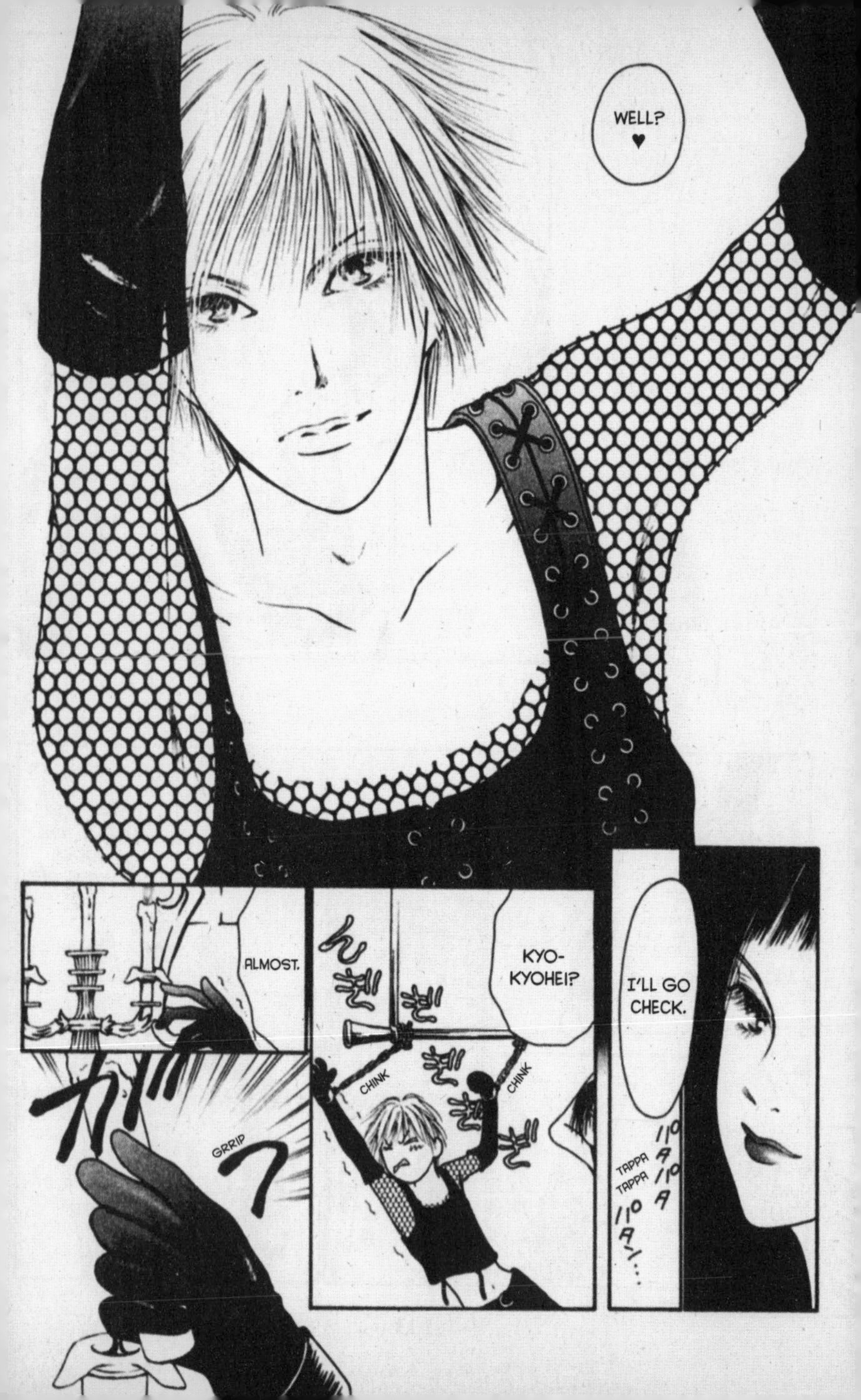
WELL? ♥
I'LL GO CHECK.
TAPPA TAPPA
KYO-KYOHEI!?
CHINK
CHINK
ALMOST.
GRRIP

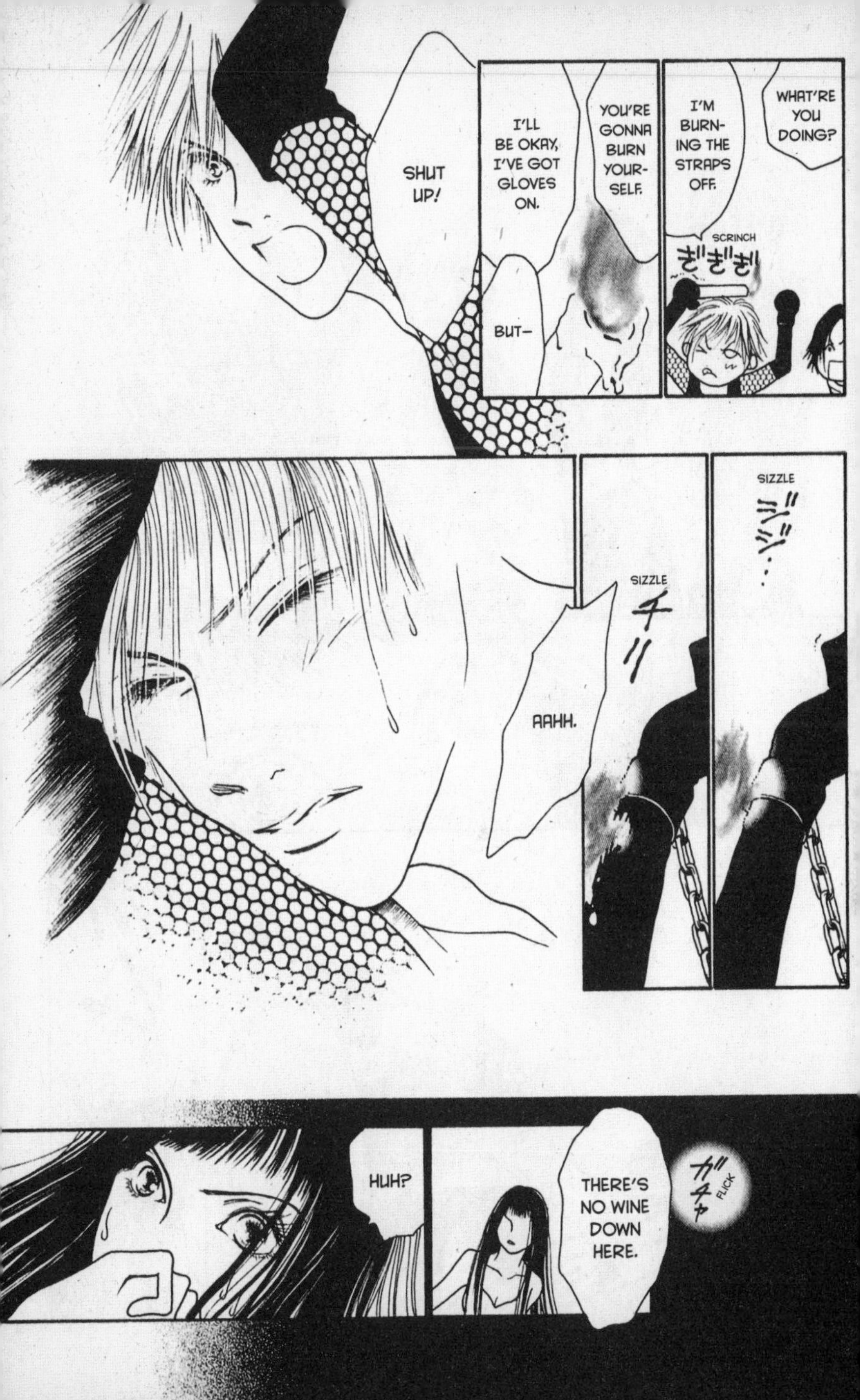
WHAT'RE YOU DOING?
I'M BURNING THE STRAPS OFF.
SCRINCH
YOU'RE GONNA BURN YOURSELF.
I'LL BE OKAY, I'VE GOT GLOVES ON.
BUT–
SHUT UP!
SIZZLE
SIZZLE
AAHH.
FLICK
THERE'S NO WINE DOWN HERE.
HUH?

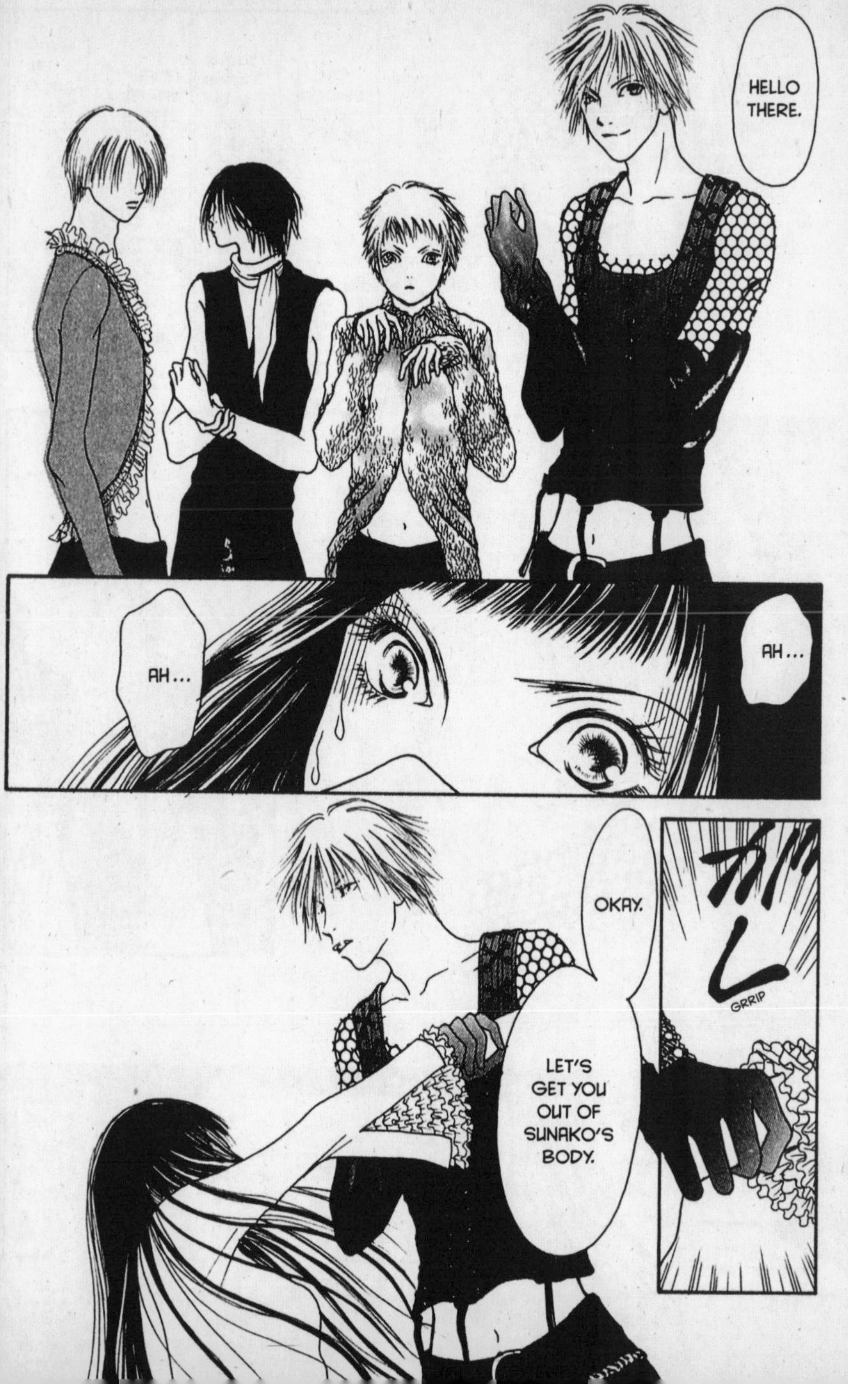
HELLO THERE.
AH...
AH...
GRRIP
OKAY.
LET'S GET YOU OUT OF SUNAKO'S BODY.

SINCE I'M INSIDE OF HER BODY...

BESIDES, HER LIFE IS HOPELESS ANYWAY.

THERE'S NO REASON FOR HER TO GO ON LIVING.

...YOU CAN'T VERY WELL KILL ME, NOW CAN YOU?

I'LL MAKE THE MOST OUT OF HER LIFE.

I DON'T KNOW HOW SHE CAN GO ON WITH HER LIFE.

...SO DARK AND SO NEGATIVE ALL THE TIME.

SUNAKO IS...

YOU'RE RIGHT.

HOW CAN YOU SAY THAT, KYOHEI?

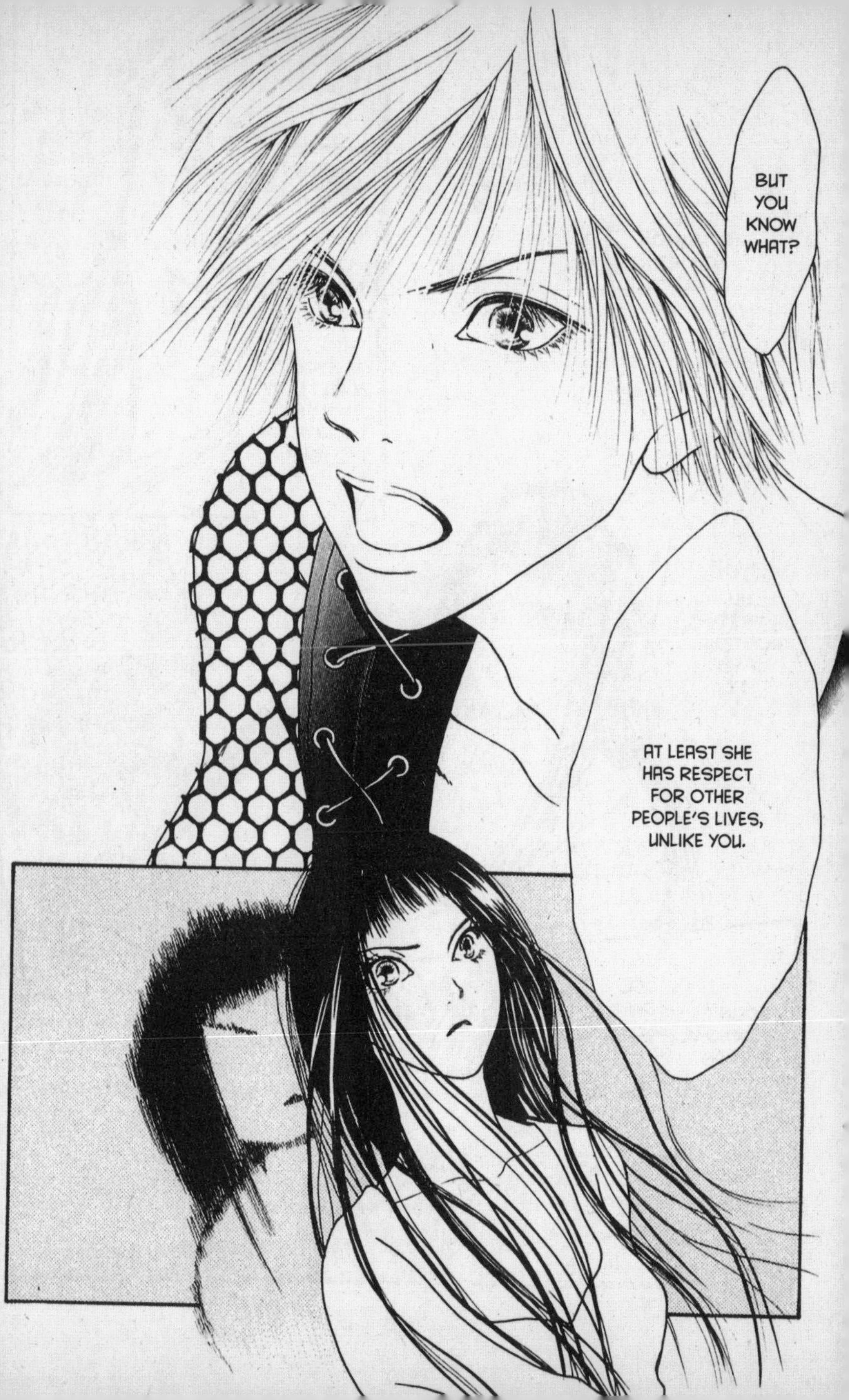
BUT YOU KNOW WHAT?
AT LEAST SHE HAS RESPECT FOR OTHER PEOPLE'S LIVES, UNLIKE YOU.

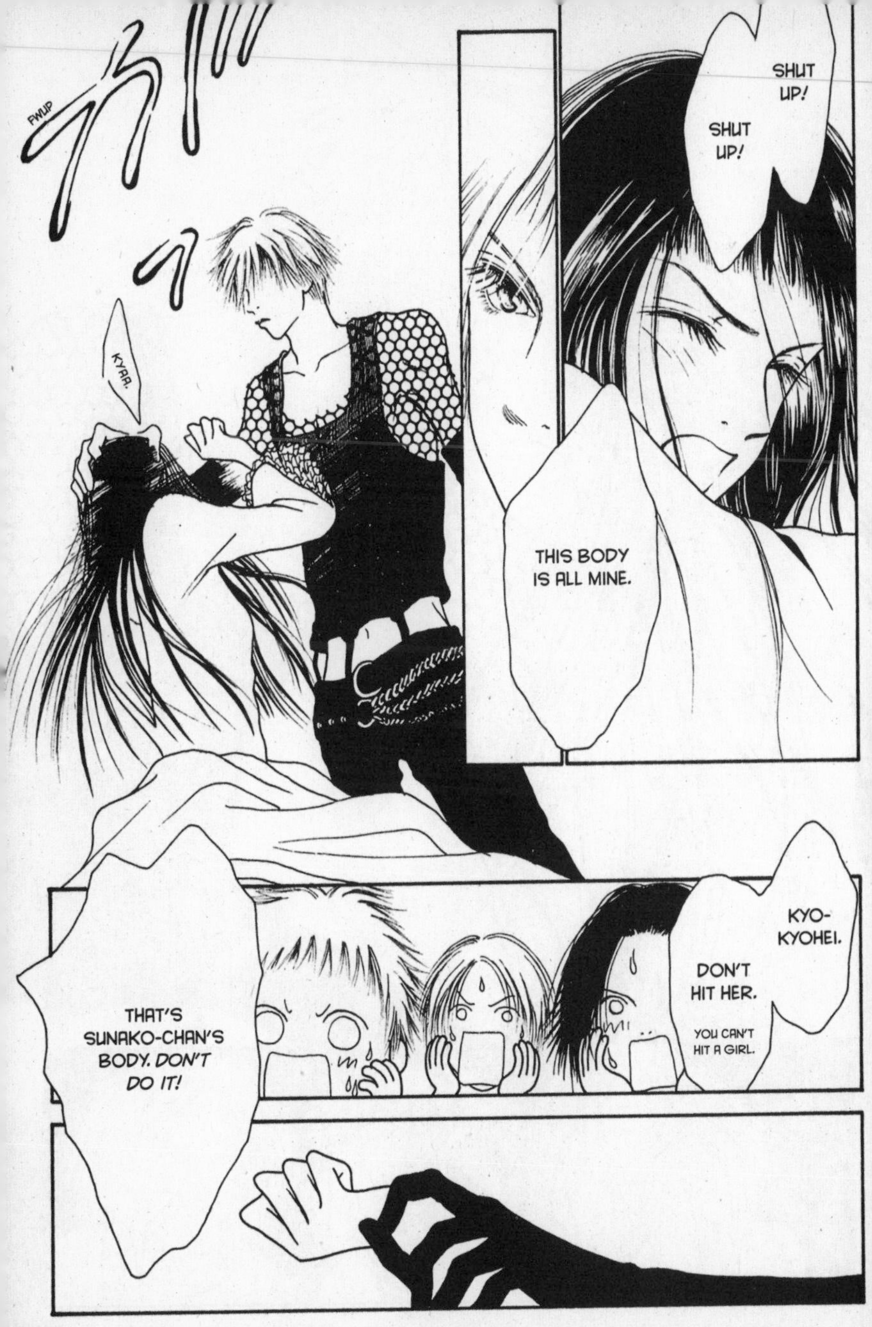
SHUT UP!
SHUT UP!
THIS BODY IS ALL MINE.
FWUP
KYAA.
KYO-KYOHEI.
DON'T HIT HER.
YOU CAN'T HIT A GIRL.
THAT'S SUNAKO-CHAN'S BODY. DON'T DO IT!

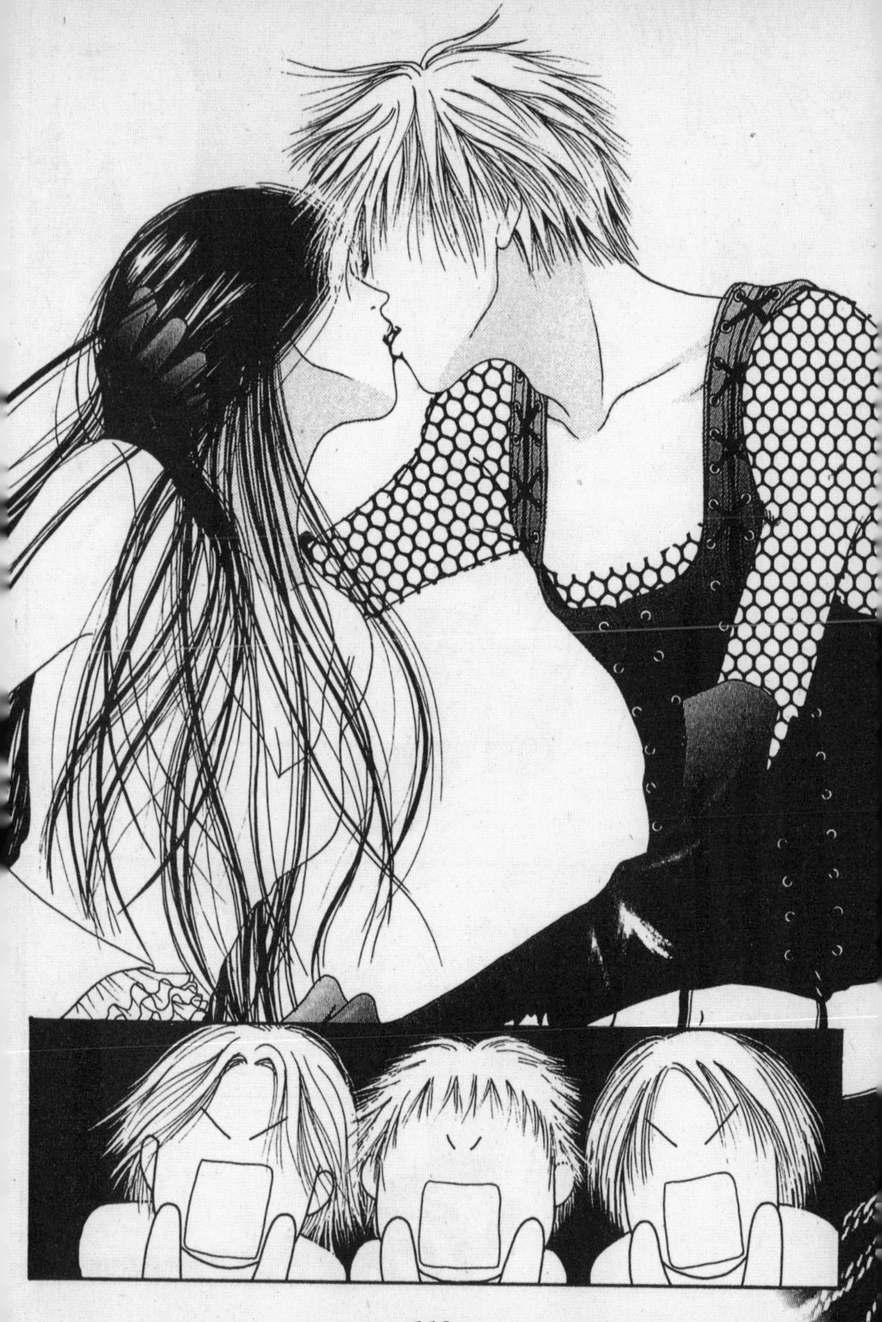

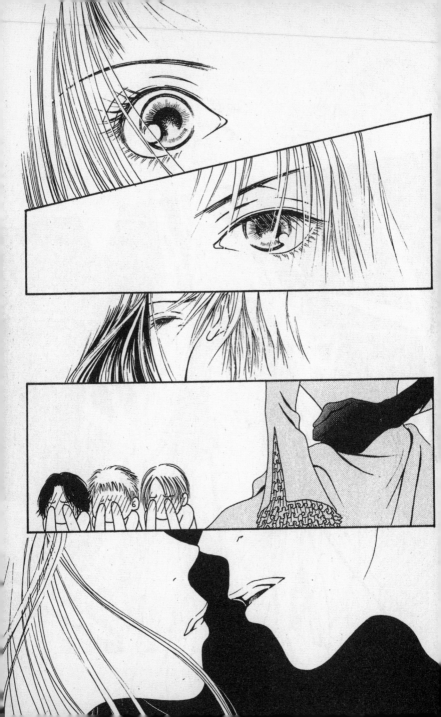

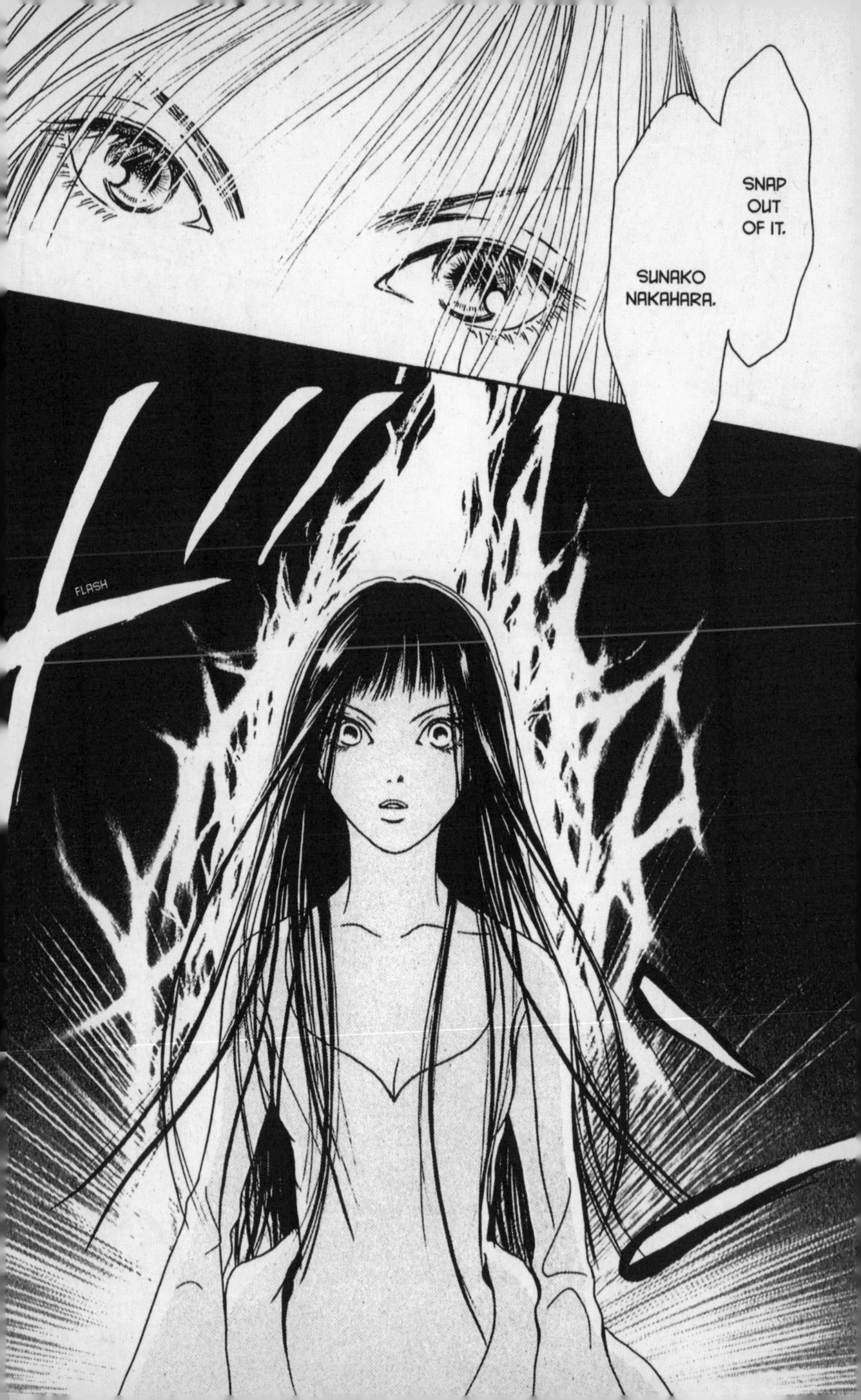
SNAP OUT OF IT.
SUNAKO NAKAHARA.
FLASH

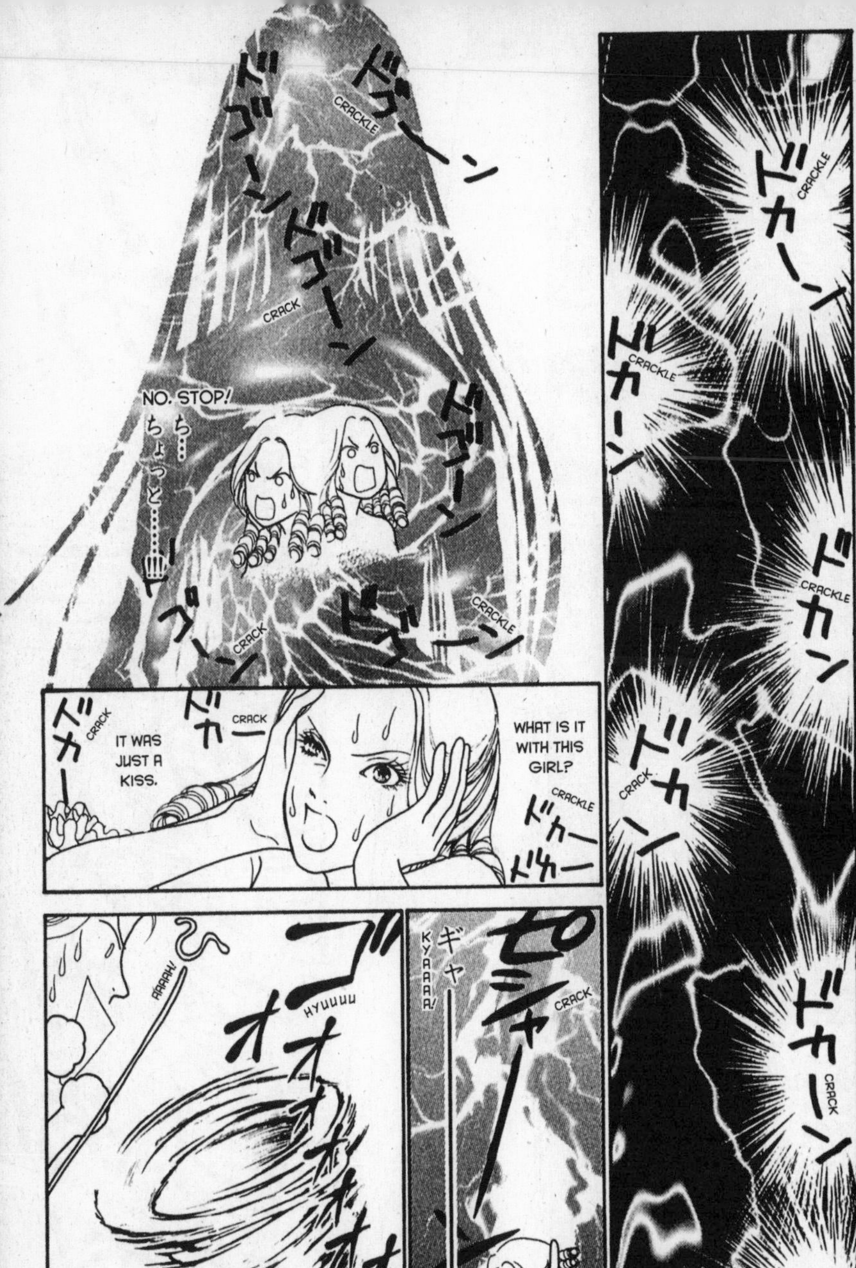
CRACKLE
CRACKLE
CRACKLE
CRACK
CRACK
CRACKLE
CRACK
NO. STOP!
ち…ちょっと…
CRACKLE
CRACK
WHAT IS IT WITH THIS GIRL?
CRACKLE
IT WAS JUST A KISS.
CRACK
CRACK
CRACK
ギャ
KYAAAAA!
HYUUUU
ひ
AAAAH!

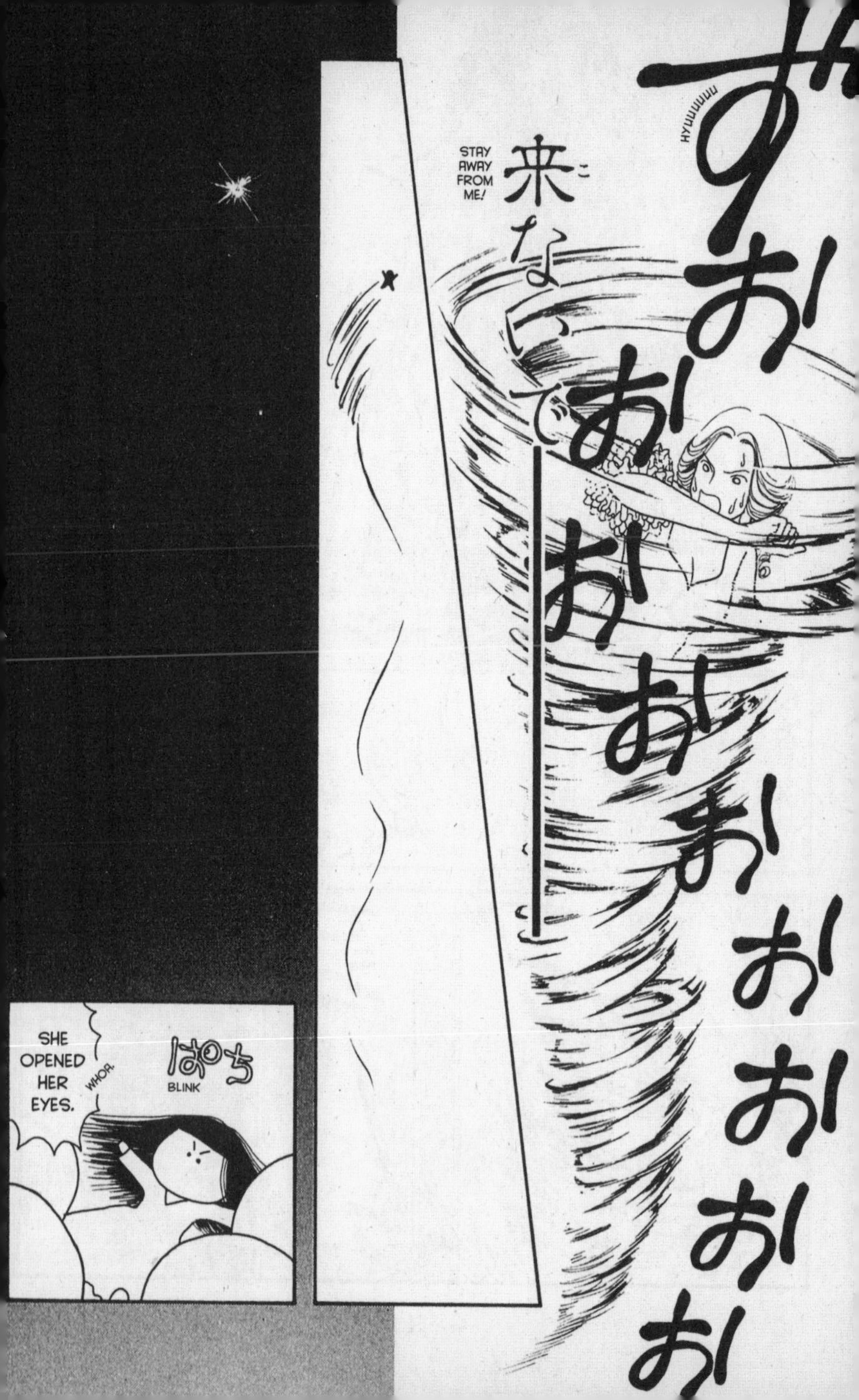
HYUUUUUU
来ないで
STAY AWAY FROM ME!
SHE OPENED HER EYES.
WHOA.
ぱち
BLINK

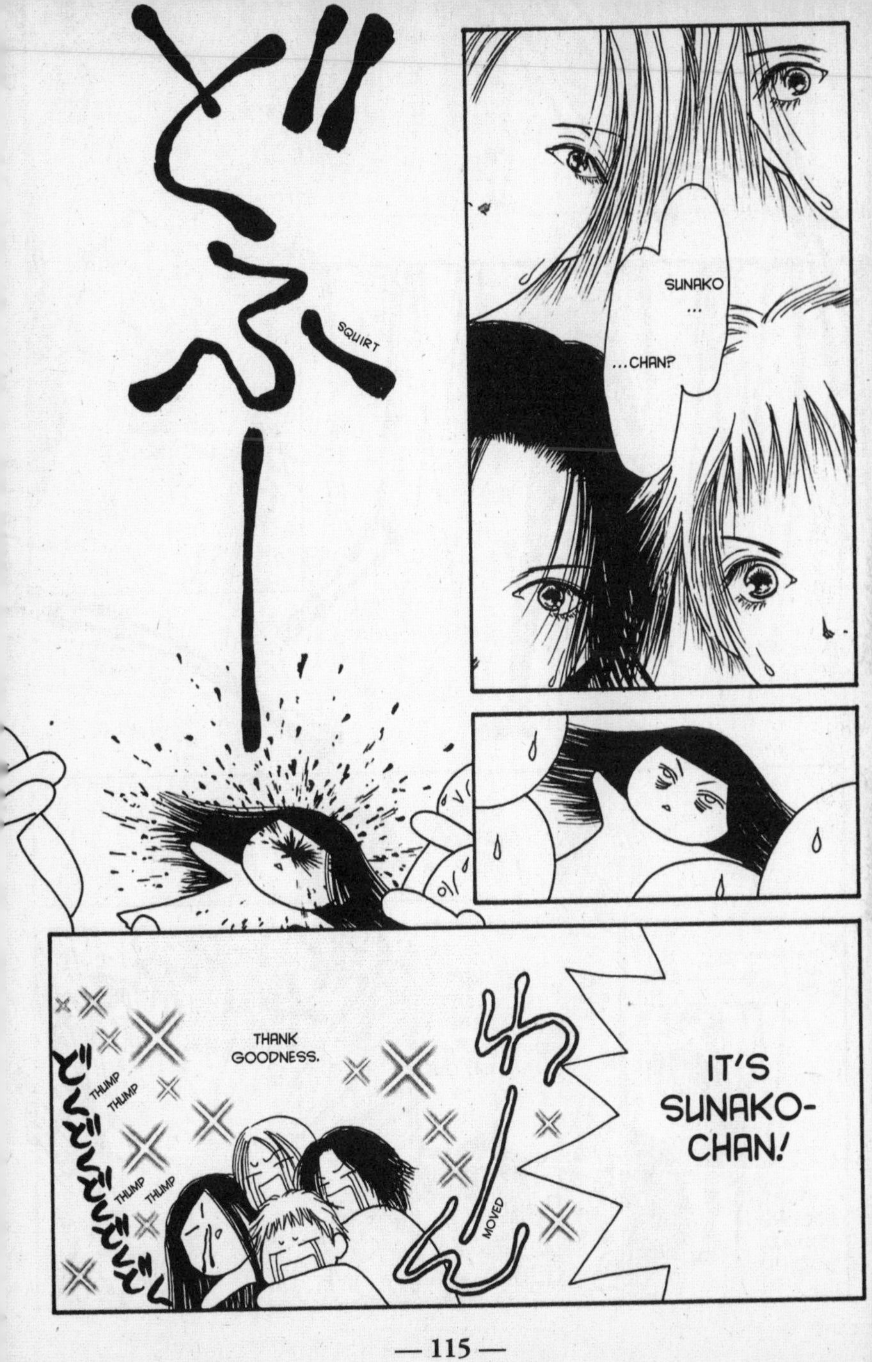
SUNAKO ... ...CHAN?
SQUIRT
IT'S SUNAKO-CHAN!
MOVED
THANK GOODNESS.
THUMP THUMP
THUMP THUMP

THUNK

LET'S GET BACK UPSTAIRS.

CLINK

"FALL APART. GO ON, AND FALL APART."

STOP FOOLING AROUND, KYOHEI.

CALM DOWN, YOU TWO.

LET'S FIND IT.

THERE'S GOTTA BE ANOTHER WAY OUT.

SHIVER SHIVER

SHAKE SHAKE

GYAAAA!

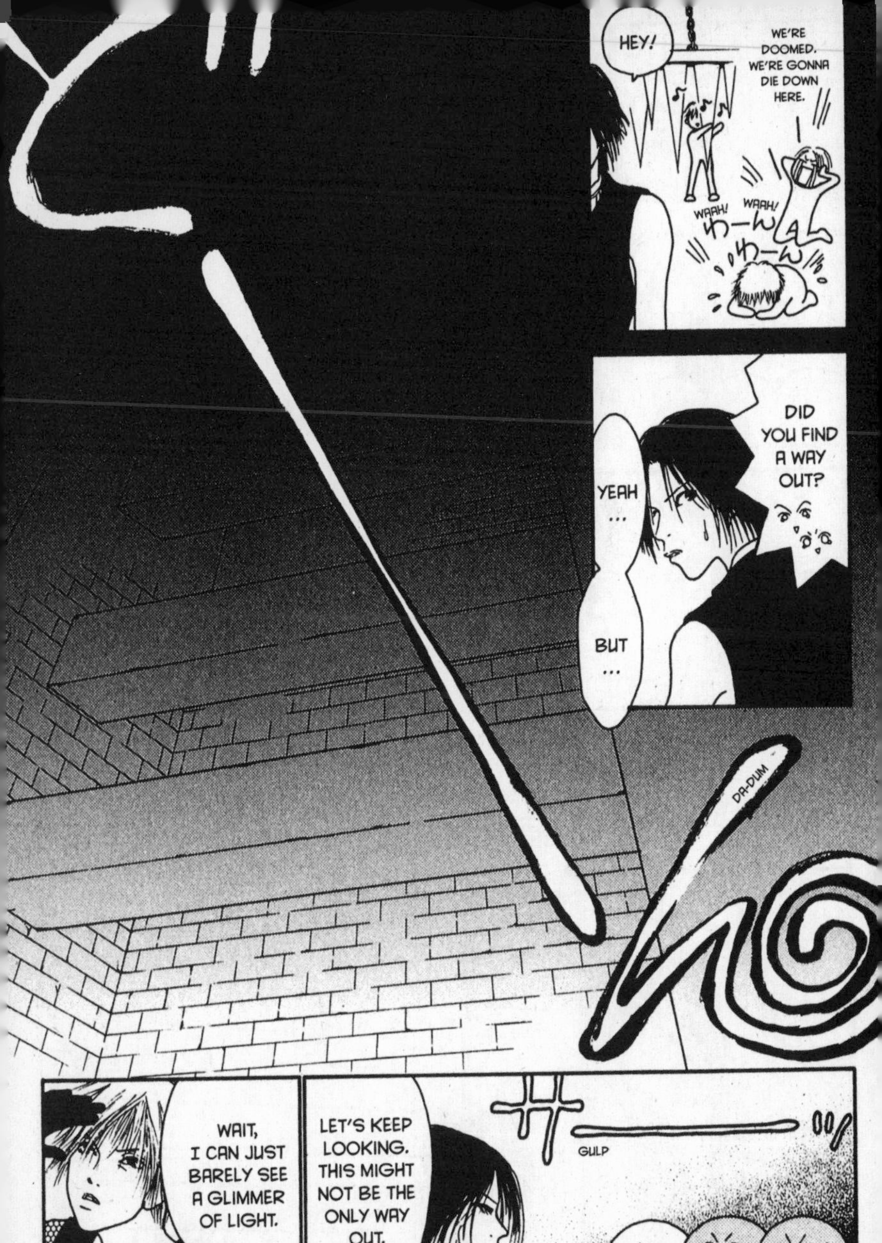
HEY!
WE'RE DOOMED. WE'RE GONNA DIE DOWN HERE.
WAAH! わーん
WAAH! わーん
DID YOU FIND A WAY OUT?
YEAH ...
BUT ...
DA-DUM
GULP
LET'S KEEP LOOKING. THIS MIGHT NOT BE THE ONLY WAY OUT.
WAIT, I CAN JUST BARELY SEE A GLIMMER OF LIGHT.

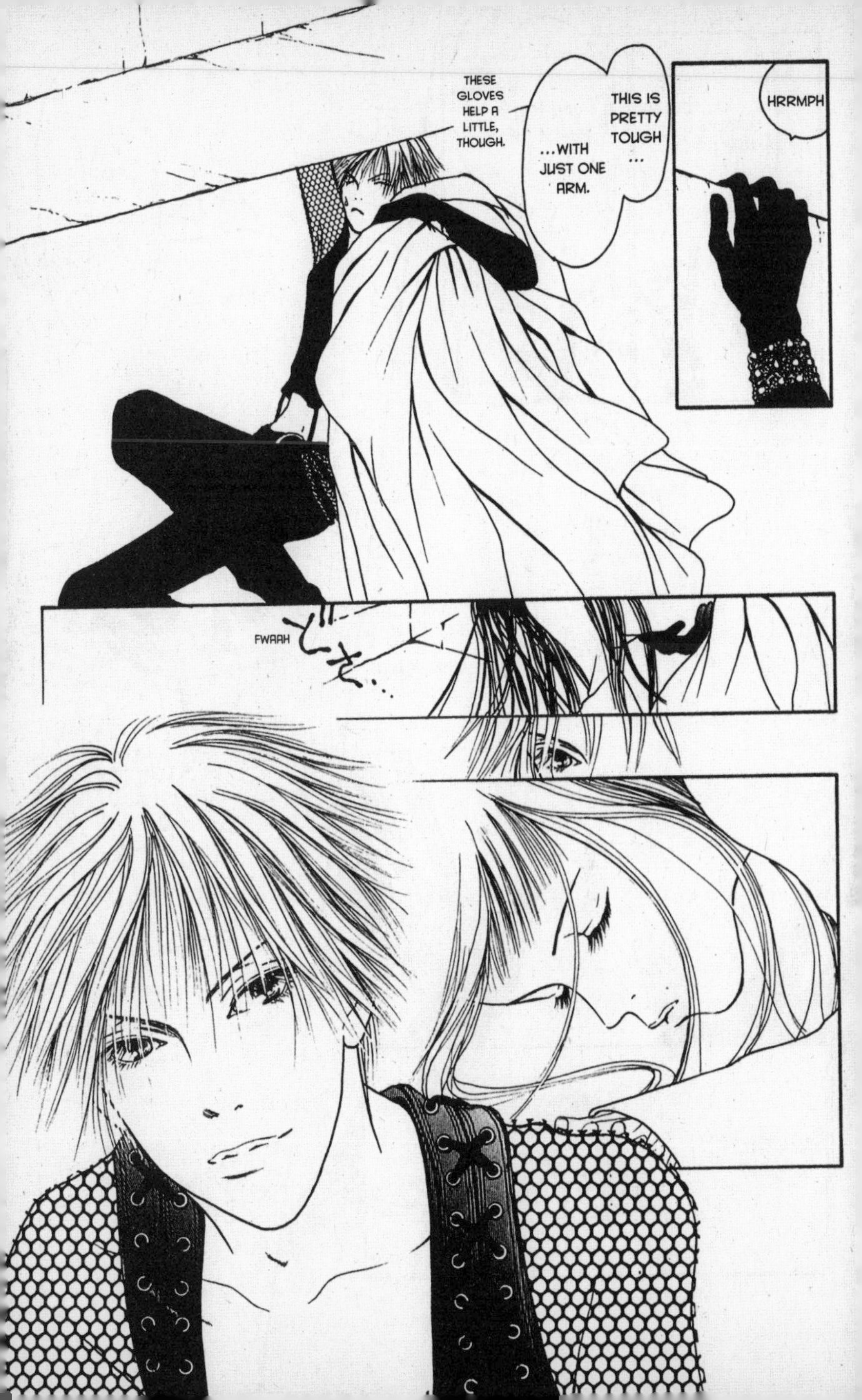
HRRMPH
THIS IS PRETTY TOUGH...
...WITH JUST ONE ARM.
THESE GLOVES HELP A LITTLE, THOUGH.
FWAAH

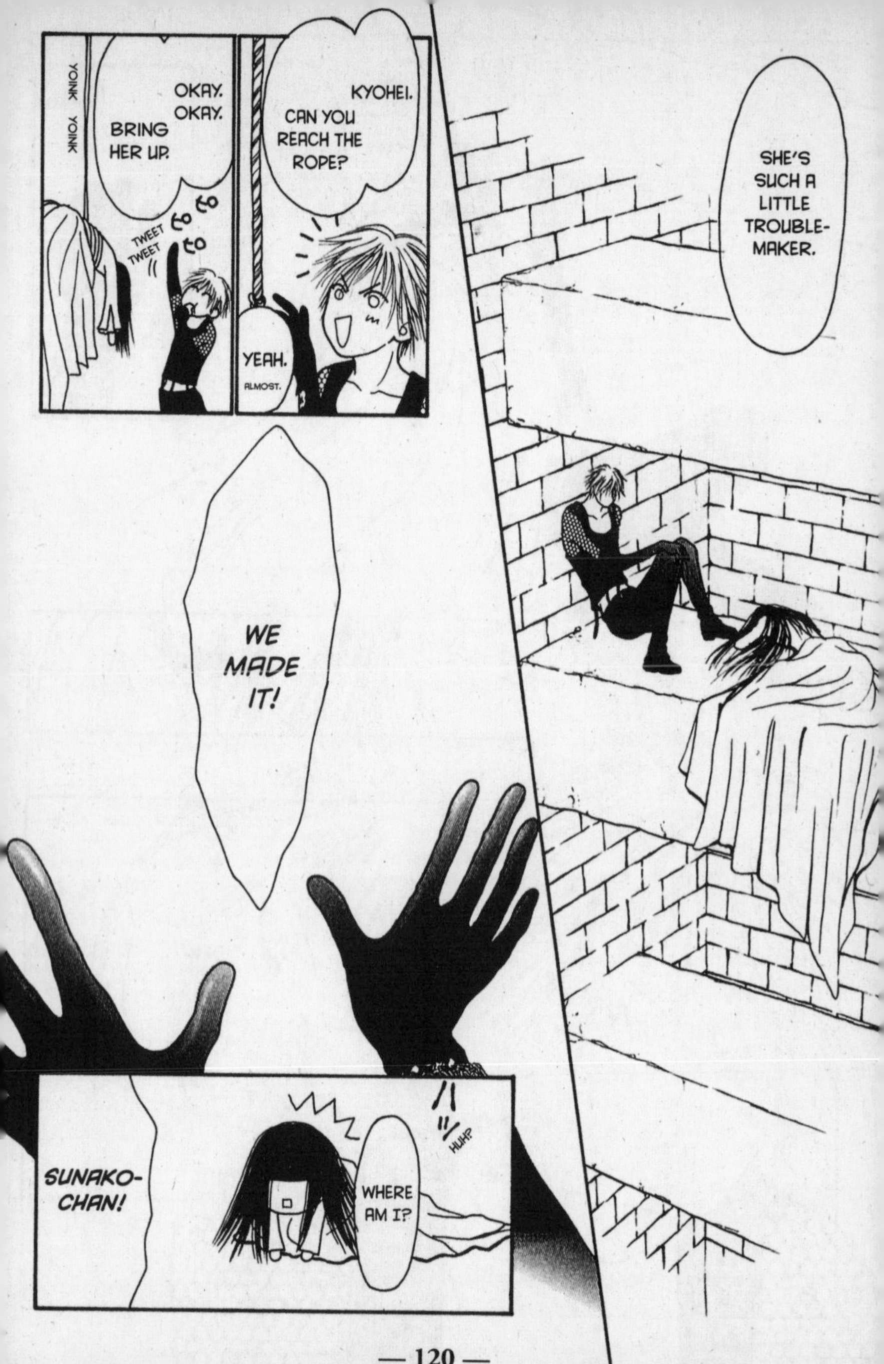
SHE'S SUCH A LITTLE TROUBLE-MAKER.
KYOHEI.
CAN YOU REACH THE ROPE?
YEAH.
ALMOST.
OKAY. OKAY.
BRING HER UP.
YOINK YOINK
TWEET TWEET
WE MADE IT!
HUH?
WHERE AM I?
SUNAKO-CHAN!

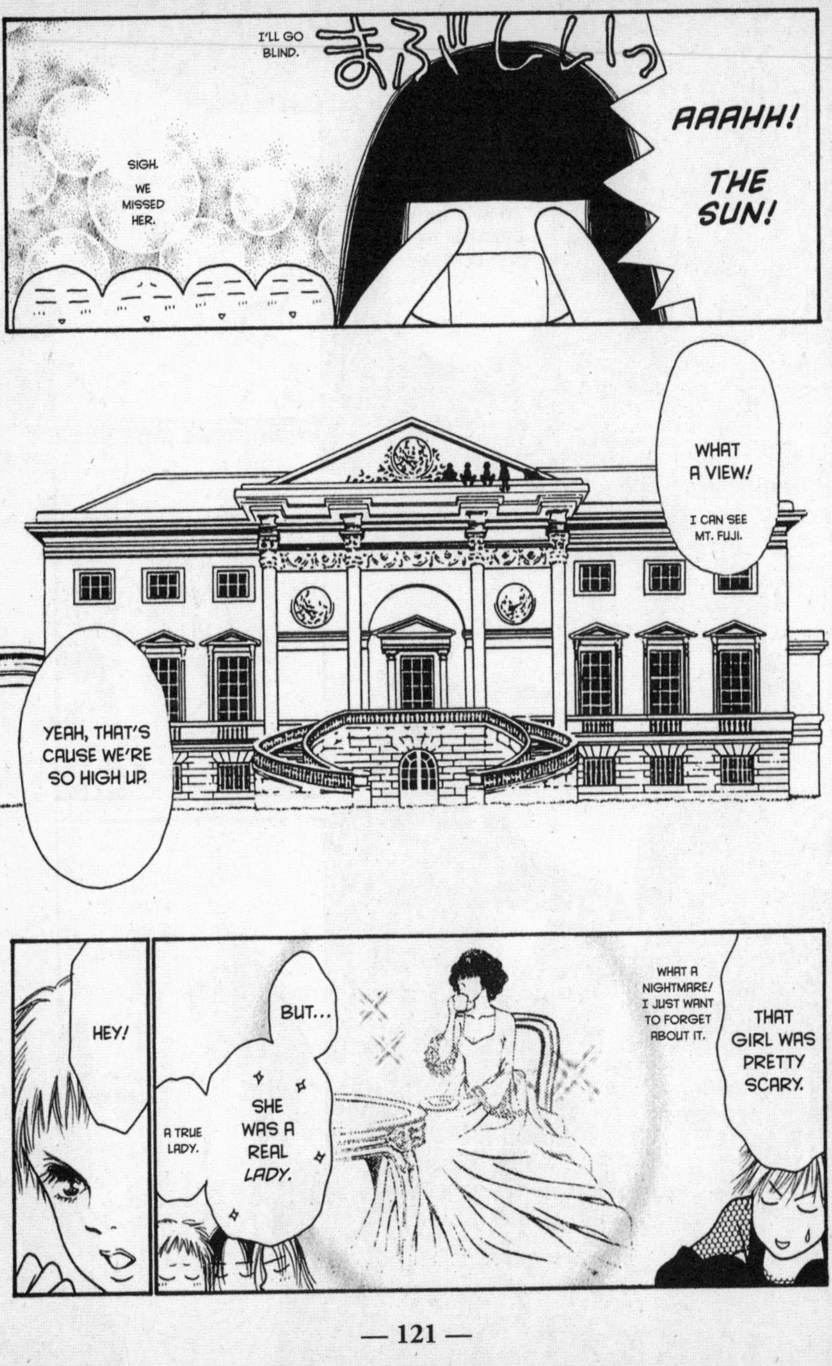
AAAHH!
THE SUN!
まぶしいっ
I'LL GO BLIND.
SIGH.
WE MISSED HER.
WHAT A VIEW!
I CAN SEE MT. FUJI.
YEAH, THAT'S CAUSE WE'RE SO HIGH UP.
THAT GIRL WAS PRETTY SCARY.
WHAT A NIGHTMARE! I JUST WANT TO FORGET ABOUT IT.
BUT...
SHE WAS A REAL *LADY.*
A TRUE LADY.
HEY!

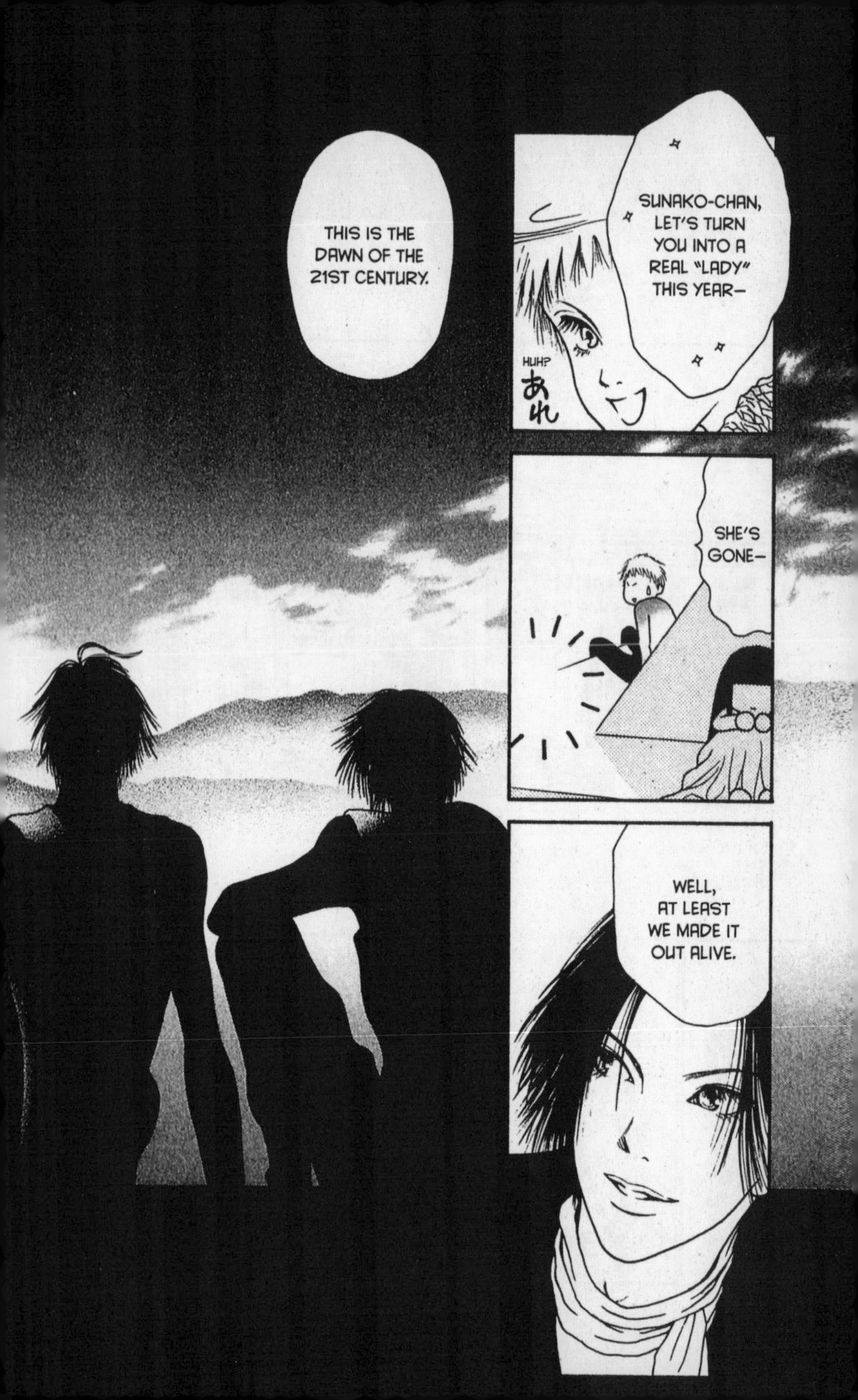
SUNAKO-CHAN, LET'S TURN YOU INTO A REAL "LADY" THIS YEAR—
HUH?
あれ
SHE'S GONE—
WELL, AT LEAST WE MADE IT OUT ALIVE.
THIS IS THE DAWN OF THE 21ST CENTURY.

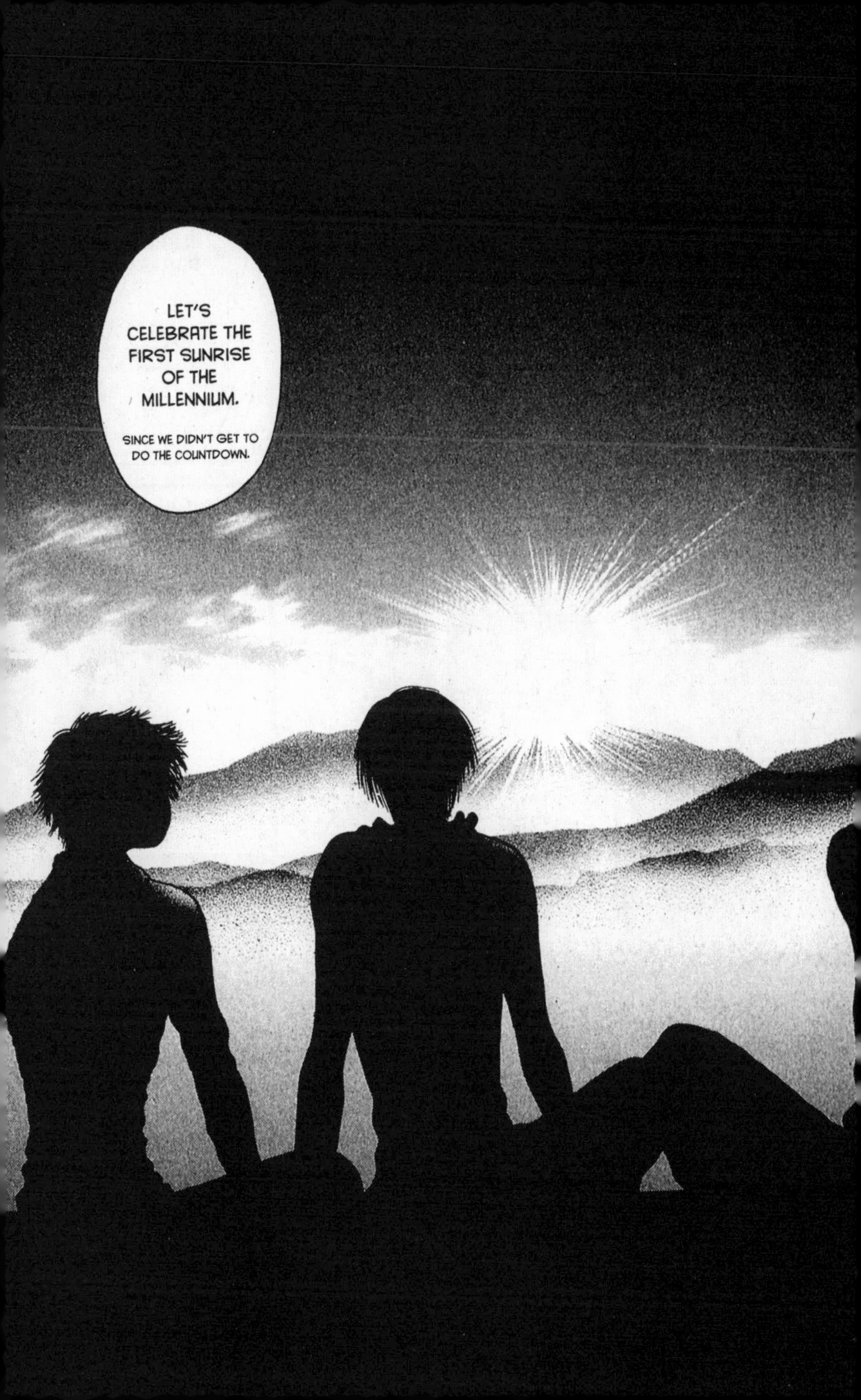
LET'S CELEBRATE THE FIRST SUNRISE OF THE MILLENNIUM.
SINCE WE DIDN'T GET TO DO THE COUNTDOWN.

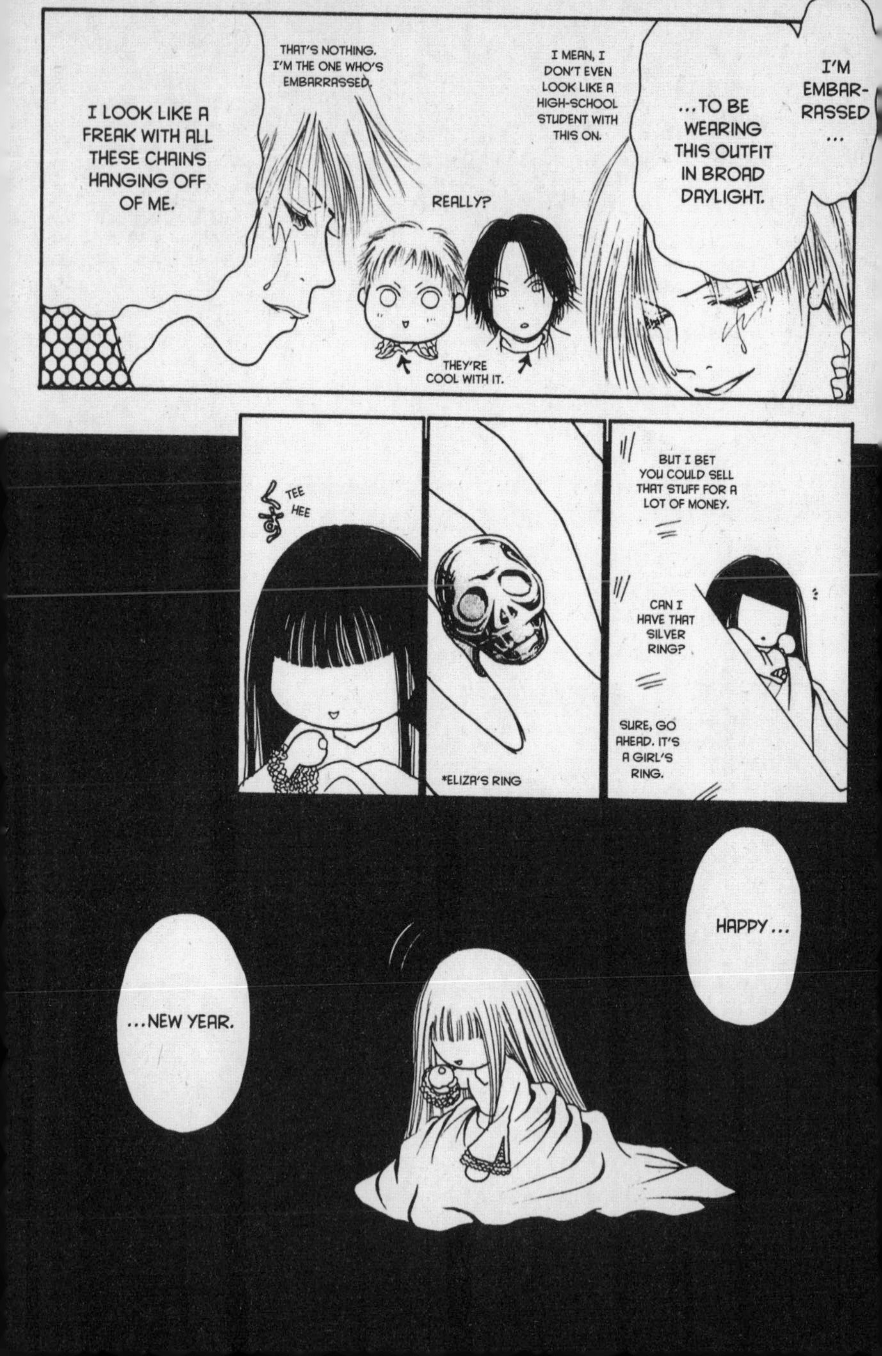
I'M EMBARRASSED...
...TO BE WEARING THIS OUTFIT IN BROAD DAYLIGHT.
I MEAN, I DON'T EVEN LOOK LIKE A HIGH-SCHOOL STUDENT WITH THIS ON.
REALLY?
THEY'RE COOL WITH IT.
THAT'S NOTHING. I'M THE ONE WHO'S EMBARRASSED.
I LOOK LIKE A FREAK WITH ALL THESE CHAINS HANGING OFF OF ME.
BUT I BET YOU COULD SELL THAT STUFF FOR A LOT OF MONEY.
CAN I HAVE THAT SILVER RING?
SURE, GO AHEAD. IT'S A GIRL'S RING.
*ELIZA'S RING
TEE HEE
HAPPY...
...NEW YEAR.

Chapter 9
Blood-Splatteringly Steamy Love at the Hot Springs
PART 1

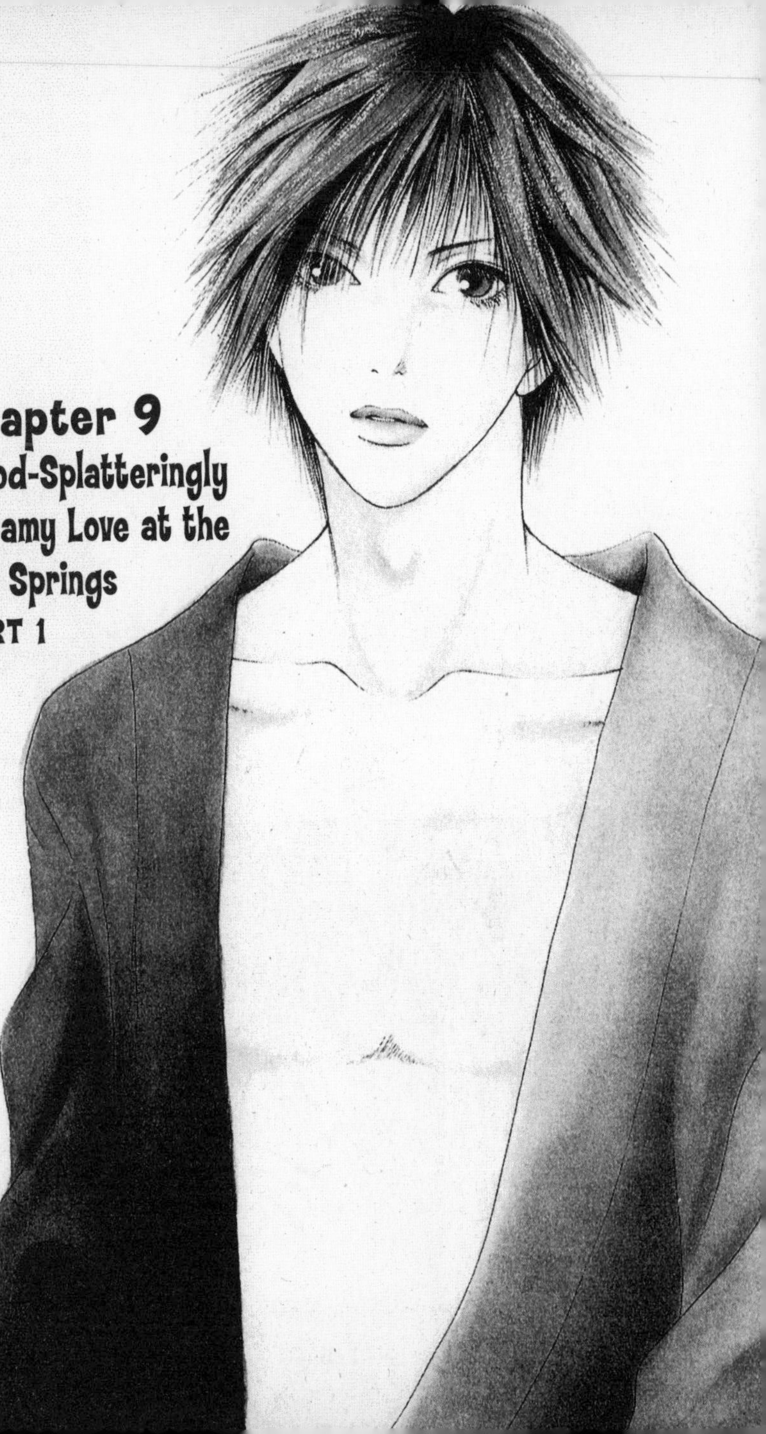

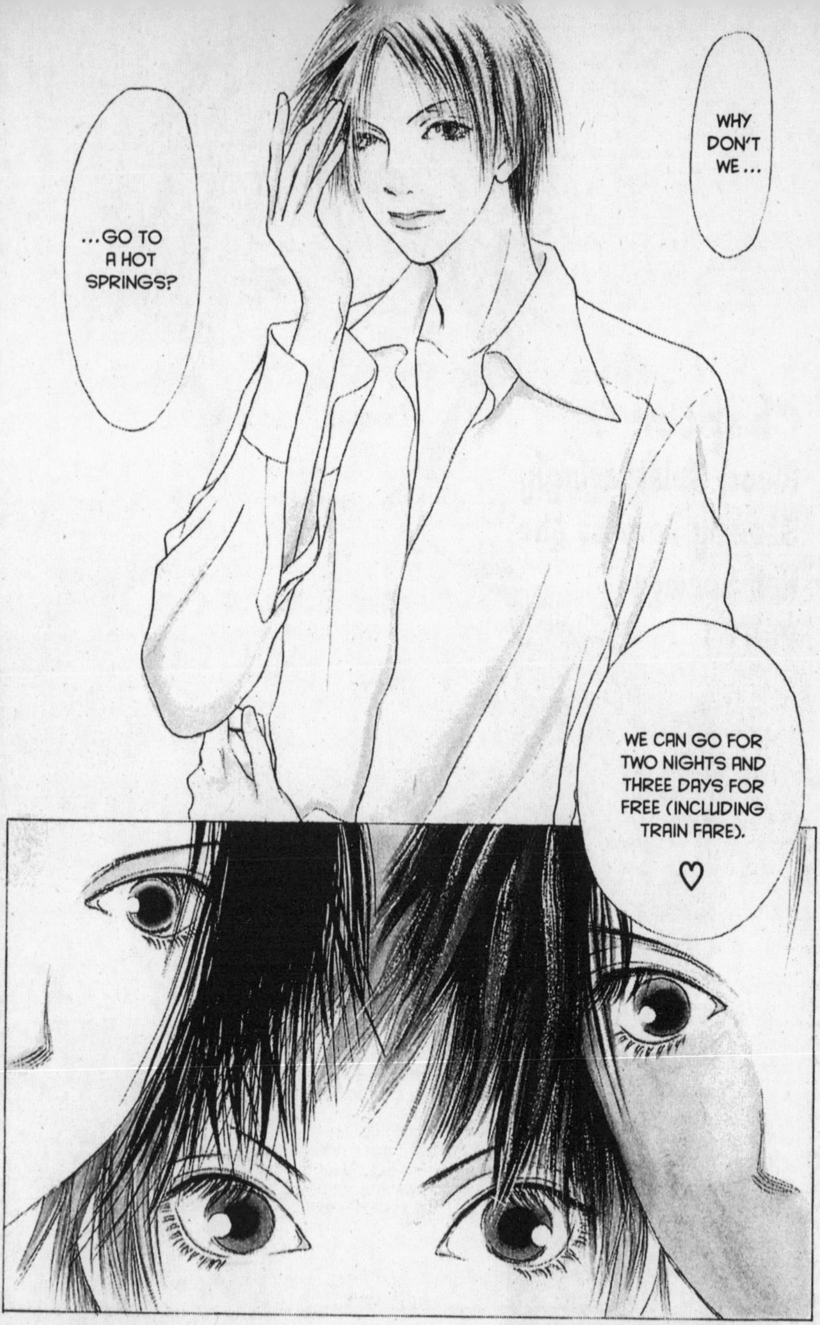
WHY DON'T WE...
...GO TO A HOT SPRINGS?
WE CAN GO FOR TWO NIGHTS AND THREE DAYS FOR FREE (INCLUDING TRAIN FARE). ♡

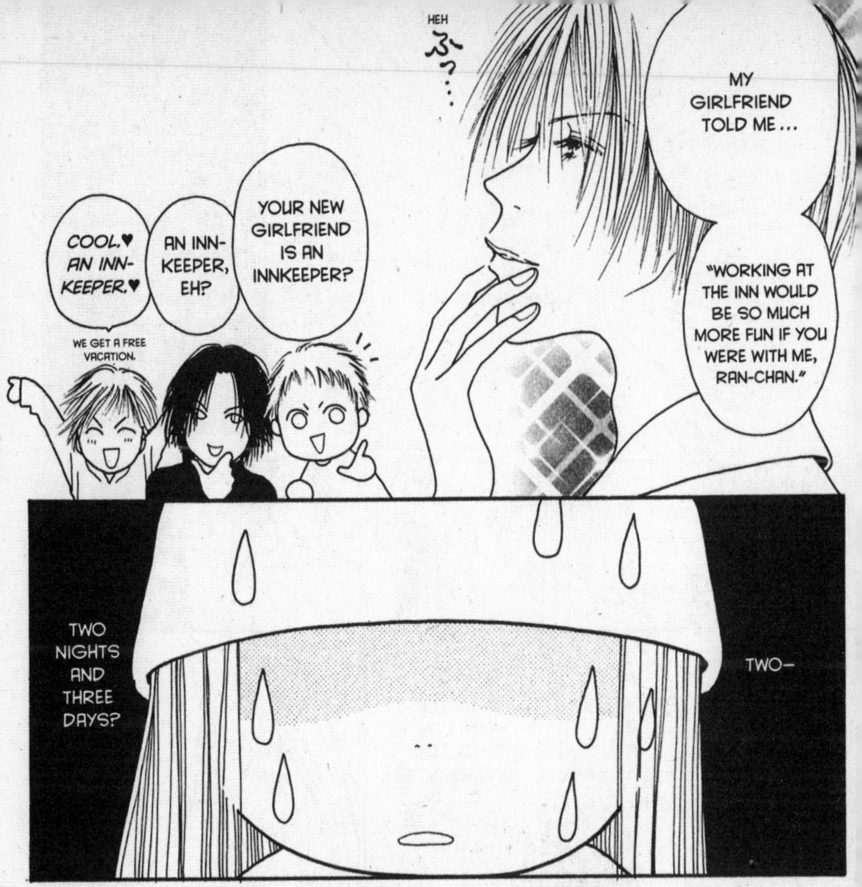
MY GIRLFRIEND TOLD ME...
"WORKING AT THE INN WOULD BE SO MUCH MORE FUN IF YOU WERE WITH ME, RAN-CHAN."
HEH
YOUR NEW GIRLFRIEND IS AN INNKEEPER?
AN INN-KEEPER, EH?
COOL.♥ AN INN-KEEPER.♥
WE GET A FREE VACATION.
TWO-
TWO NIGHTS AND THREE DAYS?

BEHIND THE SCENES

WHILE I WAS WRITING THIS STORY, I WANTED TO GO TO A HOT SPRINGS SO BADLY. (I ENDED UP NOT BEING ABLE TO GO, BUT ...) I STILL REALLY WANNA GO. YEAH. HOT SPRINGS ROCK!

YEAH. I WENT TO A HOT SPRINGS IN THE SUMMER, AND THE INNKEEPER WAS A REAL BITCH. (WE FOUGHT.)

I WAS ACTUALLY GONNA MAKE THIS STORY ABOUT AN UGLY INNKEEPER VS. A BEAUTIFUL MAID. I ENDED UP NOT USING THAT ELEMENT IN THE STORY, SO I MADE HER BEAUTIFUL INSTEAD. IF SHE WERE AN UGLY INNKEEPER, I WOULD'VE NAMED HER "YUKO." THAT'S RIGHT, I'M TALKING ABOUT YOU, YUKO! I'M NEVER GOING BACK THERE. THE MAID WAS REALLY NICE, AND SO WAS THE GIRL AT THE FRONT DESK.

WHAT? ...I'LL... ...PASS.

HEY, RANMARU. SHE'S TALKING TO YOU.

WHAT HAPPENED TO "THE ULTIMATE LADIES' MAN"?

ARE YOU SICK OR SOMETHING?

RANMARU MUST BE DYING.

SORRY FOR BOTHERING YOU.

BLAK
BLAK

I'M REALLY IN LOVE.

THIS TIME...

IF I STAY HERE ANY LONGER...

I'LL MELT.

DEAR MACHIKO, RANMARU IS ACTING STRANGE.

SHUT UP! I SAID NO WAY.

IF YOU GUYS ARE SITTING TOGETHER, OTHER GIRLS WILL KEEP HITTING ON YOU.

PLEASE CHANGE SEATS WITH ME, KYOHEI-KUN.

SCRIBBLE SCRIBBLE

LET'S SEE. SUDDEN ONSET OF INSANITY...

BLEAH

— 130 —

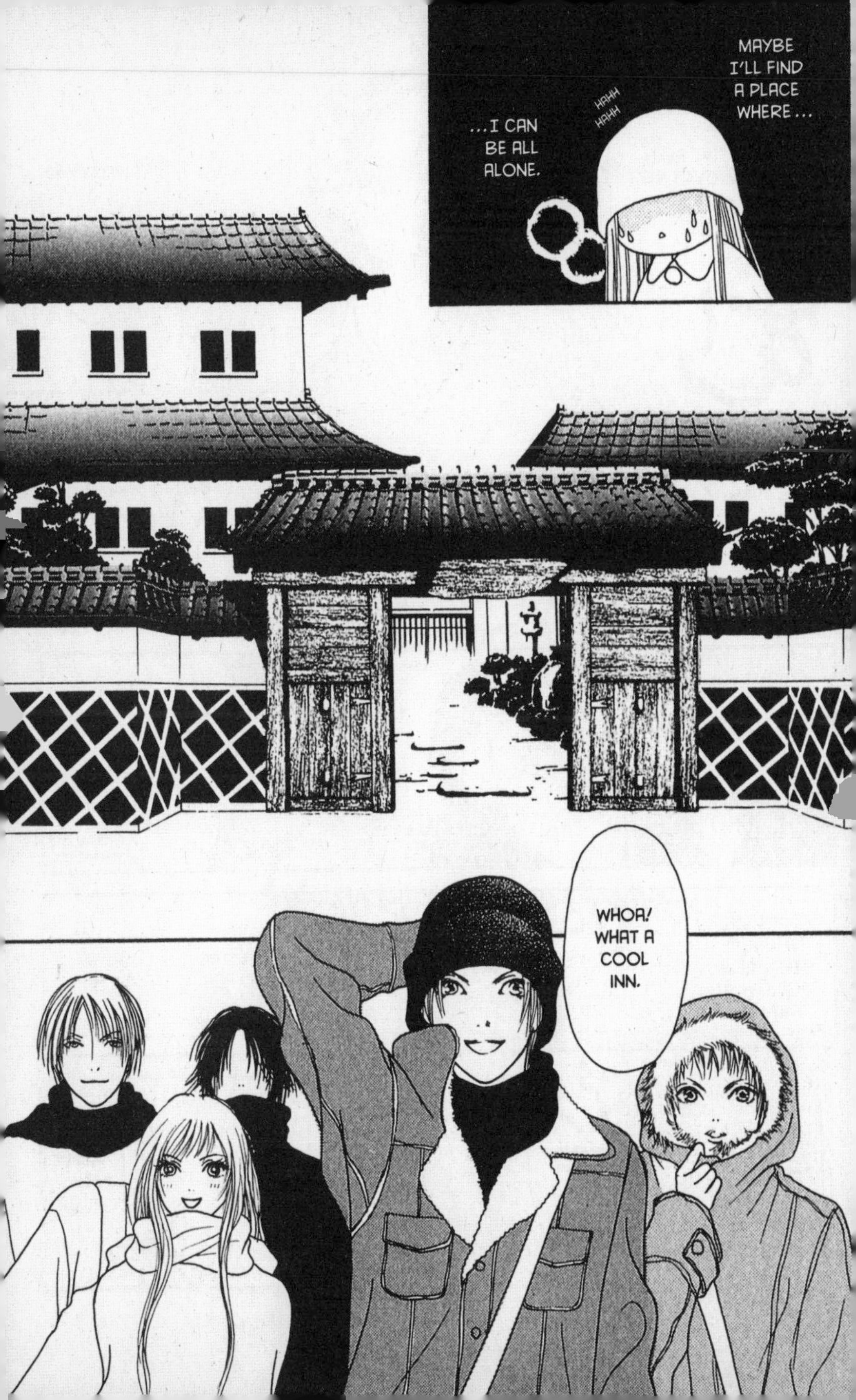
MAYBE I'LL FIND A PLACE WHERE...
HAHH HAHH
...I CAN BE ALL ALONE.
WHOA! WHAT A COOL INN.

SHE'S PRETTY, ISN'T SHE?

IT'S HARD TO BELIEVE SOMEONE SO FRAGILE CAN MANAGE A PLACE LIKE THIS.

I'LL HAVE TO LOOK OUT FOR HER.

SIGH

THEY EVEN HAVE A PING-PONG TABLE.

THEIR OUTDOOR HOT SPRINGS IS OPEN 24 HOURS.

I CAN SEE THE OCEAN, YUKI-CHAN.

WOW, IT'S HUGE.

BLAH BLAH

SHUT UP, *HOME-WRECKER.* ♥

GIGGLE ♥

QUIT IT, YOU GUYS.

STOP IGNOR-ING ME.

I DON'T KNOW.

HEY, WHERE'S SUNAKO-CHAN?

LET'S HIT THE HOT SPRINGS.

TAPPA TAPPA

GOD, IT SOUNDS JUST LIKE AN OLD LOVE SONG...

SIGH, EVEN THOUGH I'M IN LOVE WITH HER... SHE BELONGS TO ANOTHER MAN.

A GHOST. THERE'S A GHOST IN THE BATH.

SHIVER
SHIVER

HUH?

FINALLY...

FINALLY, I'M ALONE.

HEH
HEH
HEH

I SAW A WEIRD SHADOW IN THE CHANGING ROOM.

I SAW ONE BY THE VENDING MACHINES.

REALLY?

I JUST SAW A GHOST IN THE HALLWAY.

KYAAAAA!

← BATHS

THIS IS TERRIBLE.

SHUFFLE SHUFFLE

CALL THE POLICE.

PLONK

SHE TRIES SO HARD NOT TO GET ANYONE'S ATTENTION, BUT SHE ENDS UP GETTING EVERYONE'S ATTENTION.

I GUESS SO.

SHE MUST'VE BEEN TAKING A BATH.

HOW TYPICAL.

SHE'S HUMAN.

YOU PROBABLY JUST SAW OUR FRIEND.

IT'S OKAY.

HUH?

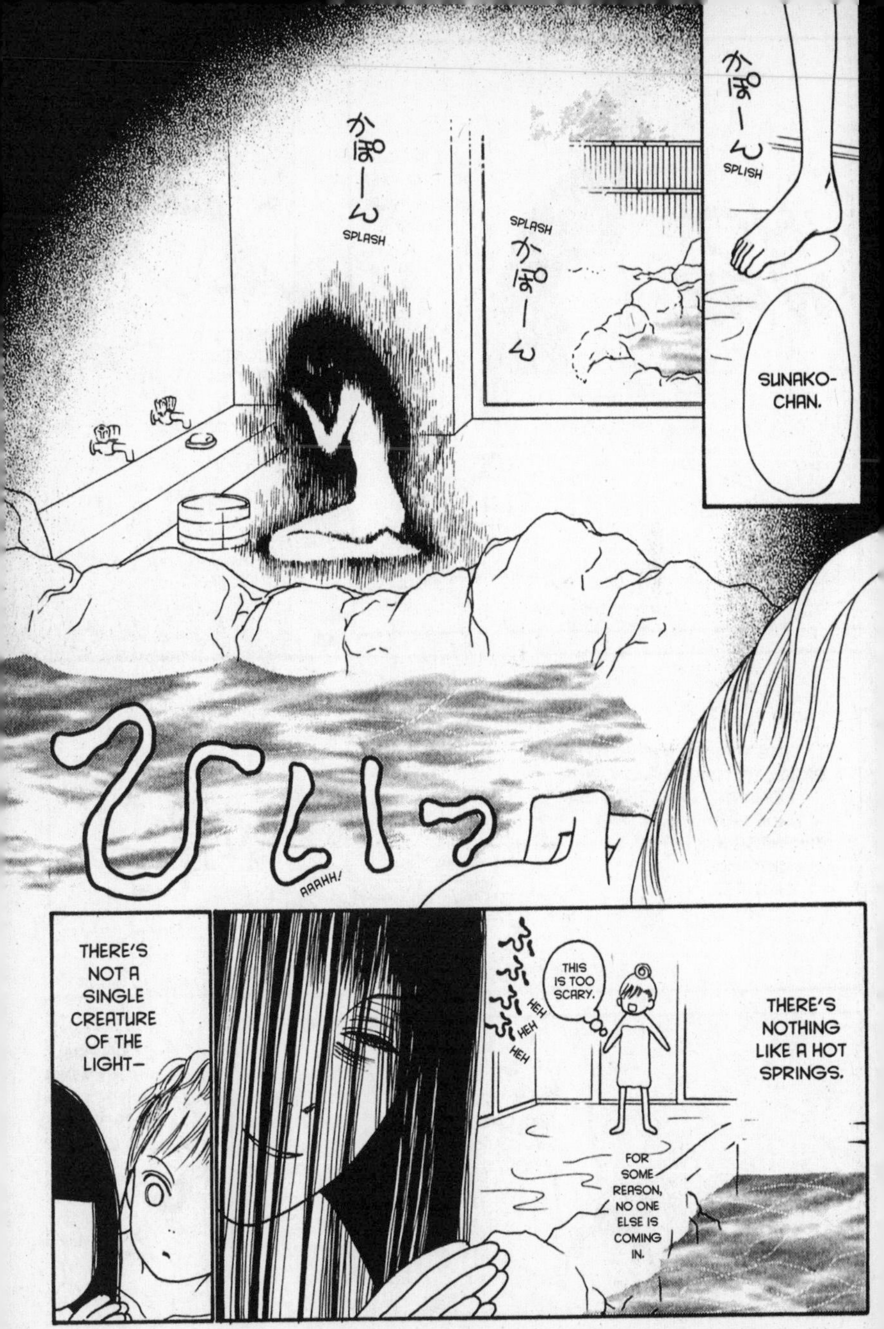
かぽーん
SPLISH
SUNAKO-CHAN.
SPLASH
かぽーん
かぽーん
SPLASH
ひいっ
AAAHH!
THERE'S NOTHING LIKE A HOT SPRINGS.
THIS IS TOO SCARY.
ふふふふ
HEH HEH HEH
FOR SOME REASON, NO ONE ELSE IS COMING IN.
THERE'S NOT A SINGLE CREATURE OF THE LIGHT—

NO WAY.

I NEED YOU TO KEEP KYOHEI-KUN BUSY.

TOWEL

AREN'T YOU OVER-REACTING A LITTLE?

ANY-WAY...

SPLASH

IT'S MY DREAM TO TAKE A ROMANTIC WALK WITH TAKENAGA-KUN IN MATCHING YUKATAS.

I JUST HAVE TO BE ALONE WITH TAKENAGA-KUN.

IGNORING HER

おねがい。
PLEASE.

HE KEEPS GETTING IN MY WAY.

AND THEN, I'LL TAKE OVER ALL YOUR CHORES.

I'LL GET TO LIVE WITH YOU GUYS (MAYBE).

IF I BECOME TAKENAGA-KUN'S GIRL-FRIEND ♥...

THERE'S SOMETHING IN IT FOR YOU TOO, SUNAKO-CHAN.

YOU'LL BE FREE FROM YOUR CHORES, SUNAKO-CHAN.

I WON'T GIVE UP.

MUMBLE
BABBLE
BLAH
BLAH

UH-OH.

NOTHING.

NOI, WHAT DID YOU SAY TO HER?

SHE-SHE'S LOST IN HER OWN WORLD!

BUT WHY?

IT WON'T WORK.

I'LL MELT AWAY INTO NOTHINGNESS BEFORE THAT HAPPENS.

SIGH, BUT THEN AGAIN...

BUT I'LL NEVER HAVE TO LEAVE MY ROOM AGAIN.

I HAVE TO STAY NEXT TO THAT CREATURE OF THE LIGHT—

...OR SPENDING THE NEXT FEW YEARS WITH HIM.

I HAVE TO CHOOSE BETWEEN SPENDING THE NEXT TWO DAYS WITH HIM...

HMM.

GRIN
ニヤ......

SUNAKO-CHAN, WAKE UP.

THUD
むた......

SHE COULDN'T TAKE IT.

I'M GOING BACK TO MY ROOM.

 WHAT?

HAHH HAHH

NO.   WAIT.

I'LL LAY OUT YOUR FUTON.

RATTLE
カラ......

SNIFFLE SNIFF SNIFF
しくしくしく

RUSTLE
バサ

RUSTLE
バサ

I-I'M SORRY.

CRACK
むぎゅ

FLOOF

バサ

GOOD-NIGHT, EVERY-BODY.

THANK GOD.

—144—

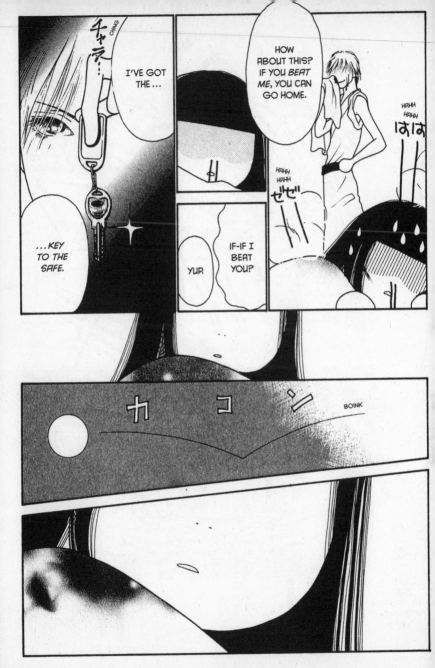

HEY, CHEF!

I NEED YOU TO TAKE CARE OF SOMETHING FOR ME TONIGHT.

OKAY.

CHING

BYE BYE.

SO, I'LL SEE YOU GUYS LATER. ♡

ARE YOU SURE?

HE'S ALWAYS LIKE THAT AT FIRST.

HA HA

RANMARU-KUN SEEMS REALLY SERIOUS ABOUT THAT WOMAN.

EVEN THOUGH SHE'S MARRIED.

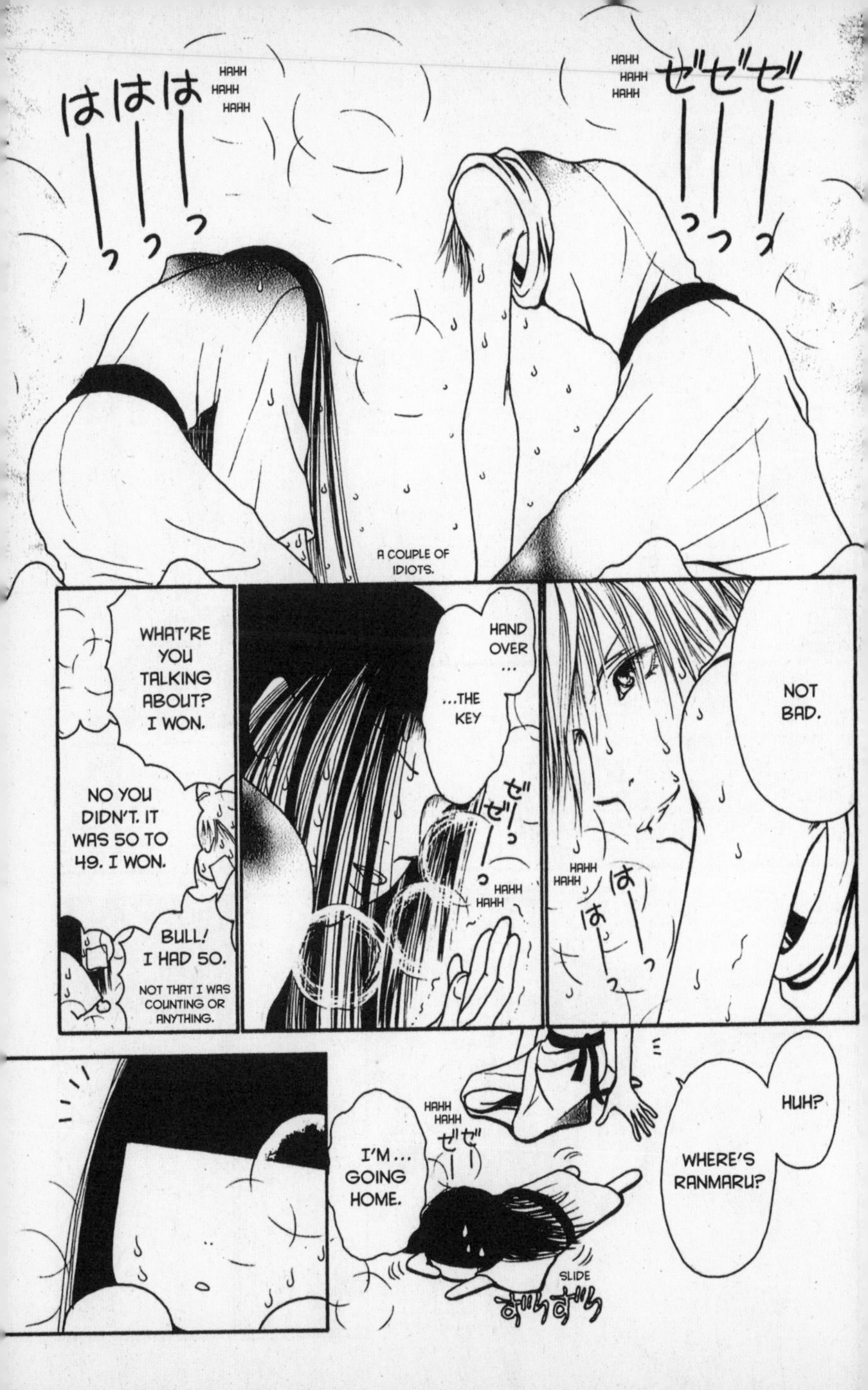
HAHH
HAHH
HAHH
ぜぜぜーーーっっっ
ははは―――っっっ
HAHH
HAHH
HAHH
A COUPLE OF IDIOTS.
NOT BAD.
HAHH
HAHH
はーっはーっ
HAND OVER ...
...THE KEY
ぜーっぜーっ
HAHH
HAHH
WHAT'RE YOU TALKING ABOUT? I WON.
NO YOU DIDN'T. IT WAS 50 TO 49. I WON.
BULL! I HAD 50.
NOT THAT I WAS COUNTING OR ANYTHING.
HUH?
WHERE'S RANMARU?
I'M... GOING HOME.
HAHH
HAHH
ぜぜ
SLIDE
ずるずる

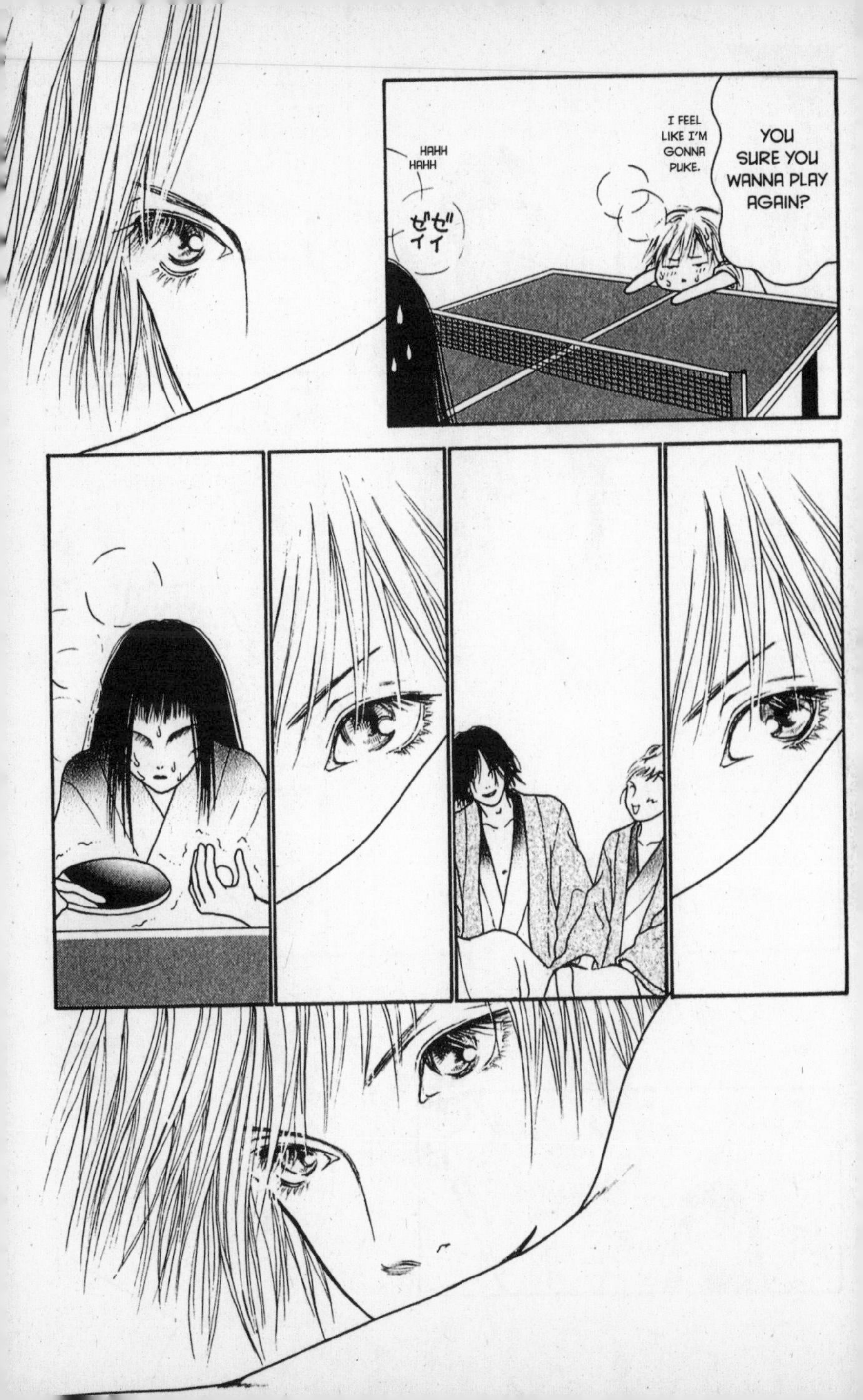
YOU SURE YOU WANNA PLAY AGAIN?
I FEEL LIKE I'M GONNA PUKE.
HAHH HAHH
ゼゼイイ

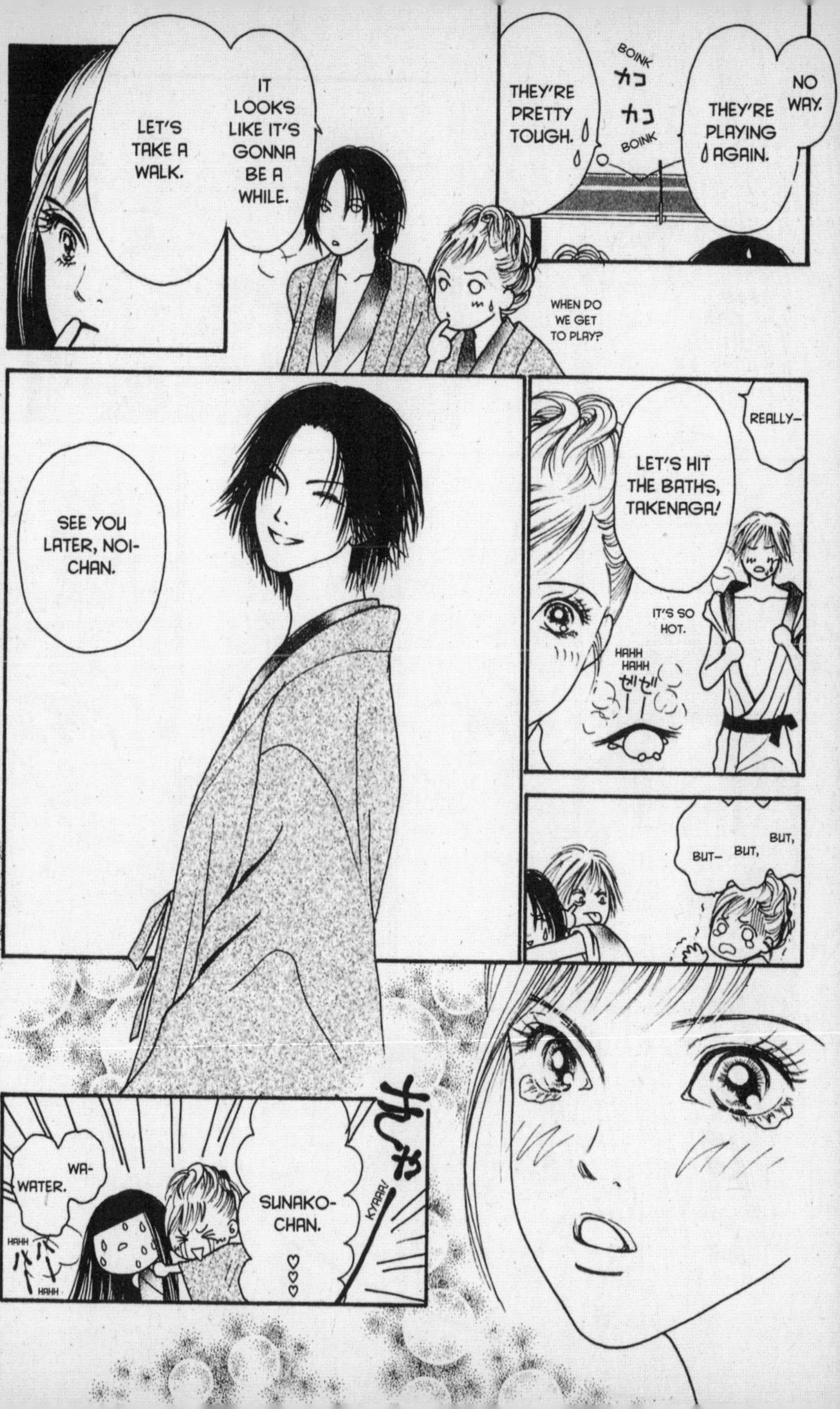
NO WAY.
THEY'RE PLAYING AGAIN.
BOINK
カコ
カコ
BOINK
THEY'RE PRETTY TOUGH.
IT LOOKS LIKE IT'S GONNA BE A WHILE.
WHEN DO WE GET TO PLAY?
LET'S TAKE A WALK.
REALLY—
LET'S HIT THE BATHS, TAKENAGA!
IT'S SO HOT.
HAHH HAHH
ぜぜ
BUT, BUT, BUT—
SEE YOU LATER, NOI-CHAN.
きゃ
KYAAA!
SUNAKO-CHAN.
♡♡♡
WA-WATER.
HAHH
ハァ
HAHH

WHAT'RE YOU DOING HERE?

OH, SHE'S UP.

FWUMP

— 159 —

THOSE TWO ARE PROBABLY OUT THERE TAKING A WALK RIGHT NOW.

IT'D BE KIND OF SCARY IF WE SAW SOMEONE DOWN THERE.

IT'S SO DARK, I CAN'T SEE.

TSS

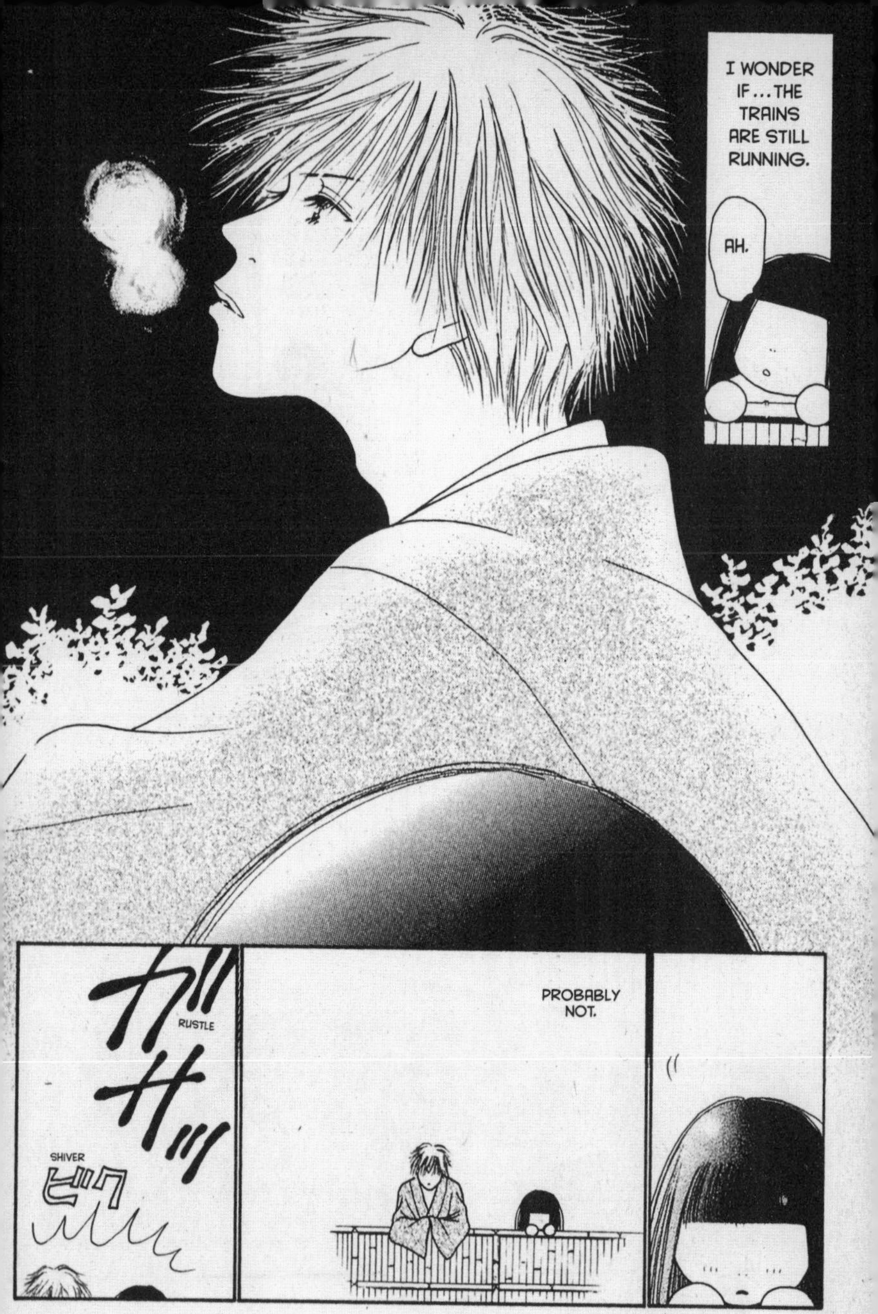
I WONDER IF…THE TRAINS ARE STILL RUNNING.
AH.
PROBABLY NOT.
ガサッ
RUSTLE
ビク
SHIVER

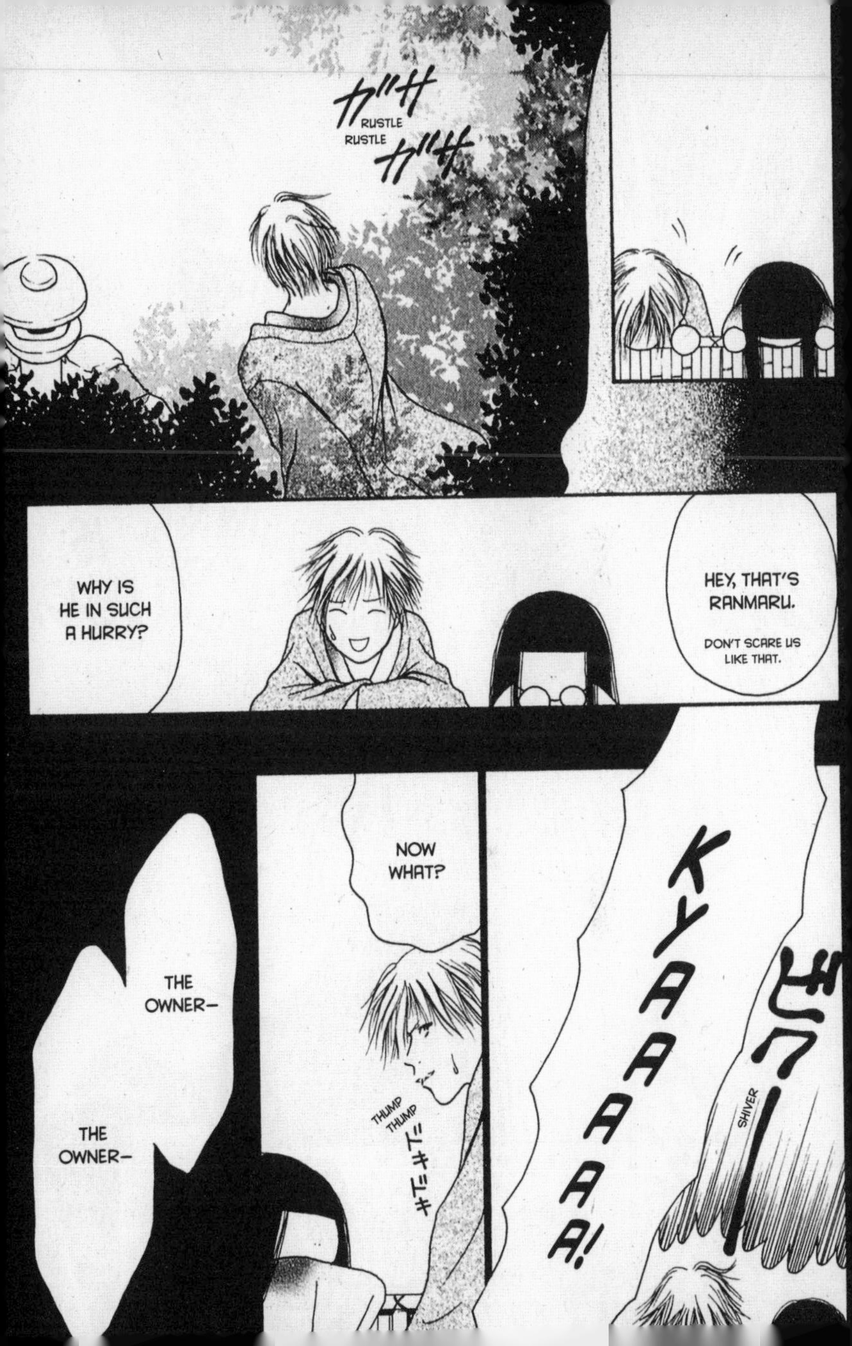
ガサ
RUSTLE
RUSTLE
ガサ
HEY, THAT'S RANMARU.
DON'T SCARE US LIKE THAT.
WHY IS HE IN SUCH A HURRY?
ビクー
SHIVER
KYAAAAAAA!
NOW WHAT?
ドキドキ
THUMP THUMP
THE OWNER—
THE OWNER—

TO BE CONTINUED IN WALLFLOWER VOLUME 3.

IT ALL STARTED WITH A CALL FROM *BEKKAN FRIEND* EDITOR, HAMANO-SAMA.

IT HAPPENED ONE DAY IN SEPTEMBER.

PHONE

I GOT A **BACK STAGE PASS** FOR THE **SADS** CONCERT.

あの
あのあのあの

CALM DOWN.

YOU MEAN—

YOU MEAN, I-I-I GET TO MEET *KIYOHARU-SAMA?*

清春に会える!?

(さま)
(SAMA)

ARE YOU OKAY?

バガーン

THUD

WELL, SINCE IT'S KIYOHARU, I GUESS YOU CAN GO.

IF I SAY NO, SHE'LL PROBABLY HATE ME.

MY BOSS WAS VERY UNDER-STANDING.

(AND SHE'S REALLY BEAUTIFUL.)

THE CONCERT WAS AT ZEPP TOKYO ON SEPTEMBER 20TH, THE DAY BEFORE MY *DEADLINE!*

THANK YOU, IZAWA-SAMA (MAIDEN NAME). EVEN THOUGH IT WAS RIGHT AROUND THE TIME OF YOUR WEDDING.

THAT'S GREAT. ♡ CONGRATULATIONS.

SO, YOU'RE NOT GOING TO THE "XXXZE" CONCERT?

I CANCELLED MY PLANS TO SEE OTHER SHOWS.

MY FRIENDS WERE NICE TOO!!

DON'T DO ANYTHING I WOULDN'T DO.

CHITOSE SAKURA

MACHIKO SAKURAI

KAI-CHAN

MADOKA-CHAN

I'LL BE AT THAT CONCERT TOO. SAY HI TO KIYOHARU FOR ME.

WELL, SINCE IT'S KIYOHARU, I GUESS IT'S OKAY.

KUMI AIKATA

SORRY EVERYBODY! YOU TOO, RUMI-CHAN.

THANKS EVERYBODY!

I WAS SO EXCITED THAT I ONLY TOLD PEOPLE WHO CALLED ME, AND I FORGOT TO CALL SOME OF MY FRIENDS. SORRY, TOBE-CHAN.

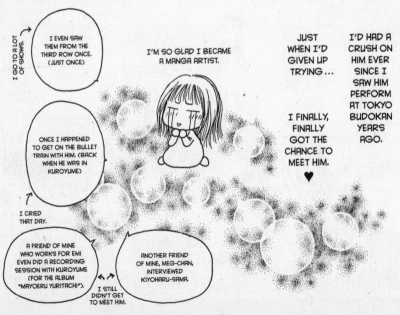

I GO TO A LOT OF SHOWS.

I EVEN SAW THEM FROM THE THIRD ROW ONCE. (JUST ONCE)

I'M SO GLAD I BECAME A MANGA ARTIST.

JUST WHEN I'D GIVEN UP TRYING ...

I FINALLY, FINALLY GOT THE CHANCE TO MEET HIM. ♥

I'D HAD A CRUSH ON HIM EVER SINCE I SAW HIM PERFORM AT TOKYO BUDOKAN YEARS AGO.

ONCE I HAPPENED TO GET ON THE BULLET TRAIN WITH HIM. (BACK WHEN HE WAS IN KUROYUME)

I CRIED THAT DAY.

A FRIEND OF MINE WHO WORKS FOR EMI EVEN DID A RECORDING SESSION WITH HIM. (FOR THE ALBUM "MAYOERU YURITACHI").

I STILL DIDN'T GET TO MEET HIM.

ANOTHER FRIEND OF MINE, MEG-CHAN, INTERVIEWED KIYOHARU-SAMA.

I'LL BE HAPPY JUST TO BREATHE THE SAME AIR THAT HE DOES.

OR I'LL JUST FOLLOW HIM LIKE A STALKER.

IT'S ACTUALLY NOT THAT LIKELY THAT YOU'LL GET A CHANCE TO TALK TO HIM.

EVERYBODY USUALLY GATHERS AT THE STADIUM, SO...

IT'S A PARTY, BUT...

AND ON THAT DAY...

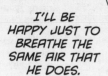

HAMANO-SAN (SHE'S SO CUTE. ♥)

I DANCED IN THE AISLE OF THE VIP SEATS. SORRY.

I COULDN'T HELP MYSELF.

AT ONE POINT, I WENT OVER TO THE STANDING ROOM SECTION AND DANCED MY BUTT OFF.

SORRY, I FORGOT WHAT HE WAS WEARING.

THE CONCERT WAS AWESOME. ♥ (AS ALWAYS.)

THEY'RE DOING IT IN THE DRESSING ROOM.

IT'LL JUST BE A SMALL GATHERING.

THANK YOU SO MUCH, MURAKAMI-SAMA OF TOSHIBA EMI.

INSTEAD OF HOLDING THE PARTY IN THE STADIUM...

HOW-EVER...

YOU CAN'T GO DRESSED LIKE THAT.

WOW, THAT WAS AWE-SOME.

I WAS SO EXCITED, I FORGOT ABOUT GOING BACKSTAGE.

THEN THE CONCERT ENDED.

DURING CONCERTS, I LIKE TO STRIP DOWN. I'D BE EMBARRASSED IF SOMEONE SAW ME.

(MY HAIR WAS A MESS, AND MY MAKEUP WAS COMING OFF.)

PLEASE CALM DOWN.

SHIVER SHIVER SHIVER

THE-THE-THE DRESSING ROOM?

UH-OH.

CIRCUITS OVERLOADING

SHE HAD TO TAKE CARE OF ME. IT MUST'VE BEEN TOUGH. ಠ

I FOUND *KIYOHARU-SAMA!*

I'M SAD THAT I CAN'T RECREATE HIS COOLNESS IN THIS DRAWING. I DON'T EVEN REMEMBER WHAT HE WAS WEARING. HOW STUPID.

KYAA

KYAA KYAA

THERE WERE SO MANY PEOPLE... I DIDN'T THINK I'D GET TO SEE HIM.

POOR GUYS. THEY HAVE TO DO THIS RIGHT AFTER THE SHOW.

IF THAT'S HOW YOU FEEL, THEN GO HOME.

I WENT INTO THEIR DRESSING ROOM.

EVERYBODY WAS LINED UP TO TALK TO THEM.

IS THAT BECAUSE HE'S A DAD? OR WAS HE ALWAYS LIKE THAT?

OF COURSE, HIS *PHEROMONES* WERE OVERPOWERING, BUT HE ALSO JUST SEEMED SO → *MASCULINE.* HE HAD A REALLY STRONG *AURA* TOO. HE WAS BEYOND ORDINARY. ♥

EUPHORIA

KIYOHARU-SAMA IN THE FLESH WAS SO, SO, SO UNBELIEVABLY COOL.

I FELT LIKE THOSE BIG PUPILS WERE GOING TO SWALLOW ME UP. ♥ ♥ ♥

I'D ALWAYS THOUGHT HIS EYES WERE REALLY BIG, BUT ACTUALLY HIS PUPILS WERE BIG... AND SO COMMANDING.

HE WAS ACTUALLY 100 TIMES COOLER THAN THIS DRAWING.

(THIS ALL HAPPENED WITHIN 1/10 OF A SECOND.)

JUST THEN, KIYOHARU...

...LOOKED AT ME!

ARE YOU OKAY?

A DRAWING OF TOMOKO HAYAKAWA STUMBLING.

ど

べ

THUD

AH.

THANK YOU SO MUCH.

I'M SURE HE WAS THINKING "SHE'S CRAZY."

THANKS FOR COMING.

REALLY.

I'LL DO ANYTHING FOR YOU. ANYTHING. WHATEVER YOU WANT ME TO DO.

あ〜 あ〜 あ〜

HAHH HAHH

HAHH HAHH

BY THE WAY...

I DON'T NEED ANYTHING ELSE.

I CAN DIE NOW.

I'M SO HAPPY.

APPARENTLY, I WAS A TOTAL MESS.

I FELT REALLY AWKWARD.

YOU GOT TO TALK TO HIM.

SNIFFLE SNIFF

あうっ あうっ

WHAT DID I SAY TO HIM?

THANK YOU SO MUCH, HAMANO-SAMA.

AND...SORRY.

I GUESS I WAS ACTING REALLY SCARY.

— 171 —

HAVE YOU EVER SWEATED FROM THE TOP OF YOUR HEAD?

IT HAD NEVER HAPPENED TO ME BEFORE.

HAVE YOU EVER FALLEN DOWN BECAUSE YOU COULDN'T WALK ANYMORE?

IT'S NOT THE SAME AS JUST FALLING DOWN.

HE TRULY IS THE GREATEST GUY IN THE WHOLE WORLD.

I'LL LOVE HIM FOREVER. ♥ ♥ ♥

BUT, BUT.

I FINALLY GOT THE CHANCE TO TALK TO HIM, AND... UGH, I'M SO STUPID.

UPSET

WHAT A WASTE.

I REALLY DID BLACK OUT.

MY MEMORY CAME BACK LITTLE BY LITTLE.

I DO REMEMBER HOW COOL HE WAS. HE WAS SO GRACIOUS, EVEN THOUGH HE MUST'VE BEEN TIRED AFTER THE CONCERT.

I'LL NEVER GET ANOTHER CHANCE TO MEET HIM... AND I DIDN'T EVEN *SHAKE HIS HAND* OR GET HIS *AUTOGRAPH*... OR GET A PHOTO.

I'D LIKE TO SAY THANK YOU, AND APOLOGIZE TO EVERYBODY WHO HELPED ME OUT.

THE FOLLOWING DAY

AFTER ALL, I DIDN'T SLEEP FOR THREE DAYS.

AFTER THAT, I HAD A REALLY TOUGH TIME AT WORK.

ARE-ARE YOU OKAY?

I'M FINE.

SCRIBBLE SCRIBBLE

HANA-CHAN, THE GENIUS

EXHAUSTED

MACHIKO SAKURAI

CHITOSE SAKURA

AS I WRITE THIS, MACHIKO SAKURAI IS AT MY HOUSE.

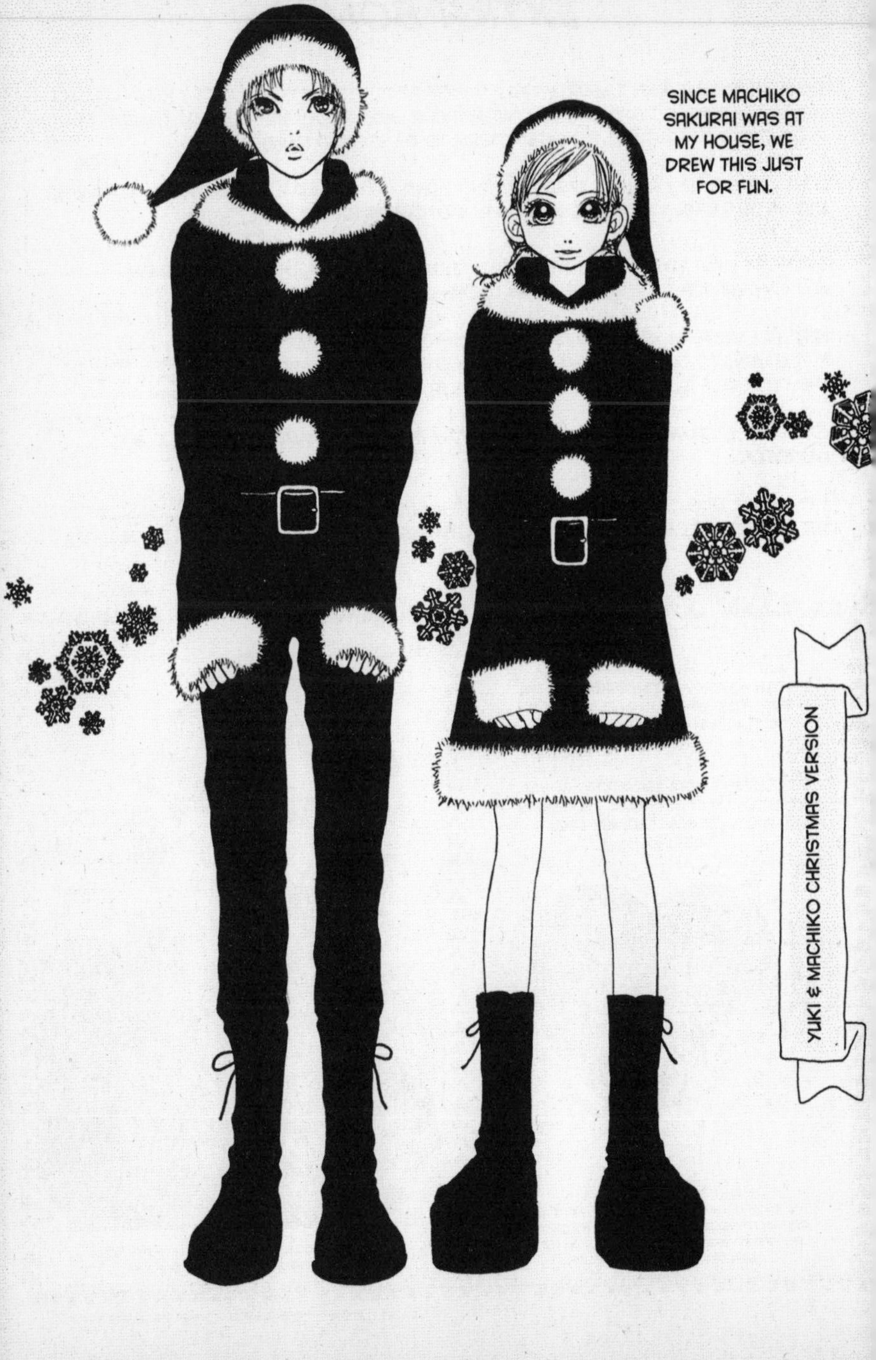
SINCE MACHIKO SAKURAI WAS AT MY HOUSE, WE DREW THIS JUST FOR FUN.
YUKI & MACHIKO CHRISTMAS VERSION

EXTRA BONUS

I GUESS IT'S BECAUSE I'M DRAWING A MANGA ABOUT "FOUR GUYS" THAT I KEEP GETTING LETTERS ASKING IF I BASED THEM ON THE "FOUR GUYS FROM THAT POPULAR BAND." PEOPLE KEEP COMPARING THE CHARACTERS TO THESE BAND MEMBERS.

LISTEN TO ME, THEY'RE NOT BASED ON THAT BAND. WHY WOULD A *KIYOHARU MANIAC* LIKE MYSELF BASE MY CHARACTERS ON SOME FAMOUS BAND?

I ALMOST WANT TO SAY THAT, OTHER THAN *TAKENAGA*, THEY'RE ALL BASED ON *KIYOHARU*. BUT OF COURSE, THEY LOOK NOTHING LIKE HIM.

HERE ARE SOME GUYS WHO *SLIGHTLY RESEMBLE* MY CHARACTERS. IF YOU WANT TO COMPARE THEM TO SOMEBODY, PLEASE COMPARE THEM TO THESE GUYS. (EXCEPT FOR TAKENAGA).

I'D BE HAPPY IF YOU'D COMPARE THEM TO BOY BANDS OR CELEBRITIES OR MOVIE STARS.

OH, OF COURSE I DESIGNED THEIR PERSONALITIES ALL BY MYSELF.

THEY'RE ALL MUSICIANS, EXCEPT FOR OGINO-KUN, WHO'S IN ADVERTISING. I GOT MOST OF THE PICTURES FROM FLYERS. THANKS FOR LETTING ME BORROW THE PICTURE, OGINO-KUN.

❧ KYOHEI ❧

MAYBE YOU DON'T THINK HE LOOKS ANYTHING LIKE *KIYOHARU-SAMA*, BUT THAT'S WHO HE'S BASED ON. IT'S NOT LIKE I'M A CARICATURE ARTIST. ↖ WHATEVER.

I COULDN'T USE A REAL PHOTO OF HIM (DUE TO COPYRIGHT RULES), SO HERE'S A PHOTO OF SOMEONE WHO LOOKS JUST LIKE HIM.

I KNOW THAT'S NOT REALLY HIM, BUT I WAS STILL EXCITED. (IDIOT)

SHE RESEMBLES HIM MOST FROM THIS ANGLE.

TAA-CHAN. ♥
SHE'S A GIRL. (SHE'S BEAUTIFUL.) YOU KNOW HER IF YOU'VE READ KODANSHA COMICS' *KIREI NA OTOKONOKO*. THAT'S RIGHT. WE TOOK THIS PICTURE IN 1998. SHE'S THE YOUNGER SISTER OF MANGA ARTIST CHITOSE SAKURA.

❧ TAKENAGA ❧

THIS IS THE VOCALIST FROM THE INDIE BAND RISK. HE ALWAYS HELPS ME OUT. I'M A HUGE FAN.

(I OWE YOU ONE.) *RISK ALWAYS PLAYS AT THE URAWA NARSIS.

RANMARU

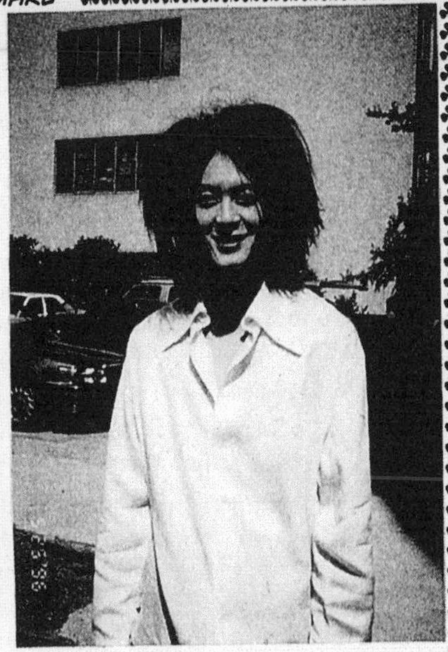

I'M SORRY, TSUKASA-KUN. I HAD TO USE A SNAPSHOT. (BACK WHEN HE WAS A TEENAGER.) HE HAD BEAUTIFUL SKIN, AND HE WAS SO THIN. I DIDN'T HAVE HIS FLYER.

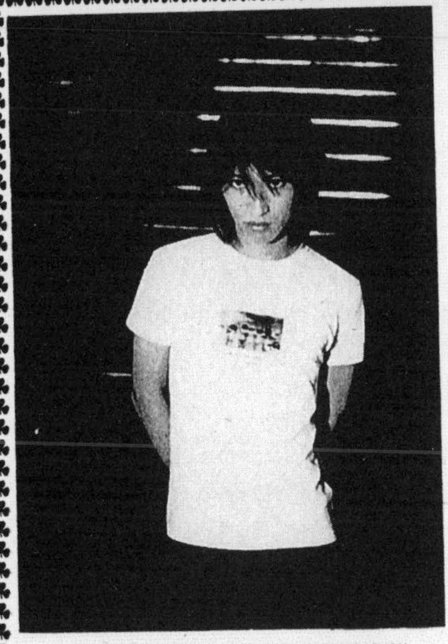

THIS IS OGIRI-KUN, THE VOCALIST FOR SHOCKING LEMON. HE'S SO COOL. ♥ HE'S REALLY A GREAT GUY. HE'S SO MANLY. HE'S NICE TOO.

YUKINOJO

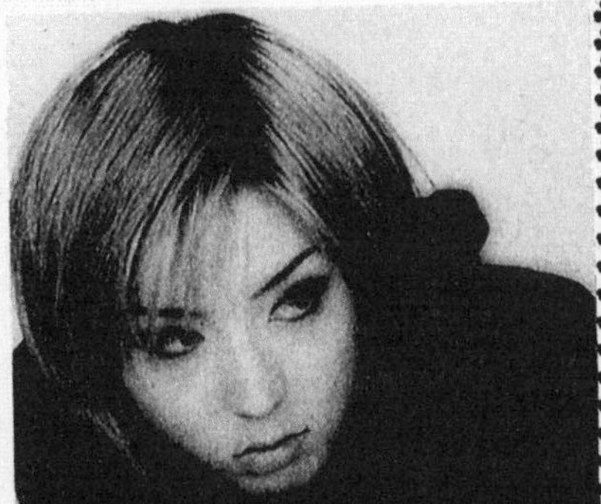

THIS IS YUKI, THE DRUMMER FROM RISK. (HEY, HIS NAME'S YUKI TOO.) HE ACTUALLY LOOKS MORE LIKE KIYOHARU. HE LOOKS CUTE WITHOUT MAKEUP ON.

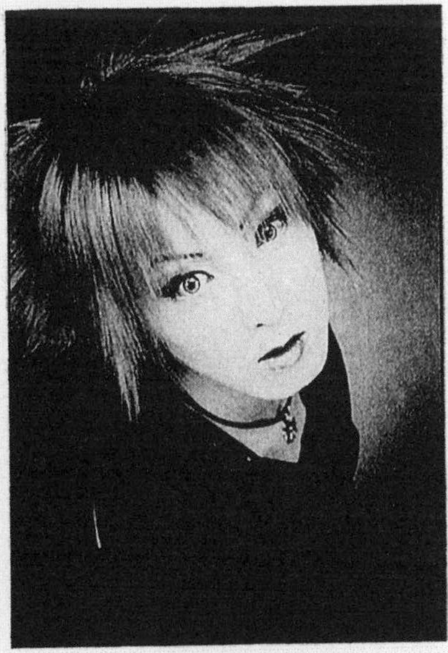

THIS IS BANSAKU-KUN. HE'S SO CUTE. (BUT I THINK HE LOOKS EVEN BETTER WITHOUT MAKEUP ON.)

THANKS FOR BEARING WITH ME. ♥

I'LL SEE YOU NEXT TIME. ♥ ♥ ♥

About the Creator

Tomoko Hayakawa was born on March 4.

Since her debut as a manga creator, Tomoko Hayakawa has worked on many shojo titles with the theme of romantic love—only to realize that she could write about other subjects as well. She decided to pack her newest story with the things she likes most, which led to her current, enormously popular series, *The Wallflower*.

Her favorite things are: Tim Burton's *The Nightmare Before Christmas*, Jean-Paul Gaultier, and samurai dramas on TV. Her hobbies are collecting items with skull designs and watching *bishonen* (beautiful boys). Her dream is to build a mansion like the one that the Addams family lives in. Her favorite pastime is to lie around at home with her cat, Ten (whose full name is Tennosuke).

Her zodiac sign is Pisces, and her blood group is AB.

Translation Notes

Japanese is a tricky language for most Westerners, and translation is often more art than science. For your edification and reading pleasure, here are notes on some of the places where we could have gone in a different direction in our translation of the work, or where a Japanese cultural reference is used.

AAAAHHH.
HOW CAN A GIRL LIKE THAT LIVE WITH SUCH HOT GUYS?
IT'S MORE LIKE SHE'S HAUNTING THEM.

Haunting (page 8)

This is actually a pun that doesn't translate well into English. In Japanese, this girl literally says, "It's more like she's *living* with them." However, the character she uses for the word "living" is one that refers to unwelcome pests.

More Haunting (page 10)

Japanese high schools hold school festivals once a year. During the festival, each class sponsors an activity such as a dance or opens a food stall or a haunted house. Sometimes guests and visitors from other schools vote on the best project. A prize is often given to the winning class.

I HEARD THAT...
...THE CLASS THAT GETS THE MOST VOTES FOR THEIR SCHOOL FESTIVAL PROJECT...
...WINS 500,000 YEN.
(APPROXIMATELY $5000)

MANGA CLUB

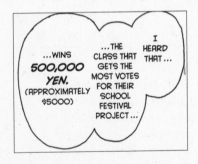

Manga Club (page 12)

During school festivals, sports teams and activity clubs usually put up signs and banners.

I HEARD THEY USED TO EXECUTE PEOPLE HERE DURING THE EDO PERIOD.
NOOOOO!
REALLY?

Edo (page 39)

The Edo period is a period in Japanese history that lasted through the mid 19th century. Edo is the old word for Tokyo.

Christmas (page 48)

In Japan, Christmas Eve is a holiday for lovers, much like Valentine's Day in the U.S. It's very important to have a date for Christmas Eve.

DO YOU KNOW WHAT...
SHUFFLE
...KYOHEI-KUN'S PLANS ARE FOR CHRISTMAS?

KFC for Everybody! (page 59)

For some reason, fried chicken is a celebratory Christmas food in Japan. KFC is always very busy on Christmas. Also, the "Sandy Claus" referenced here is a character from *Nightmare before Christmas*, one of Tomoko Hayakawa's favorite films.

SIGH
ああ
I'M SO HAPPY. ♥
SHE EVEN BOUGHT SOME FRIED CHICKEN.
CHOMP CHOMP
"SANDY CLAUS"

Hahaa, My Lord (page 72)

When Sunako gives Kyohei the chicken, she says "hahaa." In samurai times, this is what people said when they presented a gift to someone of higher status. Here, we translated it as "here you are, my lord."

Soba Noodles (page 84)

Toshikoshi soba, translated as "New Year's Soba," is a traditional soba noodle dish eaten on New Year's Eve.

Year-end Cleaning (page 86)

It's tradition to clean house before the New Year's festivities begin. It's the Japanese version of spring cleaning.

Smile, You're on Dorifu Camera (page 90)

Takenaga actually says "Are we in a *Dorifu* sketch or something?" *Dorifu* is an old sketch comedy group from the '80s.

Love Songs (page 133)

Ranmaru actually says "It sounds like an *enka*." *Enka* is a popular style of Japanese music. The songs are often about lost or forbidden love.

Yukata (page 136)

A *yukata* is a casual kimono usually worn at a hot springs resort.

Preview of Volume 3

Here is an excerpt from Volume 3, on sale now in English.

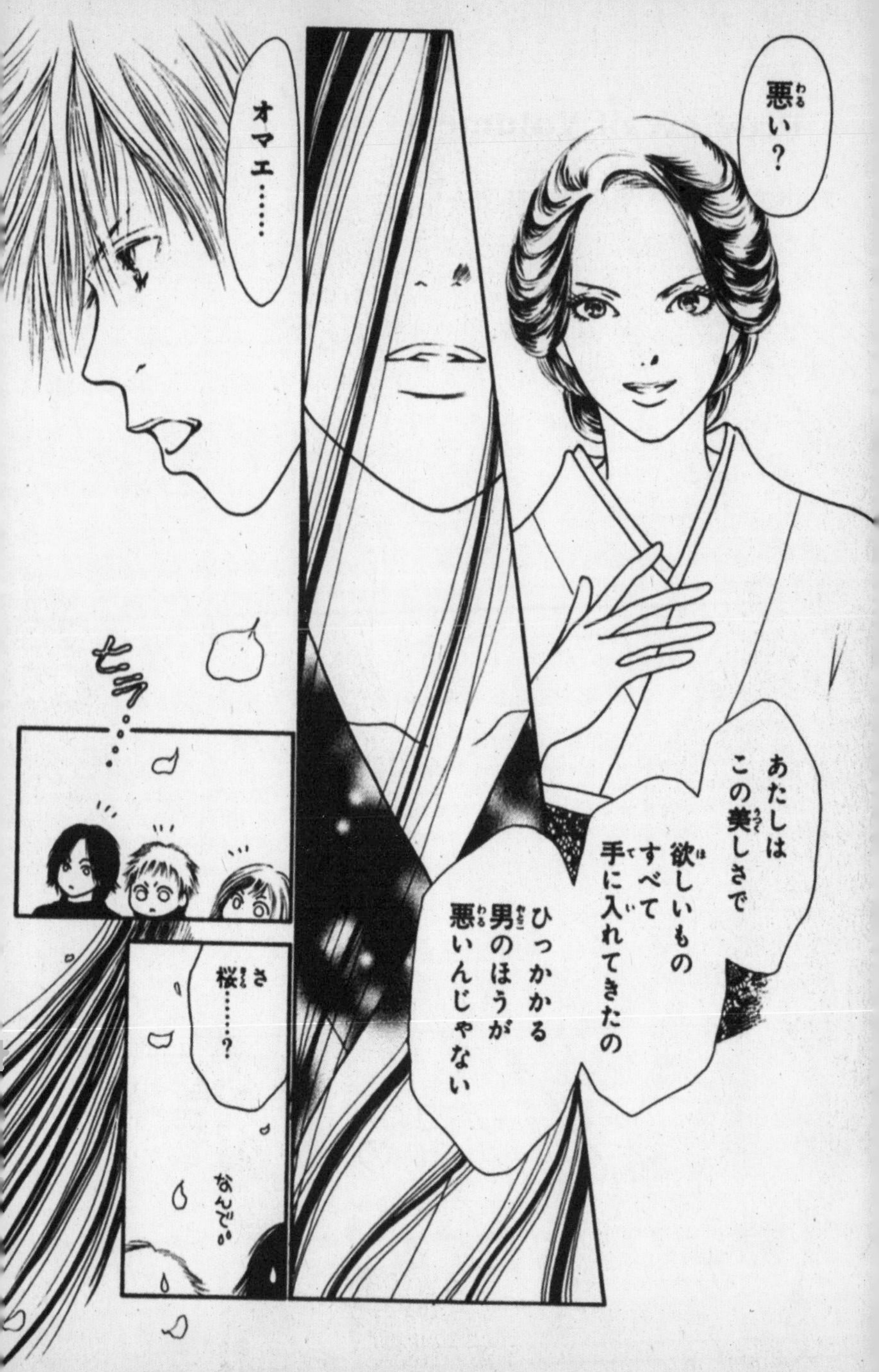
悪い？
あたしはこの美しさで欲しいものすべて手に入れてきたの
ひっかかる男のほうが悪いんじゃない
オマエ……
ヒラ……
桜さ……？
なんで。

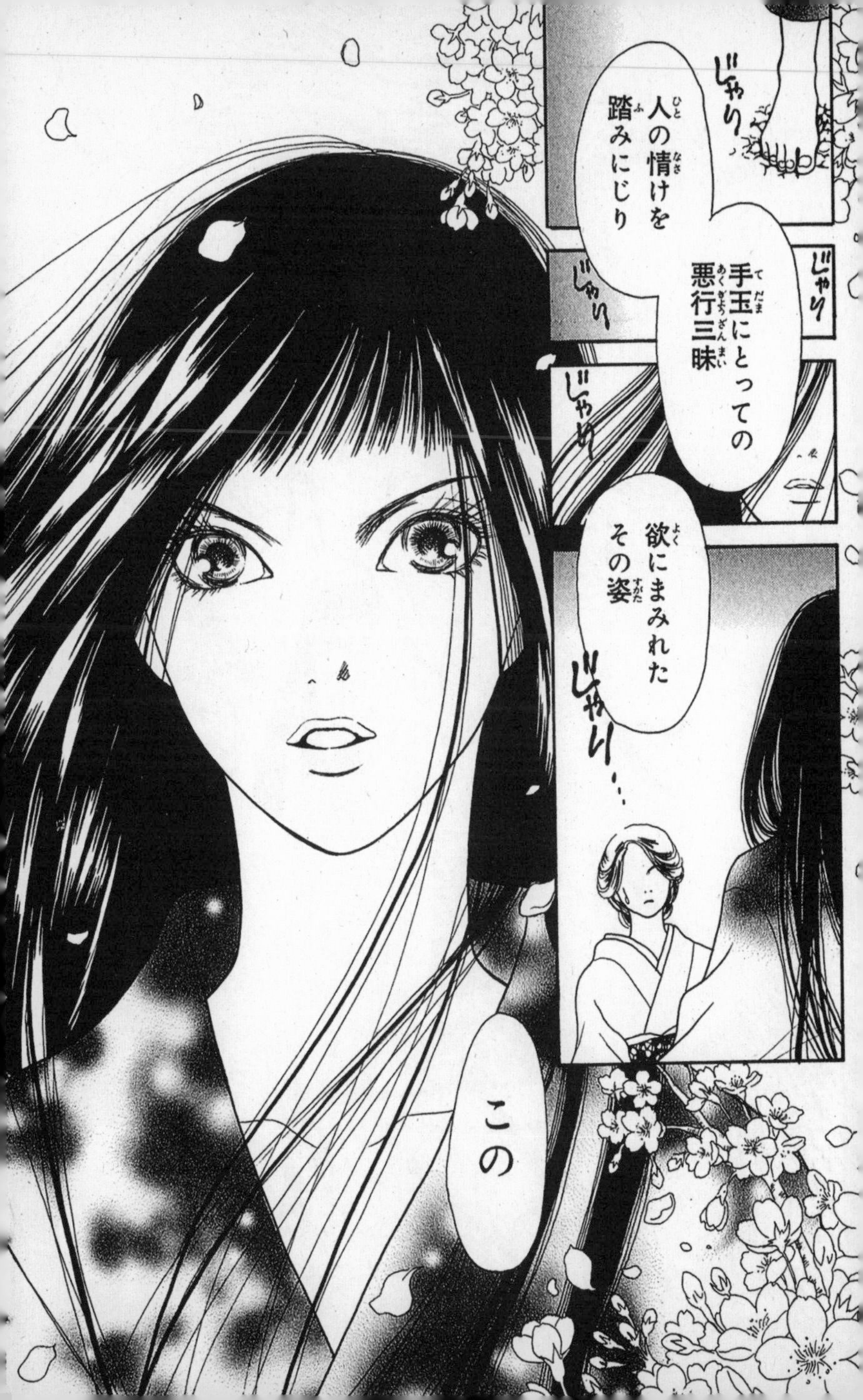
じゃりっ
人の情けを踏みにじり
じゃり
じゃり
手玉にとっての悪行三昧
じゃりじゃり
欲にまみれたその姿
じゃり…
この

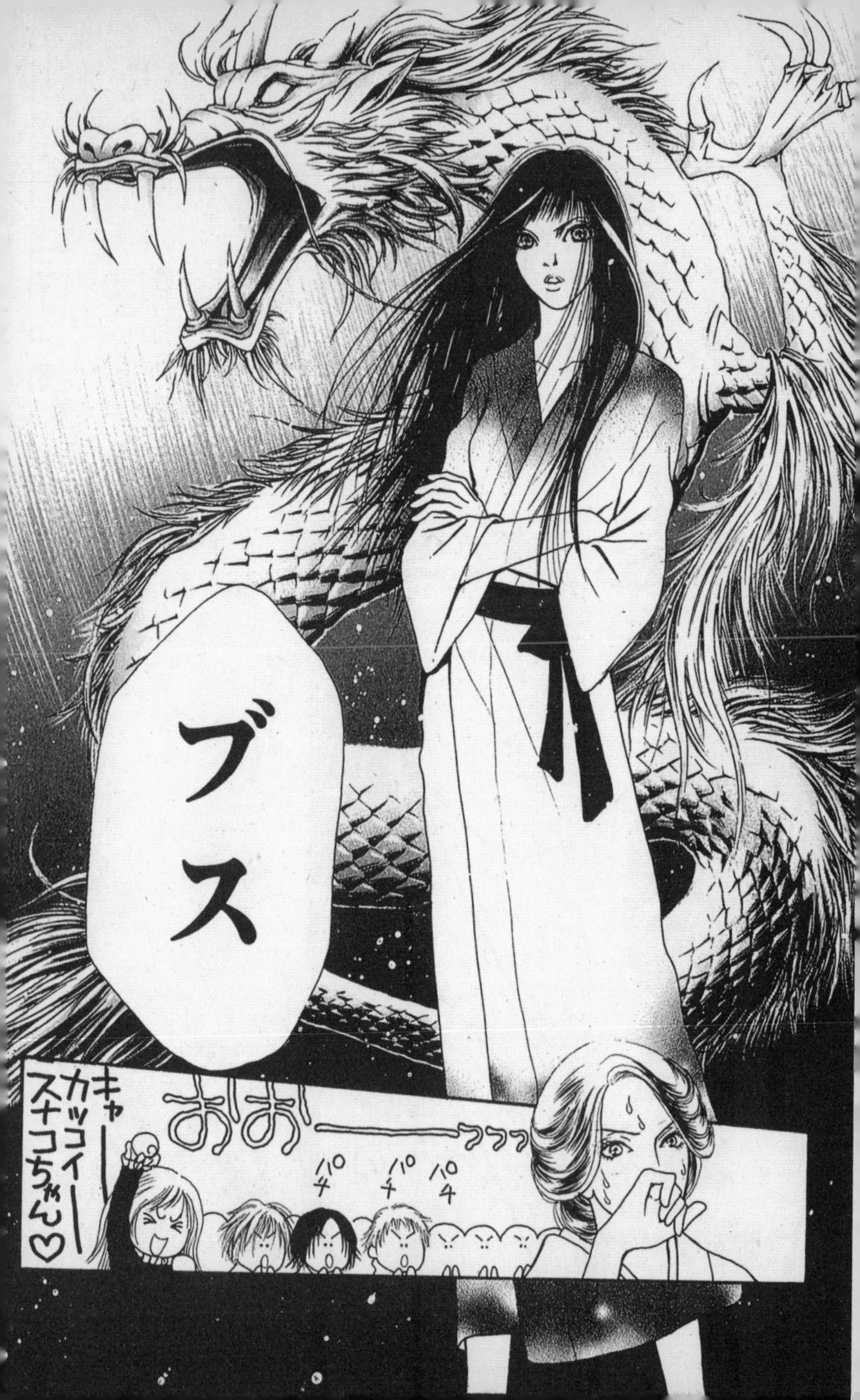
ブス
おおーっっっ
パチ パチ パチ
キャー
カッコイー
スナコちゃん♡

TOMARE!

止まれ

[STOP!]

You're going the wrong way!

Manga is a completely different type of reading experience.

To start at the *beginning,* go to the *end!*

That's right! Authentic manga is read the traditional Japanese way—from right to left. Exactly the *opposite* of how American books are read. It's easy to follow: Just go to the other end of the book, and read each page—and each panel—from right side to left side, starting at the top right. Now you're experiencing manga as it was meant to be!